Patagonia Chronicle

ON FOOT IN TORRES DEL PAINE

Patagonia Chronicle

ON FOOT IN TORRES DEL PAINE

Susan Alcorn

Shepherd Canyon Books
Oakland, California

Shepherd Canyon Books
Oakland, CA 94611, U.S.A.
(866) 219-8260 or (510) 339-3441
www.backpack45.com

ISBN-13: 978-0-936034-04-1

Library of Congress Control Number 2012909210

Publisher's Cataloging-in-Publication Data

Alcorn, Susan.
    Patagonia chronicle: on foot in Torres del Paine / Susan Alcorn.
    p. cm.
    ISBN 13 978-0-936034-04-1
    includes bibliographical references and index.

1. Parque Nacional Torres del Paine (Chile) -- Description and travel. 2. Patagonia (Argentina and Chile) -- Description and travel. 3. Patagonia (Argentina and Chile) -- Guidebooks. 4. Hiking -- Patagonia (Argentina and Chile) -- Guidebooks. 5. Backpacking -- Patagonia (Argentina and Chile) -- Guidebooks. I. Title.

F3186 .A53 2012
982/.7 --dc23   2012909210

18 17 16 15 14 13 12   1 2 3 4 5

Dedication

This book is dedicated to the dozens of trail angels who have helped us on our various treks—volunteers who build and maintain the trails; individuals (often anonymous) who maintain water caches or ice chests crammed with soft drinks and candy bars alongside the trails; people who open their doors to hikers who long for a place to shower and a comfy bed; individuals who stop to offer directions to lost travelers, and to those who transport us (sometimes hundreds of miles) to trail towns or trailheads.

My special thanks to Jeannine Burk; Lynn and Tom Cole; Andrea and Jerry Dinsmore of Hiker Haven; Diane Ely; Bob Ennis; JoAnn Michael; Donna and Jess Saufley of Hiker Heaven;[1] Sandy and Craig Simmons; "Warner Springs" Monty Tam; Walt and Laurie of Wrightwood, CA; and Jim P. of Etna, CA—all of whom have helped us in myriad ways on our long-distance hikes.

Contents

Introduction

If you are a traveler, or otherwise interested in exciting and awe-inspiring travel destinations, the Patagonian region of South America should be at, or near, the top of your list of places to explore. Notwithstanding its oft-ridiculous weather, Patagonia's magnificent scenery and exotic wildlife make it worth top billing for adventurers.

For hikers, two national parks in Patagonia stand out—Torres del Paine and Parque Nacional Los Glaciares. *Torres del Paine* (Towers of Paine, pronounced "pie-knee"), in the national park of the same name, is a magnificent mountain range rising out of the steppes in Chile. Although some of the park can be visited by car, coach, horseback, or boat, most of it is reachable only on foot.

Whether you are a hiker or not, you will not want to miss the spectacular *Glaciar Perito Moreno* in Argentina's *Parque Nacional Los Glaciares* (The Glaciers National Park). Los Glaciares is also the home of *Fitz Roy,* an 11,020-foot mountain peak that challenges mountain climbers from around the world. Trekkers can find trails and circuits that will bring them to outstanding views of Fitz Roy and the range that surrounds it.

Considering a trip to any part of South America is generally more intimidating to the independent American traveler than planning one within the U.S. or to Europe because the continent is less familiar to most of us. Planning where to visit, where to hike, and how to get around in Patagonia's vast and varied terrain can be perplexing, but this book will help you sift through the options. Its three major components—the personal accounts of Patagonia travel; the logistics of planning a trip; and the historical and background information to enrich your knowledge of this region of the world—should alleviate your concerns.

I hope that after reading the accounts of our hiking and road trips into the southernmost parts of Argentina and Chile, you'll feel both inspired and confident about embarking on your own trek in Patagonia. Even with the time and expense of getting to Patagonia, you'll soon find out that this part of the world is well worth the effort. There are good reasons to take a trip to Patagonia *sooner* rather than *later*—both because of the region's increasing popularity and because of looming environmental assaults.

I guarantee that a visit to the vast reaches of Patagonia will be an experience that you'll never forget. I'd return in a heartbeat to this most amazing, exciting, beautiful land of mystery and I hope that this book will help *you* have the grandest of adventures!

Las Torres of Torres del Paine

Points of Interest: Patagonia

1 • Journey to Patagonia

I don't remember the exact moment when I became aware of Patagonia and more specifically of Chile's *Torres del Paine,* but when the thought did take hold, images of the park seemed to start popping up everywhere I looked. Colorful photos of the iconic Towers del Paine and Los Cuernos captivated me, photo essays in *National Geographic* and on the pages of Sierra Club calendars tantalized me.

My husband Ralph and I live near the home offices of an adventure company, Wilderness Travel of Berkeley, and regularly devour their catalogs of upcoming trips. We receive announcements of programs about South America from the bustling REI stores. When we learned that Wayne Bernhardson, who wrote *Moon Handbooks: Patagonia*, was going to make a presentation on Torres del Paine a few years back, we made sure to get there early in order to get a good seat. His slides and talk about a recent trip he and his teen-aged daughter, Clio Bernhardson-Massolo, had made to Torres del Paine made trekking there look feasible.

Each photo, talk, or conversation about Torres del Paine, Fitz Roy, and other Patagonian destinations further whetted our appetites. It was only a matter of time before we decided to go for it—to load up our backpacks and head for the southernmost reaches of South America. We spent no time at all making one major decision—whether to go with a tour company or to go on our own. For us, it was a foregone decision that we wanted the flexibility and challenge of doing it on our own.

It's not that we are averse to traveling with a small group—in fact we have enjoyed a couple of guided trips—most notably with Tusker Trail to climb Mt. Kilimanjaro and with Adventurers Abroad to go to Machu Picchu, Peru and to Bolivia. However, on this trip, we wanted to set our own itinerary. Moreover, we wanted a backpacking trip to parts of Torres del Paine that few travel companies offer. (A few travel companies and personal guides are listed under *Resources* at the end of this book.)

Because it was our first trip to either Chile or Argentina and we thought it might be our only one, I had put together an ambitious three-week trip that would take us to see Magellanic penguins, to the national parks of Torres del Paine and Los Glaciares for backpacking, and to the Lake District in the midst of the Andes for sightseeing—and that did not take into account the fact that we had to fly in and out of either Santiago or Buenos Aires.

Then I met with Barbara Lee, a Berkeley-based photographer, who had been to Patagonia only a few months earlier, and heeded her advice.

"Concentrate on one area," she said.

So Ralph and I cut a few places from our three-week itinerary, discussed our priorities for what we most wanted to do in Patagonia and settled on seeing the penguins near Punta Arenas, hiking the Circuit Trail in Torres del Paine National Park in Chile, and visiting Fitz Roy and other attractions in Los Glaciares National Park in Argentina.

We reluctantly scratched the Lake District from our list and stuck a couple of extra days into our revised itinerary to cover flight cancellations, or for delays on the hiking segments. Even so, we wondered if we would run short of time. We were becoming more and more aware that our schedule had to allow flexibility, but we didn't yet have a grasp of the time that would be eaten up by getting around the vast regions using public transportation. (A condensed version of our trip is in Appendix 2, p. 257.)

Ralph, the one in our family who puts together the walking itinerary for almost all of our trips, got busy. I set about arranging flights, making hotel reservations for the first and last nights, and began writing hiking and strength training "appointments" on our calendar.

Journal

MARCH 3-4, 2009. Our trip began with the shuttle to the airport arriving at 8:45 a.m. and then the noon flight from San Francisco International Airport to Miami, Florida; our second flight was to Santiago, Chile arriving about 10:00 a.m., March 4th. (Because we were using our frequent flier miles, we had fewer choices as far as departure times and routes than those paying cash.)

Although there were no complications with the flights, it was exhausting for me because I couldn't sleep en route. I swore that I would investigate taking a sleeping pill, or getting an upgrade, before going on another long flight.

Once we reached the line for immigration in Santiago's Arturo Merino Benitez International Airport (SCL) the process was very efficient. Whenever there was an opening, a computerized signboard lit up with a number indicating which booth to approach.

We waited in line about fifteen minutes and when the sign flashed the number of an open booth, we approached the immigration officer to show our passports. Unfortunately, we had missed a previous, and *required*, stop at the cashier's window where we were supposed to pay the Reciprocity Tax.[2]

We had been forewarned that we would have to pay the tax and had come prepared with the required Chilean pesos (then US$131 each; US$140 at the time of publication). Beware trying to use torn or weathered bills; I watched a fellow traveler struggle to come up with the needed funds until he realized that he was able to use his credit card.

Paying a fee for an entry visa was new to us, but it's not all that unusual. And in this case, it's only fair that citizens of certain countries must pay a fee when arriving by air—not only Americans, but US$132 for Canadians, US$61 for Australians, and US$15 for Mexicans—because these fees are equivalent to the amount these countries require Chileans to pay. (Citizens of certain other countries, such as the UK, don't have to pay a fee.) After we paid the fee, a voucher was placed in our passports that will be good until our passports expire.

The next step was to show a completed tourist card (allowing a stay for up to 90 days). It's important to hang onto the card because it must be shown to customs when you depart.

After clearing immigration, we went to customs. Ralph had declared our backpacking food and so he had to pull out our food supply. We had known not to bring any fresh fruits or vegetables, but it was a surprise and genuine loss to have our three packages of beef jerky confiscated. Luckily none of our freeze-dried dinners attracted attention—even though most contained small amounts of chicken or other meat.

Earlier, when I had made our hotel reservations, I had also arranged for a taxi (US$30) to meet us at the airport. When we reached the waiting room, exhausted, it was a welcome sight to see a friendly face holding a cardboard sign with our name on it.

We soon arrived at the Hotel Orly, which I had found on the Internet. Since I had booked it sight unseen, it was a relief to find that the hotel was clean and comfortable. The rate seemed reasonable for such a large city—US$110, including breakfast. We showed our tourist cards and said we would be paying with U.S. dollars in order to avoid Chile's hefty 19% room tax. It didn't take long to realize that we were staying in a tourist section of town—evidenced by the fact that the hotel's menu was printed with English translations.

After unpacking and a short rest, we ventured out to take the subway downtown to the *Centro Mercado* (Central Market). The building has a graceful old rooftop supported by an iron framework and covered with glass. Making our way through the marketplace filled with butcher shops, seafood stands, and restaurants was like strolling through a carnival's penny arcade with vendors barking their offerings. We finally settled on a small restaurant near the entrance, mostly because we'd been told that there would be extras included in the price.

I ordered a seafood dish of shrimp, fish, scallops, and sea clams. Since it was our first day, we hadn't completely figured out the currency exchange rate (about 600 pesos to the U.S. dollar), so my order turned out to be more expensive than I had intended. It was delicious, but richer than I'm used to; Ralph liked his paella. With our two beers, the bill came to about US$30.

To get through the readjustment of jet lag (and lack of sleep) we forced ourselves to walk around a bit more, and then went back to the hotel for a shower and short nap. Then it was up and out a second time. We knew that the sooner we adopted the new time zone, the sooner we would feel normal.

We found a supermarket and tried, in our inadequate Spanish, to find some beef jerky to replace what had been taken at the airport. One of the clerks tried to be helpful; he led me up and down the aisles to find what I wanted, but either I didn't communicate well or they didn't have what I wanted. In any case, we never did find any dried meat. I picked up some soda, which cost just about what beer did, and then we got in line. The lines were long, except for the one with a sign that indicated that it was open to pregnant women only.

There were several other restaurants near our hotel offering indoor and outdoor dining, but at dinnertime we chose the one at our hotel. The temperature during the day had been in the 70s and it had cooled to a temperature perfect for dining *al fresco*. I had pizza; Ralph had *Camarones al pil-pil* (shrimp sautéed with garlic in olive oil). Once again, with bread and beer, our total was close to US$30—which we figured was a bit less than it would have been at home.

A street musician was working his way down the street—stopping at the cafes along the way—and stopped to play his panpipes next to our outdoor tables. In lieu of tipping him, I offered him the half pizza I couldn't eat, which the restaurant packaged up and gave to him. I wondered if he would take offense, but he seemed pleased.

I soon realized that the Andean tune the musician was playing was familiar—I knew it as *If I Could* from the Paul Simon album, *Bridge over Troubled Water,* which was a hit sensation in 1970. As the days went by, and we traveled further south, we heard the tune many times and I began to wonder why it was so popular. I later found out that when Simon first heard the tune, he was told that its title was *El Condor Paso* (roughly "the Condor goes by") and that it was a Peruvian folk song at least 300 years old (others say that it originated with the native Quechuan peoples).

Simon wrote new lyrics, but after his version was introduced, film-director Armando Robles Godoy filed a lawsuit for copyright infringement. Godoy, who was the son of Alomía Robles, claimed that his father had composed the song in 1913, based on traditional music, and that Robles owned a U.S. copyright. Thereafter, Robles was credited on Simon's album.

We had entered the land of street dogs. They were everywhere. They spent most of their time sleeping on the sidewalks or draped around trees in the wells formed by the surrounding concrete—unless there was the immediate prospect of a handout in which case they became instant friends.

Overview of the region

Some call Patagonia the "land of mystery" and a legitimate question might be, "How did the region acquire its nickname?" While it's true that Patagonia encompasses a huge area, so do the steppes of Russia and the wilds of Canada, but they don't seem to captivate our imagination to such a degree. Similarly, we may think of other large countries, or portions of countries, and realize that we don't know a great deal about them, but they seem less elusive than Patagonia. What causes the mystery? Could it be that it is distant, has challenging terrain and weather, or that it's sparsely populated? We hear little about Patagonia on the nightly news—what is its political situation?

Geography

PART OF THE mystery, for some (and that included me for a long time!) is *where* it is and *which* regions it includes. Authorities differ in defining the exact boundaries, but all can agree that it is the southernmost parts of Chile and Argentina.

Chile is a narrow country on the west coast of South America. The southern third of the country's almost 3,000-mile length is composed primarily of hundreds of mountainous islands separated by channels and fjords. Both Chile and Argentina have claims to portions of Antarctica.

Chile is bordered by Bolivia and Peru on the north, and Argentina to the east. Cape Horn, at the tip of Chile, is at the end of the region known as Tierra del Fuego. Passage around Cape Horn, where high winds and waves, icebergs and currents often combine forces, is considered by many to be the most difficult navigational route in the world.

Although Argentina's length (2,268 miles) is less than that of neighboring Chile, it is South America's second largest country and is about one-third the size of the United States. It shares borders with Bolivia to the north; Paraguay to the northeast; Brazil, Uruguay, and the Atlantic Ocean to the east; and Chile to the south and west. Argentina also has a vested interest in the oil and mineral reserves of Antarctica and claims a portion of it.

When to visit: Seasons, climate and weather

CONSIDERATION OF THE differing seasons is of foremost importance in considering a trip to Patagonia. Because it's in the Southern Hemisphere, travelers from northern countries must keep in mind that Patagonia's seasons are the opposite of theirs. In addition, the region experiences long winters and a short fall and spring.

The high season for visitors to Patagonia including Torres del Paine is November through February. October and March are considered *shoulder seasons*—expect more variation in the weather during the change of seasons. Not to put too fine a point on it, but no matter when you go, especially to the higher altitudes, be prepared for frequent changes within a day (sometimes within minutes).

As might be expected of such large countries, the climate and weather of Chile and Argentina is quite varied. The Atacama Desert of northern Chile is one of the driest places on earth, with less than half an inch of precipitation a year—and that is from condensed fog, not from rain. Its temperatures, however, are far different from those of other well-known deserts such as the Sahara of Africa or Death Valley in California. Its climate is moderated by the cool Humboldt Current that flows north along the coast, often bringing high humidity and thick clouds. Atacama's highs range from 63-76 °F (17-24 °C) and lows from 52-63 °F (11-17 °C).

In contrast to the aridity of Atacama Desert is the wetness of Chile's southern coast. It is said that in towns such as Puerto Aisén that it rains 370 days a year. In reality, the rainfall and climate can vary dramatically from one valley to the next.

The shared border between Chile and Argentina is almost all in the Andes and the boundaries are still in dispute. The Andes is the longest mountain range in the world, extending more than 4,000 miles down the western portion of South America and through seven countries. Argentina's Cerro Aconcagua, at 22,835 feet, is the highest mountain in the Americas.

Argentina's Patagonian desert, with its inhospitable 260,000 sq. miles, is the largest desert in the New World. As is the case with Chile's Atacama Desert, the Argentine Patagonian desert is considered a *cold winter desert*. Because the Andes intercept the moisture flowing onshore from the Pacific, precipitation rarely reaches the desert, creating what is known as a *rain shadow*. The high, arid region's temperatures rarely exceed 80 °F (27 °C) or dip below 32 °F (0 °C).[3]

The notorious weather of Patagonia—snowstorms in winter, gale winds most of the year in some areas—makes finding an extended window of time with clear blue skies and calm weather somewhat a matter of luck. The weather conditions and patterns vary depending on where you are.

In the Alto Valle del Río Negro area (northern Patagonia), the average winter temperature is 28 °F (-2 °C) and summer maximum temperatures can reach more than 100 ° F (40° C). The Andean Patagonia is humid; rainfall exceeds six feet (2,000 mm) a year, but becomes drier as you approach the Atlantic zone, where the average rainfall might be only six inches (200 mm). Tierra del Fuego registers approximately two feet (700 mm) of rain per year, yet at times temperatures can reach the high 80s (30° C).

Travel

MOST INTERNATIONAL TRAVELERS headed for Patagonia will go through Argentina's or Chile's gateway cities of Buenos Aires or Santiago (the respective capitals). These two cities are midway down the South American continent, but they are still far north of Patagonia. To reach the major attractions of Patagonia, one must continue on by air, bus, or car hundreds of miles farther south.

The reality of how large Patagonia is was brought home when Ralph and I made our first trip there in 2009. After flying to Santiago (flight times adding up to almost sixteen hours), we had to take another three-and-a-half hour flight to reach Punta Arenas, to be in close proximity to the park where we were going to hike. Those onboard who were continuing on to Ushuaia, Argentina, the southernmost city in the world (and then on to Antarctica), had another 125-mile hop ahead.

Additionally, because of the rugged terrain, the Patagonian regions of both countries are relatively difficult to reach. Travel between various points of interest can be time-consuming because of the great distances and/or because of a lack of highway access. Flights may be suspended due to weather, which can make on-time departures and arrivals a roll of the dice.

This remoteness of Patagonia is something most Americans and Europeans are unused to. Although we observed a great deal of road construction taking place in some parts of Patagonia—probably driven by the interest in tourism—the governments of both Chile and Argentina have had to weigh the costs of building highways in areas with few travelers when they have major cities with teeming populations demanding improved streets and freeways.

Although Patagonia's land area is huge—about one-third of both Chile and Patagonia—less than five percent of their populations live there. The population density is approximately 1.9 persons per square kilometer, compared to Manhattan, New York's density of approximately 26,879 per kilometer.

Taking into account all of these factors, it should come as no surprise that the majority of visitors to Patagonia will not be tooling around the countryside in their own (or a rental) car. They will most likely rely on public transit—taxis, buses, or subways in the cities, and vans, buses or airplanes for long-distance travel.

Politics then and now

ALTHOUGH CHILE TODAY is a country with strong democratic institutions, stable social institutions, a relatively homogeneous population, and a strong economy, it did have a 17-year military dictatorship (1973-1990) under Augusto Pinochet that left more than 3,000 people dead or missing.

Conditions have improved considerably since the 1989 election of Patricio Aylwin, who served as President from 1990-1994. This began a 20-year period of liberal leadership. In 2006, Michelle Bachelet became president, the first woman elected to that office. She is widely credited with guiding Chile through serious downturns in the world's economy and toward improvements in many pension and social programs.

In spite of her popularity, Bachelet's presidency came to an end because of Chile's constitutional limit of one four-year term. In 2010, billionaire Sebastian Pinera was sworn in as president. He's the first conservative to lead Chile since the defeat of Pinochet. Pinera is an economist, investor, and businessman, who was educated in Chile and at Harvard University in the U.S. However, his popularity has plummeted since his election. In Santiago, student protests demanding that profits from copper mining (and other resources) should be used for education, housing, and health needs have grown increasingly strident. Environmentalists, though celebrating their recent successes (see Chapter 16), continue to challenge the construction of new dams in Patagonia.

Nor has Argentina escaped protests. In Buenos Aires, thousands of people have taken to the streets protesting high inflation and the economy's slow growth. President Cristina Fernandez, who was re-elected in 2011, has seen her popularity fall.

Yet the country's government and economy are stable compared to what they were in 2001-2002, when they suffered economic and political chaos. In 2001, the head of the Economy Ministry, Domingo Cavallo, attempted to halt capital flight and to stem the imminent debt crisis by freezing bank accounts. Riots broke out in the streets and clashes with police ended with several deaths. Argentina defaulted on its international debt in 2002, unemployment hit 25%, and real wages toppled. Finally in late 2002, the economy began to stabilize and restrictions on bank withdrawals were lifted.

Whether "land of mystery" is a deserved nickname or not, Patagonia does have many layers for visitors to uncover and it may well be that many of the people who live in this harsh environment enjoy their reputation of being resilient, adventurous and slightly mysterious.

Don't be deterred by the logistics of visiting Patagonia, just keep in mind the old English proverb, "Hope for the best, prepare for the worst." Do your homework (know what you are getting into); pack well, but lightly; and allow for delays.

Santiago's 72-foot Virgin Mary

2 • Santiago: Chile's Gateway City to Patagonia

Journal

THURSDAY, MARCH 5, 2009. Santiago, Chile. I quickly adapted to the time change in one respect; I slept through the night. The hotel's breakfast was generous with a selection of fresh fruits, breads, fruit tarts, scrambled eggs, ham slices, cheeses, and yogurt. It was a welcome contrast to the "continental" breakfasts composed of cheap bagels and muffins that we had so often encountered in chain motels back home.

After breakfast we set out on foot to one of the city's landmarks—the statue of the Virgin Mary. This brilliant white 72-foot (22-m) statue was donated by France in the 1920s and sits atop *Cerro* (Hill) *San Cristobal*. Cerro San Cristobal rises almost 1,000 feet above the rest of Santiago, and is second only to their Cerro Renca in height.

It was a long road walk to the outskirts of town and uphill through the *Parque Metropolitano* (Metropolitan Park). This is Santiago's largest municipal park and contains a zoo, a Japanese-style garden, and two public swimming pools.

Most of the time we were on the roadway, but there was minimal traffic so we didn't feel at risk walking on the smooth asphalt. As the road wound up the hill, we passed many view-points and picnic tables, but the smog was so bad that visibility was limited and the views toward the Andes to the east were not very exciting. Even though there was a bit of snow on one nearby peak, I didn't take photos because I knew they'd be disappointing. (It appears that visibility is poor much of the year, but the summer months—December to March—or after it rains are the best opportunities for good views.)

When we reached the summit, we ran into several small groups of tourists. They had come up the hill on the funicular—the tram that climbs the hill on a railway. We followed the others to look at the statue of the Virgin and the church with its amphitheater where Pope John Paul II celebrated mass in 1987. Being more interested in the walk and the views, we skipped the tour. We had planned to walk to the summit and then take the funicular down, but still having plenty of energy, we decided to walk down too.

The path was signed *dificil* (difficult), but we didn't find it too bad—dirt with loose rock in parts, but steps when needed. A stray golden-haired dog kept us company the entire way. He finally left us after we were well into town. Perhaps he found someone who would feed him, or perhaps he was distracted by the teenagers running about with paint and eggs smeared on their faces, hair, and clothing (apparently part of a school initiation).

We went back to the hotel to do some final sorting of our luggage—separating the city clothes we brought for Santiago and Buenos Aires from the hiking gear. Because we will be making an out-and-back journey from Puerto Natales to Torres del Paine, we will leave excess items in the Puerto Natales' hostel to be retrieved after our backpacking trip.

IT ALWAYS MAKES me nervous to leave anything behind: "Will I be warm enough?" "Will my raingear hold up?" "Should I carry one or two paperbacks?" (I'm Kindle-resistant.) It has been more stressful than usual to pack because we haven't been in Patagonia before.

Before we left home I made a couple of difficult decisions— namely how much warm vs. cold weather gear I should bring, and whether I should bring boots or trail runners. The boots won, but now that we are walking around on hard surfaces, especially on hot days, my feet are not very happy about their unyielding surroundings. Although I also brought dressy sandals to wear when we're in cities, they aren't comfortable for walking more than a short distance.

This means I have to wear my boots when we walk around sightseeing. And, even though we see students casually dressed in Levis, or even shorts, most of the adults in the financial district are conservatively dressed. The men wear business suits or khakis, dress shirts, and ties; the women are also professionally attired—in suits, dresses, or tailored skirts and blouses. So, when we walk around downtown and run into the people coming out of their offices at lunchtime, I feel like a bit of a klutz.

FINALLY, WITH OUR backpacks and our duffle bag stuffed, we went out to eat. We were finding that Santiago, Chile and Santiago de Compostela, Spain (another remarkable place we have visited) share much more than a name—they also share many foods. We stopped at a tapas bar and ordered from the menu that was printed on the paper tablecloth. It was fun to select some unfamiliar items, and I was doubly happy when our choices turned out to be good. In this case, the meatballs, Spanish omelet, endive stuffed with cheese, gazpacho made with mango, and *profiteroles*—those decadent cream puffs drizzled with chocolate—were all tasty.

We hadn't had time to explore Santiago's museums and public buildings, but our friend Tom Coroneos, who spent several days there in 2007, had sent these comments, "More important are the changes since I was here in 1980, the prison-state time. People are happy....The Presidential palace [La Moneda/the Mint], which was bombed and strafed then...is now open, guarded by two relaxed soldiers (one a woman)."

Tom found *La Moneda Cultural Center*, which highlights Chilean art, film, and other cultural offerings, of great interest. The center is under the Plaza de la Ciudadanía, which is just north of the Palacio La Moneda. He added, "The Colonial Museum [on Londres Street] in the center of town was also rich." Indeed, *Museo Colonial de San Francisco* offers a collection of colonial and religious art. It now occupies one of the Santiago's oldest buildings—the San Francisco Convent built in 1628. Tom added, "I spent the days walking the pedestrian streets, which were closed to cars, enjoying folk music and dance and then [enjoyed] seafood and wine at the Central Market."

Fur seal pile on Isla Marta

3 • On to Punta Arenas and Puerto Natales

Journal

FRIDAY, MARCH 6, 2009. Santiago to Punta Arenas (3-hr. flight)

Our flight from Santiago was a bit late starting. Not knowing anything about LAN Airlines' on-time record (or even their safety record), at that time, I wondered how long the wait would be and hoped they were doing additional safety inspections. We had some good views of the Andes and the Patagonia range, but we would have had better views of the mountains if we'd booked seats on the left (inland) side of the plane.

We had finally arrived in Patagonia—in Punta Arenas, Chile's southernmost city. Punta Arenas (population 155,000) first became prosperous during the California Gold Rush because of its location midway between the Atlantic and Pacific Oceans on the north side of the Magellan Strait. Clipper ships made stops there to take on coal and other cargo. Later, the city became the center for Chile's wool industry and a wealthy set of landowners developed, which created a wealthy enclave. Today, Punta Arenas is home to a mix of cultures including the descendants of Croatians, Portuguese sailors, and English sheep ranchers. It's also a good place to begin a trip to Torres del Paine National Park and for voyages to Antarctica.

We took a taxi into town and checked into the Hostal Patagonia (US$60) for which we had reservations. The room was not fancy, except for the satin trim on the bedding, but it was fine because it was safe, clean, and quiet. The location was convenient; there were several restaurants within walking distance and we were only about five blocks from the main street and central square.

The main thing we wanted to do in Punta Arenas was see penguins. We'd read that Punta Arenas, which overlooks the Strait of Magellan, is a good jumping off spot for day trips to their rookeries. We wanted to visit *Monumental Natural Los Pingüinos* (Penguins Natural Monument), which is a protected site composed of two islands—Magdalena and Marta. Both are in the strait about 20 miles offshore of Punta Arenas.

The owner at Hostal Patagonia, Rosa, spoke English, and was very friendly and helpful. She sold tickets to various area excursions and for buses, so we inquired about tours to see penguins and wondered aloud if we should go today or tomorrow.

"The weather is good today, I can't tell about tomorrow," she said.

This wasn't just a salesperson's pitch, "get it while it's hot!" We knew that the weather was both unpredictable and rapidly changed, and so we decided we had better go right away. We collected our jackets and cameras; I took an anti-seasickness pill and hoped for the best. The shuttle picked us up at the hostel at 3:40 p.m., and we zipped into the center of town to an adventure center to pick up another eight people.

On our ride along the highway to the launch site, Ralph and I both became aware that our orientation to our surroundings was awry. We felt like we were headed south, when we were actually headed north. It was a strange feeling: the path that the sun *appears* to travel when you're in the southern hemisphere is opposite what it appears to travel in the northern one. The sun appears to move in an arc to the north—whereas at home it looks like the sun is traveling along a southern arc. Because we don't ordinarily think about it consciously, but just expect things to follow what we are used to, it felt topsy-turvy.

I had envisioned climbing on a large ferry and then jockeying for position on various levels of decks. I was rather shocked, therefore, when the van pulled off the highway onto a gravely shoulder in front of a small dock with faded a canvas sign read-ing "Visit Isla Magdalena."

A couple of small motorboats were tethered to the pier's bleached posts. We were going to be navigating the infamous Strait of Magellan in a semi-inflatable boat? The fact that it had been modified by the addition of a cabin on top added to my concern. Wouldn't adding weight to the top of the boat make it even more unstable? As I watched the weathered boat bobbing in the water, I wondered what I had gotten myself into.

For me, the Strait of Magellan has always been a place that conjures up images from earlier times—of sailing ships tossed about by enormous waves, crews lost at sea, and shipwrecks on sharp rocky shores. When Portuguese explorer Ferdinand Magellan and his crew made their way through the strait in 1520, the world then learned that sailing ships had a shorter route available than the Drake Passage off of Cape Horn. However, it still took Magellan 38 days to sail the 354 miles of the new route: the narrowness of the passage, the currents, and the horrendous weather combined to make it a harrowing voyage.

Even though I still wasn't convinced that I wanted to venture out in a small, dilapidated-looking boat, no one else seemed to be turning back. Don't they read the news reports about unregulated, overloaded boats sinking in foreign lands as they ferry people across dangerous waters? I wondered. Then, as we clambered onto the boat and entered the cabin, the odor of diesel fuel hit me. I felt like Kathryn Hepburn joining Humphrey Bogart on the African Queen.

With barely any headroom and windows so dirty that we couldn't see out, I wondered again what we had signed on for. As soon as the boat left the dock, I found out why the windows were opaque. After a few minutes of hydroplaning through the waves with the salty ocean spray drenching the bow and windows with every dip, I realized that washing the windows would have been a waste of time.

We sat inside, twiddling our thumbs, wondering what lay ahead. The captain introduced the crew (two hands) and then explained—first in Spanish, then in English—where we were headed. Instructions included the admonition to don life vests before going topside.

It took an hour to reach Magdalena Island, but at least while moving, we had fresh air and the thrill of zipping through the water. As we approached the island, I grabbed a life vest and headed forward to take photos. It was hard to maneuver around the others to take my shots and difficult to deal with the rocking of the boat, but at the same time, I was determined to make the best of our short opportunity to watch the penguins.

When finally I realized that we were going to be allowed on shore, I was overjoyed. We disembarked and walked on to the island. We had just an hour to explore this precious Chilean national reserve for the Magellanic Penguins with a population of 120,000 of these flightless birds.

An eight-foot-wide roped off path—ostensibly protecting the penguins from us—led up the gentle grade to the lighthouse. We took our time, taking photos by the zillions. Although the visitors followed the rules about staying inside the ropes, the penguins casually ignored them and walked ahead of us up the trail. You can't keep a straight face when you watch their antics on land—their waddling gait and clumsiness. This awkwardness—even to the point of falling on their faces—is in sharp contrast to their agility in the water where they can reach speeds up to 15 miles per hour. Adding to my delight was the fact that the penguins had to cross our dirt trail to get to the water and indeed, there was a small group hanging out on the sandy shore.

We learned about their life cycle. The eggs were laid in nests underground in mid-October and carefully tended by both parents while hatching into chicks and then becoming more independent fledglings. Now in March, the adults had entered prime molting season. Feathers were everywhere. Their unkempt appearance due to the loss of feathers made them even more adorable.

We saw lots of *allogrooming* (tidying one's partner; can't let your partner go out in public without every "hair" in place!), and snuggling, and so forth—it seemed as if everyone was out and about. The burrows, which were created for nesting purposes, and to which the young ones retreated when they sensed danger, were now little used. The colony would be deserted in another month when the penguins began their seasonal migration. When they returned from their long journey, sometimes up to 2,000 miles in length, many would return to the same site, and the males may reclaim the burrows they used previously.

One of the distinguishing features of the Magellanic Penguin is the double band of black feathers on the front of its neck that resemble a necklace. I could see why they are sometimes called "jackass penguin" (though that name officially belongs to a species found in Africa). Charles Darwin in *Voyage of the Beagle* wrote, "This bird is commonly called the jackass penguin, from its habit, while on shore, of throwing its head backwards, and making a very loud strange noise, much like the braying of an ass."

It was not particularly windy or cold near water's edge, but as we made our way to the island's high point, the breeze picked up. We spent a few minutes at the old lighthouse, which also houses the small museum, but we were much more interested in spending our short time on land watching the penguins' antics than we were in looking at historic documents and exhibits of local fauna.

After our tour of Magdalena, we climbed back into the boat for a fifteen-minute ride to the other island of the preserve, Isla Marta. There, on the beaches and in the coves were hundreds of raucous fur seals—from the huge males to the young black pups. On many of the sandy or rocky surfaces, there were bright blotches of red color; some of the blood was placental, some was from the dueling males. It's a wonder that any of the pups or weaners (*pups* are still nursing; *weaners* have been weaned) survive, not only because of the elements, but also because the males literally run right over them to reach other males to fight and establish dominance, or to claim females for mating.

On the top of the island, safely above the activity near the water, were thousands of sea and shore birds—cormorant, skuas, and gulls. Because Marta is a much smaller island than Magdalena, visitors are not allowed to go on land in order to protect the animals.

Going back to town was faster it seemed, sort of like every horse I have ever rented returning to the stable double-time. Even so, it was an exhausting day and I fell apart at dinner. I'm certain Ralph was embarrassed that I was crying at the dinner table—the wine probably contributed, but mostly it was that I was overly tired.

Penguins

Chile and Argentina each have four species of penguins. Chile has the Magellanic, Rockhopper, Macaroni, and Humboldt; Argentina has the Magellanic, Rockhopper, Macaroni, and Gentoo.

Magellanic penguins live on the Pacific and Atlantic coasts of Chile, Argentina and the Falkland Islands. In spite of population declines in northern Argentina due to oil pollution and tourism, and in the Falkland Islands due to commercial fishing, their overall population has increased in recent years to approximately 1,800,000 breeding pairs. Both Argentina and Chile protect the birds' colonies from commercial fishing. Besides Isla Magdalena and Marta that we visited, tourists in Chile can visit Seno Otway and Playa Mar Brava near Ancud on the island of Chiloé. Visitors to Argentina can visit penguins in Chubut and Punto Tumbo.

The *Rockhopper* penguins are found at 15 offshore sites on islands in Chile and Argentina. Isla Pinguino near Puerto Deseado, Argentina is said to be the only place where tourists can view them. The world's breeding population of Rockhoppers is 650,000. Chile's population is stable; Argentina's is increasing overall and it's thought that some increase may be from many coming from the Falklands. Although the Falkland Islands has 280,000 pair remaining in 36 breeding sites, the birds' overall population has been decimated because of fishery practices.

Macaroni penguins are found at nine breeding sites around Argentina and Chile, all on remote offshore islands inaccessible to tourists. They number about 12,000 breeding pairs, a small fraction of the world's population of around nine million breeding pairs.

Humboldt penguins are found along the Pacific coast of northern Chile and Peru, with one tiny colony further south on the Island of Chiloe. The total world population of Humboldt penguins is around 12,000 breeding pairs, with about 8,000 of those breeding pairs in Chile. Populations have dropped severely due to the loss of food resources caused by commercial fishing, damage to breeding sites through the removal of guano, and non-native predators.

Gentoo penguins have established two small breeding colonies in Argentina. One colony is on Hammer Island and they can be reached from Ushuaia. They are a bit larger than the Magellanic Penguins and have reddish-orange beaks and orange feet.

Journal

SATURDAY, MARCH 7, 2009. I pried myself out of bed in order to have breakfast, then insisted Ralph go for a walk while I rested until nine. Yesterday, while on the shuttle that took us down the highway to see the penguins, we had passed a cemetery on the outskirts of town. When Ralph returned from his short stroll, we decided to walk to see it.

THE CEMETERY ECHOES the riches that once were here—when sheep barons owned the land in the years before the Panama Canal was built and ships frequently took this more southerly route. Richly decorated crypts and white marble mausoleums remind us of the lavish lifestyle of previous generations. Bronze angels and wrought iron railings abound; cypress trees and plastic flowers provide proof that past and present family members tend the grave sites. When we peek through some of the small glass windows into the large mausoleums, we see photos of the deceased. To me, it is an eerie, but fascinating custom.

The surnames—primarily of German, British, and French origin—tell us of the cultural background, as well as of the present diverse population, of this part of Patagonia. Wanting a less somber set of memories, we head uphill to the mirador, Cerro La Cruz.[4]

FROM THE VIEWPOINT, we had breathtaking views of the Strait, Tierra de Fuego across the water, and the streets and colorful tin roofs and painted houses of Punta Arenas. From there, we headed back down to the city's new waterfront park, and walked along the shore. I appreciated the visionary planning; they've built bike and pedestrian walkways and installed shelters and benches along the way. I considered myself blessed because we were able to enjoy all this with blue skies and minimal wind.

Next time around, I want to visit the *Museo Salesiano de Mayonino Borgatello*. It was started by an order of Italian missionaries in the 1890s. The *museo* (museum) is in a two-story building at 374 Avenida Bulnos. It has exhibits such as a re-creation of the *Cueva de las Manos* (Hands Cave) with its ancient, stenciled handprints, and displays depicting the way of life of the region's indigenous peoples, later explorers, Gold Rush miners, and settlers.

I'd also visit the *Centro Cultural Braun-Menendèz*, at 949 Calle Magallanes, which is housed in a mansion formerly owned by one of the city's most prosperous families. The house, built in 1904, reflects their wealth and style—rooms filled with European antiques and decorated with Italian marble floors and stunning ceiling frescos.

We had a dinner at La Mamacita. It's one of the newer trendy places to eat and serves freshly-prepared seafood. There were also numerous and inexpensive eateries with pizza or breaded or fried cutlets of one kind or another.

Sunday, March 8, 2009. Punta Arenas to Puerto Natales. We caught the 8:30 a.m. bus to Puerto Natales. Very comfortable with a bathroom, AC. There weren't many passengers, which meant that we could move around to look out the different windows. We saw few settlements; mostly we were in open scrubland interrupted occasionally by a cattle or sheep *estancia* (ranch).

After we got to Puerto Natales, which proclaims itself the gateway to the Torres del Paine National Park, we bought tickets for the next stage—another bus ride—to the entrance of the park. From Punta Arenas to the park is approximately 195 miles (315 km.), from Puerto Natales it's about 70 (112 km.). (The Baguales Group site has the clearest bus info that we've found.[5])

We had a couple of hours between bus rides, so we located Casa Cecilia, the hostel where we want to stay after we visit Torres del Paine. We left a deposit for a room (of 32,000 pesos per night) and then were able to put our duffle bag full of city clothes in their storage locker.

Puerto Natales's population is only 18,000. It's a fairly quiet town—that is until a boat comes in with a new shipment of visitors. Then the 200 or so tourists disembark, the local women run down the hill to offer rooms to those without reservations, and it becomes a more chaotic scene. Tourism, fishing, and cattle are the town's chief economic supports.

We walked alongside the *Ultima Esperaza Sound* (Last Hope Sound), an inlet that drains most of the water from Torres del Paine. While following the main road that comes into the center of Puerto Natales, we spotted a giant statue in the center divider. It looked like a bear, but when we got closer, we found out that it was a *milodon* (a prehistoric sloth). The remains of these animals from more than 10,000 years ago were found in a nearby cave in the late 1800s. The cave, the *Monumental Natural Cueva del Milodon,* is only about 15 miles from here.

I was struck by how remote Puerto Natales felt until I considered the fact that it's a seven-hour bus drive[6] from Ushuaia at the southern end of the continent, five or six hours to go the paved 250 miles (400 km.) from Rio Gallegos in the east, or about three hours (15 miles/24 km.) from Punta Arenas to the south. The Navimag ferry from Puerto Montt, Chile takes three nights.

After reaching the edge of town, we turned back in order to find lunch. There were few people on the streets, but we enjoyed looking at their homes. Most are tiny and quaint with

rusted metal roofs, paneled doors, white lace curtains hanging inside the salt-sprayed windows, and surrounded by white
picket fences.

We walked through the Plaza de Armas, passing the ancient
train engine within the city center park, taking a couple of photos of the old blue and white colonial church across the way,
and reached Masay on Manuel Bulnes. The café's décor wasn't
exciting—a utilitarian stainless steel counter, Formica tables
with chairs that could have come from the fifties, and linoleum
floors, but the turkey sandwiches were excellent. They were
made with generous slices of roasted turkey rather than those
awful ultra-thin slices you often get in delis. (I loved the fact that
avocado was plentiful and commonly added to the sandwiches.)
I noted that pizza was also on the menu, and that everything
was budget-priced.

We walked back to the bus station to continue on our
journey to Torres del Paine. Some might find the undulating land
through which we traveled on our second bus ride of the day
boring, but I thought the countryside was beautiful—treeless
plains stretching into the horizon, clear blue skies, and incredible views of mountain ranges. We passed many small herds of
guanacos, small groups of rhea (flightless birds known as *ñandú* in
Spanish), and a lake dotted with pink flamingos. I had been reading about them, so I knew that flamingos are filter feeders and
the microorganisms they eat determine their color—the more
nutrients, the richer their color.

They have a unique process by which they eat. When they
lower their heads into the water, they turn their heads upside
down and move them from side to side to collect a mixture
of water, mud, and food. Then they use their tongues to force
the slurry past what are called the *lamellae* (finger-like projec-
tions) inside the beak. By this process, they filter out the food
particles. Obviously we couldn't see all of this from the bus, but
the next time I go to the zoo, I'm going to watch more carefully.

4 • Adventures in Torres del Paine

The Paine Massif mountain range that composes Torres del Paine National Park differs from most other renowned mountain ranges in that its mountains sit close to sea level. For hikers this makes life easier—they don't have to be concerned with adapting to altitude. The Torres del Paine is a magnificent mountain range within the park of the same name.

The three spikes of *Las Torres del Paine* are Torre Sur, Torre Central, and Torre Norte. The highest is Torre Sur (also known as Torre d'Agonsti), which is 9,350 feet (2850 m). Torre Central is 9,186 feet (2800 m) and Torre Norte (also known as Torre Monzino) is 8,530 feet (2600 m).

Another iconic sight within Torres del Paine is that of *Los Cuernos* (the Horns). These spectacular twisted peaks that we admired for their beauty are also a fine example of how the mountains here were formed by different processes. The lighter color of rock is of volcanic origin. This granite, which is seen in the park's sharp peaks, was once an underground magma chamber. The darker rock, which you see at the tips of Los Cuernos, is layers of softer sedimentary rock.

Erosion of the softer rock by glaciers, water, and wind has created the valleys between the peaks and allowed the system of hiking trails to develop.

Torres del Paine National Park has many hiking trails, but the most popular are part or all of the "W" route and the Circuit (illustrated on the Chapter 12 trail maps—pages 168-169). The "W" consists of three legs (hence its nickname) centered on exploring the valleys and vistas of three spires of the Paine Massif that rise 7,000 feet above the surrounding plains. The left leg (westernmost) goes alongside the Lago Grey to Grey Glacier. The middle leg climbs into the Valle del Francés where at trail's end you'll be in an awe-inspiring cirque formed by towering cliffs. The right leg—which most judge the most difficult hike, climbs to the towers of the Torres del Paine. The vast majority of the park's estimated 130,000 annual visitors do tours, day hikes, or overnight trips that focus on exploring this granite wonderland.

As you'll read about in more detail in Chapter 12, there are some options for seeing the beautiful views that the "W" route offers. Although the trails into the mountains can be covered in three long hiking days, taking five (made possible by staying in refugios or by backpacking and camping along the way), will allow more time to soak in the experience. You will find elevation profiles of both the "W" and Circuit routes on page 164.

The Circuit, our destination, is a multi-day trip that takes you on a circuit around the Torres del Paine massif. It offers views of the mountains that can't be had on the "W" route and it takes you through the more remote backcountry.

A highlight of the Circuit, which those who do only the "W" route miss, is the stiff climb over John Garner Pass and the magnificent views of Glaciar Grey and Lago Grey from that perspective. (John *Garner* Pass is often called John *Gardner* Pass—both on signs in the park and on the official CONAF map—however, the pass was named after British mountaineer and explorer John Garner, who with two local rangers, pioneered this circuit in 1976.) www.smh.com.au/travel/ice-bold-20081113-645i.html

For the Circuit route, you'll need to carry a backpack with supplies for camping or for staying at the refugios along the way. The route is much less crowded than the "W" route. It's only when the trail comes down from Garner Pass and joins with the westernmost leg of the "W" route that backpackers will begin to see dozens of other hikers. That will be a big contrast to the handful of others encountered during the first few days of the circuit.

We discovered early on that most people backpack the Circuit *counter clockwise* and there are several reasons to do so:

- to avoid the strong headwinds that would hit them on the John Garner Pass if they went clockwise;
- to ease into the trek more gradually rather than doing the steepest climbs first;
- because the ascent of John Garner Pass is easier when tackled from the east because it's less steep. (However, this also means that the descent from John Garner will be more difficult and dangerous.);
- because it saves the spectacular panorama of Glaciar Grey from the John Garner Pass for later in the trip.

Journal

March 8, 2009, resumes. Puerto Natales to Torres del Paine. Because the bus had a schedule to keep, there were no stops for photos. It was one of the few times that I wished that we were driving our own car.

After arriving at the Porteria y Guarderia Laguna Amarga entrance station, we had to get off the bus to register and pay entrance fees, which were about 15,000 Chilean pesos (required pesos!) (US $28) each. This is the fee for tourists during the high season, but it's good for the length of your stay. We were relieved to see that there wasn't a long line to do the paperwork because the shuttle to take us into the park was already there and we didn't want it to take off without us.

We noticed that although officially solo trekking is not permitted in the park, there were people traveling on their own. Those who want to backpack alone (not advisable) might not want to mention it at the gate because they might be denied permits. During the height of the season, it should be relatively easy to link up with a partner. (In earlier times, people entering the park without the proper camping equipment were sometimes turned away, but those rules have been eliminated.)

Having already ridden several hours on buses as we made our way from Punta Arenas to Puerto Natales and then Puerto Natales to the park entrance, we were relieved that our third ride, which would shuttle us to our first night's campground, would be a short one. We loaded our backpacks on top of the mini-bus. It was one of those times that you pray that all the connections will mesh and that there will be room for all. Just about the time that everyone had loaded their backpacks atop the van, Ralph remembered that we had put our fleece and rain jackets in the overhead compartment on the bus we had just left. Unfortunately, the bus was gone; it was on its way further into the park.

The good news was that the bus was going to drop people off, then return to our entrance station; the bad news was that the return would be in about four hours. The other bad news was that we had to ask the driver of the shuttle to retrieve our backpacks, which were now buried under a couple dozen other packs. We tried to convince ourselves that this incident did not portend further disasters. We remained optimistic that our clothing would still be where we'd left it when the bus returned.

With most passengers now gone, the entrance station became quiet once again. We poked around the visitor center, which had little more than a couple of faded wildlife posters and a display case filled with insects held in place by straight pins. Judging by the dusty glass and the disintegrated condition of the bugs, I'd guess the natural history display was older than the guards were.

Since we had plenty of time to kill, the guards/rangers suggested we climb the hill behind the station to see the wildlife. We could see a couple of guanacos standing on jutting points high up. We followed a marked trail that took us away from the roads and indeed found many of the camelids grazing. They were quite unconcerned about us and didn't seem to object to posing for photos, but always with their backsides towards us.

"What are we going to do if are jackets aren't on the bus when it comes back?" I asked.

It was sort of a rhetorical question when I made it; neither of us really wanted to think about the steps involved in returning to Puerto Natales or anywhere else to replace our jackets.

"Maybe they'd have something at one of the lodges inside the park," Ralph answered.

We let the topic drop.

Guanacos

Guanacos are native to South America and are found in Bolivia, Peru, Ecuador, Colombia, Chile and Argentina. Torres del Paine and the surrounding arid, mountainous regions have large populations. They are camelids and related to the new world llama, alpaca, and vicuña, and to the old-world camel and dromedary. And like their relatives, guanacos will often spit when threatened. I didn't want to get too close.

They are social animals that live in herds composed either of females, their young and a dominant male, or of bachelor males. They have few predators; however, pumas (mountain lions) will prey on the young. Humans are a threat to some extent—the soft inner hair of the llama's coat is finer than cashmere and the leather of the young is prized. The other human threat is encroachment on their territories. However, there are currently 400,000 to 600,000 guanacos.

Guanacos are well-adapted to their environment. Although they primarily eat grasses and shrubs, they also can lick nutrients and dew from desert cacti. Their red blood cells carry more oxygen than any other mammal —enabling them to survive at high elevations.

Journal resumes

WE CAME BACK down the hill and sat on the wooden steps of the entrance station. The guards, certainly more bored than we, had decided to play soccer. The five-eighths diameter rope that they had strung across the roadway to remind vehicles to stop served as a centerline and they launched into their game.

They were all pretty good, but it's beyond my comprehension how anyone can stop, and return, a ball by using their head. I flinched the one time that the ball came flying my way.

Eventually the big bus returned. We were extremely relieved to find that our jackets were just where we had left them on the rack above our seats. (We vowed never to put anything overhead again, but of course we've broken that promise many times since.)

When the last shuttle of the day returned, we hopped on. After a 20-minute ride, we were dropped off in the camping area near the Refugios Torre. We easily found a campsite. Though the ones with tables and fire pits were taken, there was plenty of room for additional tents in the large grassy area dotted with many trees. We registered at the office, which was in the same building as the showers, toilets, and clothes-washing tubs.

After getting the tent set up and our bags unpacked, we found a shortcut over to the refugio. It was only a five-minute walk on a dirt path through a rocky wash to reach the rustic lodge for dinner. Unfortunately, we were too late for dinner, which had been served in two seatings.

Our only option for dining out was to sit at the bar. We were handed a menu and studied our choices. The server could have saved us the trouble, because when we went to place our order, we were informed that all that was available was a huge plate of French fries topped with three sunny-side up eggs. We each ordered a plateful and quenched our thirst with a beer.

After dinner, Ralph and I discussed our schedule for our time in the park once again. We knew that we wanted to see many of the points on the "W" route as well as complete the Circuit route, and it was time to decide which trail to take first. We decided that tomorrow we'd make the hike in to the Torres Towers (part of the "W" route) because it's often hidden by clouds and right then the weather was perfect. From where we were camped, the trail to the Torres Towers was the closest of the three legs of the "W."

Monday, March 9, 2009. We slept well, except for our restlessness from anticipating the alarm going off; we had a breakfast reservation for 7:30 a.m. Our plan for this part of the trip was to eat breakfasts and dinners at the hostels whenever possible so that we didn't have to carry extra weight in our packs. It was quite a surprise to run into a problem getting dinner last night because we didn't have a reservation. It must be even more crowded at mealtime during the height of the tourist season in this park, which was November-February. Things might have been winding down, but there were still plenty of tourists in the "front" country.

We had just crossed the rocky field separating the campground from the refugio when we turned back to catch a glimpse of the peaks of the nearby mountains. The sky had begun to lighten and we were soon treated to a spectacular sunrise with a red glow reflected onto the Torres Towers.

Ralph tried to hurry me along so that we wouldn't be late for breakfast, but I insisted we stop and take photos. Who could guarantee that we'd ever see such a spectacular sunrise again? This was our real introduction to Torres del Paine, a spectacular mountain massif shaped by glaciers, wind, and water.

When we reached the building, we saw that there was no point in rushing—the kitchen staff had assembled outside to watch the brilliantly-lit sky and mountains.

We were directed to our seats. Seating was on hard, varnished benches on either side of long tables. We were elbow to elbow with whoever appeared. Luckily, we were seated with a couple from Colorado with whom we established an immediate rapport. Deborah and Dennis shared many of our interests; they knew of the Camino de Santiago and have also hiked on it. They have a home near Cahors, which is on the French LePuy route that we have hiked.

I was intrigued with the way that they had arranged their lodging before embarking on this trip—they had set up house trades in both Santiago and Buenos Aires. I was also envious of the fact that they had a month to spend in each place.

Deborah and Dennis also shared our interests in writing and publishing. He had recently published a book about an Iraqi woman being saved by a New York attorney dealing with international matters. *A Thousand Veils*, by D. J. Murphy, may not have been autobiographical, but I'm certain it drew on some of Dennis's experiences while a practicing attorney in Cincinnati, New York City, Paris, and Saudi Arabia.

Servers brought scrambled eggs, small bowls of cornflakes, platters of toast, and pitchers of coffee and plopped them before us. "Do you want hot milk or cold for the cereal?" asked the waitress.

"Cold," I replied. Hot milk on dry cereal sounded yucky to me. But, whichever one you chose, it was poured for you. There was obviously a tight rein on portions!

When we set out on our day's hike, we carried our backpacks—with camping gear and food—in order to be prepared for whatever conditions we found on the trail. We had a couple of alternatives in mind. We either could hike up the right hand leg of the "W" route to the viewpoint of the Torres and all the way back down to our campsite here at Campamento Torres, *or* hike all the way up, but stop midway down at Campamento Chileno—which has both a hostel and a small camping area.

It took us about two and a half hours of hiking to reach Chileno. We were in spectacular country—magnificent scenery everywhere we looked—the rolling hills, the gorge that contains a huge river flowing from the glaciers, the waterfalls, the mountain peaks. I especially liked the forested section near the river, and crossing the wooden bridges that swayed as we crossed was particularly fun—and exhilarating!

Even though we hadn't decided whether to go all the way up to the viewpoint of Torres and back down or not, we decided to set up our tent behind the Chileno refuge. The place allocated for camping had some trees to provide shade, but the ground was nothing more than a dirt patch. There was no windbreak and gusts of wind blew dirt into our faces as we were working. A young man was attempting to sweep the loose dirt into piles, but it seemed like a lost cause. We put most of our gear inside our tent and with lighter loads continued uphill. Besides the obvious advantage of having less weight to carry, we had guaranteed we'd have a camping spot if we did decide to stay at Chileno overnight.

Our climb continued. I began to feel just awful. I could tell that my pulse rate was way too fast; it was pounding in my temples. I tried to measure it, but it was erratic and too fast. I thought I had counted more than 200 beats per minute. Confused, I gave up trying and attempted to resume walking, but I was winded and dizzy and had to stop frequently.

Finally I had to face that fact that I couldn't go on. When we reached the spur trail to the viewpoint, I told Ralph to go on ahead without me. He took some convincing because he wanted us to mark this achievement together, but I finally was able to talk him into doing it for both of us.

I felt pretty devastated at having to give up, but I knew that I couldn't keep up the pace that would be required to go the whole way. After he went ahead, I slowly continued to make my way uphill, but at four o'clock, I stopped and turned around. I asked some other hikers heading up to tell Ralph that I was going back down the hill. The guidebook had suggested allowing two and one-half hours to get back down to Chileno and I knew that it would be dark by eight.

I started down, stopping periodically so that Ralph could catch up. Eventually he did and we continued downhill together. He reported that he had been able to get to the *mirador* (viewpoint), but he said that the last quarter-mile had become increasingly steep and turned into more of a scramble on the loose rock than a hike. He wasn't sure that I could have done it even if I had been feeling well.

It was the first time in my life that I have felt like I was going to pass out while hiking. Even though the trail was trending downhill, there were still brief uphill stretches and even taking six steps uphill would make my heart beat faster than normal. I'd find myself out of breath and have to sit. It couldn't have been the elevation—it's only 2,000-3,000 feet.

By the time we made it back to Chileno at a quarter past seven, I was bushed. Ralph went in to say we'd like dinner in the shelter. At first they refused him because we didn't have reservations. We knew that they had limited food supplies and we could see that most of the places at the long tables were already filled, but Ralph persisted.

"My wife isn't feeling well and needs food," he said.

So, they relented and let us in. Dinner was considerably better than our previous meals in the park had been—or perhaps I was desperately hungry. We had tomato soup, chicken and rice, flan, and rolls. We were all seated at the family-style tables scrunched together—I think the distance between the settings would have failed Emily Post's recommendations for spacing; in fact I think we were closer than we usually are with coach seating on the airlines.

Nevertheless everyone was having a good time—animated gestures, laughing, all talking at once. The young couple seated next to us—he from Belgium, she from Portugal—were friendly and I was glad we could keep up our end of the conversation because we knew something about Fado music from our Camino hiking trip to Portugal in 2007. They talked enthusiastically about trekking in Nepal and I was reminded of another place that I'd like to explore.

Most people were staying in the rooms of the refugio; we went to our tent. It was raining—so at least the dust was no longer an issue. From inside the tent, it was hard to say how much rain was falling because the water first hit the trees, and then plopped onto us.

Tuesday, March 10, 2009. After breakfast of oatmeal, eggs, toast, and juice inside the lodge, we packed up our wet tent and headed back out to Campamento Torres. It may have been downhill overall, but there was a lot of up involved too.

We set up our tent close to where we'd been the first night, and waited to see how I would do. The only thing that bothered me was my bunions. My last-minute switch from trail runners meant that my feet hadn't had enough time to adjust to the heavier, stiffer boots.

My pack had felt heavy all day because of all the extra cold-weather gear I was carrying, but I hadn't had any episodes of being out-of-breath or rapid heartbeat like I did yesterday. My pack was probably close to 30 pounds, more than I had carried in 10 years. I tried to shave off some of the ounces, so I trimmed off the margins of our maps and other papers. I was still wondering if I dared give away any of my warmer clothes.

Dinner was fairly good; we had a huge serving of curry-flavored lamb and rice, with pudding for dessert. Always served with bread and butter, but the bread does not compare with the artisan products we can get in the Bay Area. *Cena* (dinner) was 9,000 pesos each.

I'VE SEEN THE other levels of accommodation. First are the regular shared rooms with bunk beds. At Refugio Torre, there are eight bunks to a room—and I figure it is about US$35 per night. And then there is the Explora lodge across the way that charges a couple of thousand dollars (including meals and guided trips). The Explora also offers its guests massage and other spa treatments (at rates similar to home). While I can't say I hate being pampered and having my every desire taken care of, in this park I prefer to rough it. I want to immerse myself in the unique surroundings and to experience the wilds of the park on our own. One thing I know is that while the views that the Explora's guests have are spectacular, so are ours. And I guess I can put up with being grubby for a while and save two grand a night. Goodness knows if we were staying in the lodge, I'd be stewing about eating too much anyway. Of course I may feel differently if we have rain for hours on end. We are now seeing the hardier types—or at least those with more time. Before we started, it seemed everyone was planning to do the "W" route. That's challenging, but I'm proud of us for attempting the even more ambitious Circuit.

WEDNESDAY, MARCH 11, 2009. Campground near Refugios Torre to Campamento Serón. Our first real day of the Circuit. 10.23 miles (16.5 km.). It rained again last night, but all went well. We also slept well, waking about seven, which allowed us to get to the 7:30 breakfast at the Refugio Torre Central before we left.

BREAKFAST IS ALREADY getting boring—corn flakes, scrambled eggs, weak juice, tea and powdered Nescafé. However, for us the benefits of eating in the refugios whenever possible outweigh the costs. We'll have less weight to carry, and save time and energy by having someone else prepare our meals. Part of Ralph's pre-planning involved researching which refugios along the way (see Chapter 12 for details) *served food and had groceries available.*

We are carrying lunches and snacks for the eight days that we expect to be on our Circuit hike and with a three days' supply of breakfasts and dinners for times when we will be camping without any services nearby. He determined that some of the places we plan to stay had not only campsites, but also lodging. However, we want this to be more of a camping trip than a hostel-to-hostel trip, so we're carrying our tent and plan to camp out all along the route.

We are very excited about starting out on the backpack part of the trip and we weren't disappointed with what we found. The vast expanses and the mountains around us reminded me of Alaska. How is it possible to be so small and insignificant, yet at the same time feel powerful because you are moving through it?

THE HIKE FROM Torres to Serón was not at all difficult. There was some climbing, but most of it was relatively level. The sun was either fully out or peeking through clouds all day. At one point, it was raining on a nearby peak and we felt some of the mist, but luckily we never had to put on more clothes. I wore my T-shirt and long-sleeved blouse the whole way.

The massive Monte Almirante Nieto was the dominant feature for a while, and then we followed the Rio Paine the rest of the way. The river appeared to be running very high—even flooded in places. It was a dark gray-green from the glacial silt it carried. The water was moving very fast; you wouldn't survive very long if you fell in. Luckily the several fords we made weren't of the river, but of its tributaries. The water was only a foot deep at most and the crossings weren't dangerous.

Our time was good. The guidebook said to allow four hours; Ralph had estimated we'd need a bit more than five based on our usual speed, so when we arrived a bit earlier than we'd expected, we were pleased.

When we arrived in camp, there was only one other couple there. Campamento Serón offered meals and what they called a store, but it was quite the outpost. There was one small dilapidated, corrugated metal building. Inside were a kitchen with a long wooden table and benches where meals are served and a private bedroom for the camp host. From the outside, we had access to a small stall with a toilet and another stall with a shower. The washtubs were outside.

It's 4:00 P.M. and there are now nine tents set up. Several parties have come through without stopping. Perhaps they are going on to a free, but unofficial, campground that one of our guidebooks mentions is about three miles ahead.

I keep expecting huge winds. When we arrived, we saw that the picnic table had three huge rocks on it. Silly me, I wondered if they were to hold the table down in a gale. Now I realize that they are a windbreak for the cook stoves.

Everyone else is cooking their own food; we are going to eat inside so we'll have the luxury of someone else preparing our hot meal and of sitting while we enjoy it.

I feel great today—even experienced a runner's high at one point—and can't believe it after Monday's horrible experience. I'm now thinking that it was the result of overexertion—even dehydration—due to the difficultly of the climb of the first day—combined with the heat and humidity.

THURSDAY, MARCH 12, 2009. Campamento Serón to campground at Refugio Dickson. 12 miles (18 km.). Breakfast was again cornflakes, milk, scrambled eggs, juice and tea and toast. My poor stomach. Our host at Serón, Felipe, was an interesting duck—rotund with wild red hair. He's taking a break from teaching high school and college history in Santiago. He nodded his head when I asked if he had to deal with as many behavior problems in Chile's schools as we do in the U.S.

Before he came to this camp, he worked at Camp Chileno (where we had been on Monday night) on the "W" route. Felipe commented, "A madhouse," he commented, "too many people."

He was going to be here for two more weeks. Interesting that the staff is often in the midst of transition, not just the hikers.

Our hike today to Refugio Dickson was through incredibly beautiful country. We were on the trail from nine in the morning to five-thirty in the afternoon, but that allowed for plenty of stops for snacks and photo taking. We hiked along lower slopes of the mountains or on the valley floor with huge mountains—snowcapped or holding glaciers—seemingly everywhere. The vegetation was tough. Although the scrub looked similar to Hebe, or other varieties we might see at home, this one had sharp thorns. The trees had leaves rather than needles.

We never saw the "unofficial" campground along the way. It was interesting to speculate what happened to any hikers who had expected to stop there overnight. Perhaps there used to be more campsites when this area was still in private ownership, but nowadays the park undoubtedly keeps a tighter rein on who camps where. Wildfires are probably the largest threats to the park and the increasing number of visitors to the park increases the risk of such disasters.

The hardest part of the day's hike was going down some of the slopes; several sections of the trail were steep and were of loose rocky soil or rock. It was very scary at times—especially when we were above a cliff where a fall would be disastrous—but Ralph talked me through the bad stretches. The worst one was at the last; we had to get off the *moraine* (an accumulation of rock and other debris deposited by a glacier) that sits above this camp. I couldn't face doing the steep, gravelly downslope upright; my knees were just too tired after twelve miles of hiking. Ralph took both of our packs down and I scooted down some of the way in a crouched position.

There were even fewer campers at Refugio Dickson than there had been at Campamento Serón; no one was staying inside. Tents were hidden amongst the trees, which provided good protection from the elements in the very windswept place. The lake was next door and we were in a bowl surrounded by mountains with their frigid glaciers.

The shower was horrid. The shower stall was enclosed on three sides, but the door looked like something that could have been used in a Western bar. There was a big gap at both top and bottom and the wind whipped through. There was no place to hang my towel or dry clothes inside the stall, so Ralph had to stand outside in the cold wind and hand me things as I needed them.

I so wanted a hot shower and to wash my hair. My hair was a mess not only from hiking and sweating, but also from the grit that the wind carries. The water was warm for about ten seconds, and then turned cold.

But all was saved with a tasty, warm dinner of lamb, veggies with mushrooms, and canned peaches. After dinner, we moved to the upholstered chairs so that I could read and write in my journal. Being indoors with the cozy woodstove was a lot more enticing than returning to our tent, which was sitting in the rain and wind.

Two *joven* (young men) ran the whole operation—the store, the cooking and serving, and the issuing of bunks. One showed me a game called, appropriately, the Ring Game. (Here it's used to while away the hours, but after we saw it again later on during our trip, I realized that it's a popular bar game, too.) On one wall was a metal hook screwed in about six feet off the floor. A string with a metal ring on it hung from a rafter in the middle of the room.

To play the game, you sit opposite the wall with the hook on it and release the string with the ring on it so that it swings as a pendulum toward the hook. If you manage to get the ring on the hook, you win the game.

When I made the catch on the third try, everyone applauded! No one was more surprised than I was; you can be sure I didn't try to repeat my feat.

(I later learned that this game has been played by Patagonian gauchos for generations. Like any game played in a bar, it was not unusual for the contest to end in a dispute and sometimes the fights ended in a death. Traditionally when someone managed to make the ring in three or less attempts, they get a free shot of a sugar cane drink.)

When we made our way back to our campsite, we noticed that the stars were hidden behind dark clouds. We collected the damp laundry from the line, checked that the tent stakes were securely in place, tucked our hiking poles and water bladders (flat water containers) close to the tent, and zipped ourselves into our warm bags. During the night it started to rain like mad—torrential—beyond anything I'd ever seen. I started to wonder if the river could flood, so of course I had to wake Ralph and ask him. "No," he answered.

But, as usual, I wasn't convinced. It might be the case that he is usually right about such things, but I'm always anticipating a time that he'll be wrong and I'll perish.

I started feeling around the floor of the tent on my side to see if there was any water seeping underneath. I pressed down; it felt like I was pushing down on a waterbed. Oh! my god, I thought. I switched on my flashlight to see if the tent was leaking or where else the water might be coming from.

Ralph leaned over and pressed down where I had been feeling the accumulated water.

"I think it's your water bladder," he said.

Oh! disaster averted. At times like these, I wonder how my husband puts up with me. We both slept well after that.

Friday, March 13, 2009. Dickson to Los Perros campground. 5.4 miles (8.7 km.). According to the Lonely Planet guidebook, the hike was to take three-and-a-quarter to four-and-a-quarter hours, but it took us more than seven. We had no way of knowing ahead of time how well the suggested times would work for us, but luckily Ralph had had the foresight to anticipate this kind of situation; he had allocated about half again as much time for each day's hike. This much longer hiking day came as a surprise, but it wasn't disastrous. (We have since learned that we weren't the only ones that ran into this.)

There were several factors that contributed to our slower-than-expected progress. It wasn't the elevation gain—although the path follows an uphill, undulating course the entire way. Primarily it was the condition of the trail. It rained most of the day and that, combined with last night's deluge, turned the trail into a watercourse. We spent a lot of time picking our way around the puddles. This wasn't strictly necessary, we could have waded through, but we weren't in a hurry.

Even with the rain, it wasn't unpleasant hiking. Most of the time we were going through forest, so we were at least shielded from the brunt of the wind. At lunchtime the rain conveniently stopped for a short time, and we were able to sit trailside for our snacks. A trio of Magellanic woodpeckers was hard at work high up in a nearby tree searching for grubs and insects. I tromped through the wet vegetation to take photos. These are large birds, almost 15 inches long. And like Woody of cartoon fame, they (the males) are almost all black with a red head and crest.

Woodpeckers can be such a pain. Most birds fly away when they feel you are too close, but woodpeckers seem to be a tease. Just as you locate them and try to take a photo, they spiral around to the far side of the tree. If you try to move around to a better vantage point, they once again move so that the tree shields them from you. I managed a few blurry shots for the collection.

The drizzle started again after lunch. My rain jacket works well, but I don't particularly like wearing the hood, so whenever the rain decreased, I would throw back the hood. Invariably then the wind would rustle through the trees and the leaves would dump cold water down the back of my neck. Nevertheless, I was content because I was warm and dry underneath.

After the third bridge crossing of the raging river, we reached timberline and lost the protection of the forest. Ahead lay a ridge of rocks—a moraine at the base of Los Perros glacier—that we had to make our way over. The wind, hitting us from ever-changing directions, was intense. I couldn't make any headway. The trail, which had been obvious in the forest, became a faint network of paths and we couldn't pick out which was the best one to follow. Ralph went ahead following a few fluorescent pink plastic flags that indicated one path.

Tiring from my struggle, I made the mistake of sitting down—a mistake because the wind wouldn't let me get back up. As I surveyed my surroundings, the thought came that I was going to have to spend my night on the rock pile. For an instant I was okay with that, but then reality took over and I knew that I had to move on because I wouldn't be able to survive an overnight stay in such an exposed, cold, and windy place.

Since Ralph was ahead of me, he hadn't realized for a few minutes that I wasn't right behind him. When he saw that I had stopped because I was struggling, he came back to help me regain my footing. For sure, getting up from a sitting position in a gale wind was no picnic.

"I'll go ahead and take my backpack over the top of the moraine and put it in a secure place. Then I'll come back and help you with your pack," he said.

While I waited for him to come back again, I had time to wonder if I would be able to ascend further and into potentially stronger winds. But, when Ralph came back to lead the way, I managed to make it up and over the rocks.

After passing over the ridge, the winds decreased and we were able to continue on more easily. We soon reached the section of the path alongside the river. We thought we had about 30 minutes more of hiking to get to the camp at Los Perros.

A man came down the trail toward us; I asked how far it was to the camp. At first I thought what he had said was, "Fifty minutes," and I was crushed.

Then it registered, he had said, "Fifty meters." He added, "You get to have the seat closest to the stove."

When we reached the campground, we found a sheltered site amongst the trees, and set down our backpacks. We paid the camping fee at the *tienda* (store) and Ralph started to set up the tent. I headed for the shelter.

All of the locations on the Circuit so far had had shelters, outbuildings that might also be called warming huts, where you could get out of the wind and rain and cook your meals and dry out a bit, perhaps even sleep in an emergency. So as I approached the entrance to the large, green metal hut of Los Perros, I expected to find a couple of people sitting by the fire. I opened the door and was hit with a blast of moist heat.

There must have been twenty people inside either sitting at the long, wooden picnic tables cooking dinner over their camp stoves or standing near the wood-burning stove warming their bodies. Clotheslines of twine or cord were strung around the perimeter of the circular hut with rain jackets, shirts, and socks hung up to dry. Heavy boots were resting by the fire; the hikers had traded their wet boots for Crocs, sandals, or trail runners.

I was so happy to be safe, dry, warm, and in the company of others.

Fine dining - a tablecloth

Lago Paine

5 • Retracing our Steps

Saturday, March 14, 2009. Los Perros to Dickson. Last night I collected names from several of the hikers because I wanted to write about this trip. It was the best evening of the hike so far because we were all jammed in together and I finally had a chance to talk to everyone. There were some that we had seen before and thought were snobbish—including one of the German women. Now that I've had a chance to be around her more, I've decided that she just isn't as comfortable with English, or perhaps not just as outgoing as her husband. She has been, however, friendly. It was a reminder to me not to be so quick to judge.

I talked with a group of three backpackers, Rose, Henry, and Susan, from the Monterey area on California's Central Coast. It was going to be their second night at Perros camp; they hadn't set out in the morning because it had been snowing on the pass. They weren't the only ones to stay put, several people had.

Some in the group were concerned about the well-being of a couple of men who had set out in the morning in spite of the poor conditions. The two were wearing cotton T-shirts, no boots, and were inexperienced. Word had yet to come about their progress.

Ralph pointed out that we were lucky that most people had English as a second language, because otherwise we wouldn't be able to talk to anyone. We'd met mostly Germans, but also hikers from Norway, Belgium, and Portugal. I had expected most hikers to be either European or South American, but we've seen a higher percentage of Americans than I thought there'd be.

This morning our alarm went off at 6:40 a.m. I hate having to wake to an alarm any time, but even more so when we're on a trip. Yet we wanted to get an early start and that meant getting up before the sun. It hadn't rained during the night, but due to the early hour and the sky being its usual gray, we couldn't tell what the weather would bring.

Ralph and I had to make a final decision—whether or not to proceed. We'd known from the early days of planning this trip that the weather or the trail conditions could be against us. As with any trail that we've taken, we'd had to evaluate prior to the hike whether or not we could do it. Obviously we wouldn't have started out on this one if we hadn't thought we were prepared, but I have had a degree of uncertainty about this route all along.

Further, I'd had three episodes that had eroded my confidence. First was the hike that we tried on the first day—hiking to the Towers of Paine—where I had experienced the yet unexplained fatigue and weakness. Second was going down the steep slope into Refugio Dickson—where I had to slip and slide because my knees weren't strong enough for me to handle a controlled descent. Third was yesterday's incident on the moraine—my difficulty dealing with the wind.

(author's note: Two years later we figured out what probably caused my weak spell. After a brief reoccurrence of the symptoms the following year, and numerous tests including a heart rate stress test, EKGs, echocardiogram, etc., it was determined that this had been an episode of atrial heart fibrillation. Luckily, since that time, I've backpacked hundreds of miles of demanding trails, and my doctor not only approves, but also encourages me to continue.)

We re-evaluated the facts. At 3,872 feet (1,180 m) high, the John Garner Pass is the highest and most remote point of the Torres Del Paine Circuit. Yet, it's not the elevation that's an issue for me—I've been at four times that altitude and had no ill effects—it's that I don't think that I'm strong enough to buck the winds going up the pass much less handle snow and wet trail on the descent.

Ralph mentioned that because we hike more slowly than the twenty- and thirty-year-olds, we would be in the exposed sections a longer time. I think he was being kind; he's in his 70s and doesn't show much sign of slowing down. It's me, at age 68, who has slowed down and has less strength than I used to. Having experienced how exhausting it is struggling against the winds for even a few minutes, I was not willing to put us in that situation for a couple of hours.

Everything we had read to this point said not to try to go over the John Garner Pass when it is raining or snowing because you might be exposed to gale force winds, and because of the slippery, steep descent. I recalled that some of the hikers we talked to last night in the warming hut had said that the blizzard conditions they encountered trying to cross over the pass had forced them to turn back.

So ultimately, I had to make the final call. I was the one who would have the most difficulty. I didn't want to put my well-being at risk; I didn't want Ralph to put himself at added risk trying to help me. We agreed to turn back.

We went into the hut to fix breakfast and take down our somewhat drier laundry. Word had come that the two ill-equipped hikers had made it safely over the pass. Everyone but us was going to go over Garner Pass. It was hard to hold back the tears while I told a few people we weren't going, but it helped when Rose, part of the three-some from Monterey, said, "Too much fun for one day?" Laughing was better than crying.

IT IS MY *birthday and backtracking to Dickson isn't how I thought we'd spend the day. We are supposed to be congratulating ourselves on making it over the pass. But, although I am shedding some tears about our disappointment, our descent is spectacularly beautiful. Our sense of missing out on what would have been the next exciting point on the trail is more than compensated for by the fact that we can now see the surrounding snowcapped peaks, several glaciers, and waterfalls. Yesterday they were hidden by the rain and fog.*

SINCE WE WEREN'T feeling any time pressures—turning back would take fewer days than continuing on would have—and because it was a sunny day without a cloud in the sky, we were able to take our time and take lots of photos. There was no cold water dropping from the trees and down our backs, and surprisingly, the mud puddles had drained a lot.

We had fun making tons of stream crossings on logs and rock hopping—always challenging and exhilarating at the same time. I was very proud of myself for doing all of the stream crossings on my own, and I was able to walk across on the logs without having to take off my backpack. The only bad thing that happened was that I dropped my prescription sunglasses somewhere along the way and even though I back-tracked a half-mile, they seemed lost forever. I didn't have spare ones, but luckily, I had the glacier glasses that I used on Kilimanjaro.

Back at Dickson, we were served seafood stew over mashed potatoes, bread, and canned pineapple for dinner. It might seem less than gourmet, but the stew was delicious and any fruit when we were camping was a genuine treat.

Sunday, March 15, 2009. Hike Dickson back to Campamento Serón. We set out at ten in the morning, and except for the last half hour before our five o'clock finish time, it rained the entire day. We had plenty of water puddles to avoid, so considering that, I think we did pretty well time-wise.

The rain could have made the hike miserable, but since it was light and we were warm, we were fine. Ralph had been perfectly happy in his trail runners—sometimes with regular socks, sometimes with his liner socks. I, however, was glad that I made my last minute decision to wear boots. For the most part, I had no problems with my feet. I occasionally had some pain from my bunions, but no blisters. Perhaps because it was not hot?

The only animals we saw today day were two birds—a raptor while we were leaving Dickson and a small bird on the trail near here that we couldn't identify. It seemed unusual to encounter birds so unafraid of humans; I was able to get within twenty feet of the *Carancho* (also called the *Caracara*, which means carrion hawk). It looked somewhat like a large chicken. With its bright coloring—long yellow legs and an orange and white band on its beak—it was hard to miss.

So now we were back at Campamento Serón with Felipe. It was breezy and sunny for a couple of hours, so we were able to dry our stuff out somewhat. We met Mara, a very forthright woman, from Boston, who is camped near us. She was going to turn back because of a knee injury. Her hiking credentials are impressive: she's done the Appalachian Trail one-and-a-half times and the Pacific Crest Trail from Campo to Mt. Whitney. She was very self-sufficient and a bit pushy, but she was friendly with everyone and I enjoyed talking with her.

I'm SURPRISED HOW *many people are still coming in. There are more tonight than when we were here before—perhaps 25-30. The refugio is festooned with wet clothing hung by all of us. It's so humid inside the kitchen that I feel as if I am in a sauna.*

Felipe's kitchen is messy, but he cooks a good meal on the antiquated cast iron stove. We're having tomato soup, chicken, mixed vegetables, and fruit cocktail. We're splurging on beer.

MONDAY, MARCH 16, 2009. Campamento Serón to Refugios Torre. Last night was "just right" (sort of like Baby Bear's porridge!) in the tent. We had gone from hot to close-to-freezing while doing our semi-circuit and needed a different mix of clothing each night. The vapor barrier liners that we slipped into our sleeping bags were not only to keep us warmer, but also to prevent our sleeping bags from becoming damp from condensation (which would reduce their efficiency). We learned that it was important not to breathe into the liners or to wear so much clothing that we started sweating. When we introduced too much moisture into the liners, we felt as if we were in wet cocoons. Once we figured that out, the system worked great.

Ralph crawled out of the tent during the wee hours. When he came back, he said, "I got up to pee and, of course, I tried to keep my back to the wind. By the time I finished, I had done a complete circle!"

I started out today wearing rain pants, but the skies mostly stayed blue, and it became hot as the day wore on, so I soon packed them away. As we climbed up the hills from Serón, I felt increasingly felt guilty about something I said to another hiker a couple of days ago. The woman, who was exhausted from that day's hike, asked about this part of the trail and I told her that it was "pretty flat and easy." I wasn't lying to her—it was how I remembered it.

Now that we have done it a second time and the memory is fresh in my mind, I realize that though it was the easiest day, it was certainly not flat. All I could do was hope that she was rested enough the next day and that the ups and downs were not a problem.

We had strong winds in a few sections, but since we weren't near any drop-offs, it was not a big deal. We took about six hours because there were tons of stops for photos.

The vegetation had been all new to us—the deciduous trees, the profusion of white blossoms that look like daisies but have fern-like leaves, and plants that look like Hebe, but have sharp spiny thorns. When I had on my rain pants today, I noticed that I have a rip that I must have gotten from those thorns. The thorns of the shrubs, the rounded shapes of other plants that can better withstand the wind, and the vegetation that has fleshy leaves that can hold moisture are all adaptations to the climate.

IT'S WONDERFUL TO be back at Refugio Torre with a few of the amenities of the front-country. This time we're staying inside in Refugio Torres instead of camping at the nearby Torres campground. There are ten rooms, each with three sets of bunk beds, so we might have roommates, but so far so good.[7]

The best part is being able to take a hot shower without freezing in the process. I have managed to wash almost all of my clothes and they are drying in a hidden spot behind the building. It's also nice to discard the pee-pots (repurposed quart-sized yogurt containers), but how I loved having them so that I didn't have to get out in the weather in the middle of the night.

WE WERE GOING to be here two nights and we'd decided to take an expensive tour—a van ride to see more of the park and then a boat trip on Lago Grey. It was going to cost about US$360. If we'd continued on the Circuit, we would have seen Lago Grey and Glaciar Grey from the trail, but since we didn't continue, this is our only option with our limited time. We have to get back to Puerto Natales on Wednesday.

It was hard to spend that much money when we'd been doing the economical hiking and camping, but not knowing what next year will bring—if we'd be able to return to see the tremendous amount we'd not seen—and considering the effort and time involved in getting here—I can at least rationalize such an expense. I'm feeling pulled between the two major groups of travelers here—those who'd think nothing of dropping thousands of dollars to stay at Explora—and the hitchhiking set that wouldn't dream of it.

OUR TIME HERE has flown by. It feels unreal; I love this park and wish we could spend months down here. It's strange to consider how rapidly the weather changes and that this is only the end of summer; winter must be brutal. Ralph and I joke about how people from Germany, Holland, England, Norway, and the other northern countries as well as those from much of the U.S. are much more accustomed to this sort of harsh weather than we Bay Area folk are. We're definitely spoiled.

TUESDAY, MARCH 17, 2009. At the Refugio Torre. Our first night back in "civilization" reminded us of one of the reasons we like to camp in the wilderness—we can usually avoid inconsiderate people. There was no one in the dorm room when we checked in or when we went to bed, but a few hours later, a guy came in, flipped on the overhead light (instead of using a flashlight), and went about noisily unpacking and apparently oblivious to the fact that we were trying to sleep. Luckily I had earplugs and was able to sleep fairly well even though he snored all night.

Today's guided van tour took us along the south side of the park. Our tour guide, Francesco, was quite knowledgeable and we gave him a workout because although the one other couple also spoke English, the woman traveling on her own spoke only Spanish. Francesco had to repeat everything.

We stopped at a couple of lakes and drove by others. The Pehoé area was interesting and we saw that there was a boat ride available on that lake, too. We took a brisk walk to viewpoints of Salto Grande and Salto Chico. They are both wide waterfalls and carry an impressive amount of water. What makes them unusual—at least for this park—is that they are basically at your feet rather than coming off a distant mountainside. The site is popular with tourists, but it was extremely windy and most people took a look and then scurried back to their cars or coaches. We lingered a bit longer and were rewarded by seeing a rainbow form over Salto Grande.

The tour gave us a glimpse of some of the other lodges and accommodations including the luxury hotel, Explora, and some of the newest campgrounds, which have shelters complete with roofs to shield tents from the weather.

When we were on the steppes, the grassy open areas, Francesco pointed out a particular thorny, rounded shrub—one that we had seen numerous places during our circuit. He told us that its nickname is "Pillow of mother-in-law." It seems that mothers-in-law are regarded as prickly in many cultures!

We saw a few kinds of birds and dozens of guanacos. Francesco was quite knowledgeable about the guanacos. We learned that they live in the steppes where they can eat the yellow grasses, and they take dust baths much the same as llamas do. They mate December to February, and the female ovulates at the time of mating. During the mating season, the males will gather a harem of up to 25 females. It reminded me of the harems of Tule elk at Point Reyes National Seashore in Marin County, California.

Francesco said that the major threat to the guanaco is the puma. Pumas can be found in both forests and steppes. They hunt solo and make their nighttime kills in a distinctive manner. Although usually they strike at the back of the neck, sometimes they rip out the front of their prey. The male and female have different ways of making use of a kill—the male eats the thighs of the guanaco, and the female eats the other parts.

We had lunch near Portería y Guardería Serrano, the southernmost entrance station of the park. From the picnic tables at Posada Serrano, we were able to watch the ducks and other water birds in Lago Toro.

We continued on to the hostería at Lago Grey where we were to start the tour of the lake and the glacier. The lodge sits on the lake, so the views were amazing; from the dining room we looked through large windows at the lake and the surrounding mountains.

Francisco went to the reservation desk to register us for the boat ride, but apparently there had been some mix-up. My Spanish failed me, so I never did understand the details, but we could see that there was quite a heated discussion. It was all sorted out and then Ralph and I were directed to the boat ramp.

It wasn't a simple matter of walking down a nearby ramp and boarding—rather, we had a thirty-minute hike to reach the ramp. We were along the shoreline most of the time, but then we had to cross a wooden bridge. We were only allowed on the bridge six at a time—sort of like soldiers breaking cadence—so that the bridge would not fail. I was glad that there was safety netting on the sides because the water was choppy and cold.

When we reached the Lago Grey's boat ramp, we were issued lifejackets and put on a Zodiac to be ferried to a catamaran. It was fun bouncing through the water on the Zodiac—even when a wave hit us broadside and drenched those of us in the front. Luckily, it was only a short ride to reach the larger craft. Hands reached out to firmly grip our arms as we climbed aboard the rolling catamaran. None of us had our sea legs, so we all staggered forward to grab hold of anything to steady ourselves as we headed out to see Glaciar Grey.

The first half-hour of our catamaran ride was against the current and it was both exciting and a bit unnerving. As we made our way through it, the water continually splashed over the forward deck and completely over the front windows. We were told that no one could go outside while we were underway. However, the guide told us that these conditions were normal and I felt reassured. The boat seemed stable and was making headway.

After we went through a narrow passageway between rocks, the water became calm. Most people climbed topside to take in the scenery and to take photos. We were able to pick out Refugio

Grey on the shoreline, one of the places we would have stayed if we had continued the Circuit, but we couldn't see the trail.

It was thrilling to come right up to the foot of Glaciar Grey. We were on a good-sized vessel, with dozens of passengers, but we were a minute speck in comparison to this river of ice. The glacier was stunningly beautiful. The closer we got to it, the more clearly we could see the unique twisted shapes that form in the ice as it is pushed forward by the force of the ice field behind it. The boat moved slowly alongside the base of the glacier and allowed us different vantage points from which we could peer into the intensely dark blue recesses.

I'd walked on glaciers before, but this was not one a novice would go on unassisted. The guided glacier hikes on Glaciar Grey offer participants crampons, ropes, and other specialized climbing equipment. I thought they were kidding when they said we were going to have Pisco Sours made with chunks of ice that had fallen from the glacier, but it was true. I could learn to love Pisco Sours.

We had one hour alongside the glacier, which seemed to zip by in a millisecond. We took lots of photographs, but I know that they can never capture the emotions that being next to the glacier brings forth—mainly joy and awe. I felt so incredibly privileged to have been able to be there.

Our return trip was another hour and it gave us amazing views of the side of the Torres range. Being able to see the iconic chocolate-colored peaks of Cuernos and have views toward the Valle del Francés was such an intense pleasure that I could have died right then with no regrets.

We got back in time for a dinner of focaccia (pizza), chicken, potatoes au gratin, and pudding. We took showers and washed clothes. It had been a long day, but amazing. I was relieved that we didn't have a roommate again.

Wednesday, March 18, 2009: Torres del Paine to Puerto Natales. After our good night's sleep and breakfast, we packed and walked to the Las Torres Hostería (hotel).[8] It was not far from where we had stayed—less than a mile on level ground. We had a few hours to kill because we'd checked out of the hostel and the shuttle van wasn't due until 2:00 p.m. It would take us back to the entrance station at Laguna Amarga to meet the bus to return us to Puerto Natales. Tomorrow we plan to go on toward Los Glaciares (home of Fitz Roy and Glaciar Perito Moreno), if all goes according to plan. One never knows.

While waiting, we used the hotel's computer and I sent a mass e-mail and personal notes to a couple of people. It was a relief that the keypad had the characters in the location we were used to; we've taken trips to European destinations and found the keys in different configuration, which is very frustrating.

We ate our lunch snacks on the hotel's porch, and then walked over to the stables. There were about twenty horses, including two frisky colts, and it was captivating to watch the gauchos working them.

The three gauchos were training some of the horses inside the corral, and then leading them out. Finally the men let all of the horses out and chased them up the hill behind the building. The dreamlike image of the running horses, manes and tails flowing behind them, the colorfully-clad riders shouting and spurring the beautiful animals on with their lariats was transfixing.

While I stood there trying to keep the menagerie in sight as long as possible, Ralph was watching condors over a more distant hill. We tried to photograph them, but our cameras weren't up to the challenge of shooting from so far away.

There was some sadness about leaving; I could easily have spent six months. It reminded me of Alaska's interior in that everywhere you looked was drop-dead gorgeous. On top of that, we had met many fascinating people. When we heard about other interesting places they had visited, we wanted to add a few new destinations to our wish lists.

The shuttle arrived on time and took us the short distance to the entrance station. My favorite part along the route was when we had to go over the narrow suspension bridge. Because the shuttle bus had only a couple of inches clearance on either side, the driver had to stop the bus, hop out and pull in the side mirrors, then jump back in the bus and continue on. Interestingly, there was a sign posted on the bridge indicating that passengers should climb out when buses crossed the bridge, but that warning apparently is sometimes heeded and sometimes ignored.

After safely arriving at the entrance station, we joined passengers from other coaches and climbed onboard ours from the Gomez line. This bus challenged the stereotypes about buses in South America. The upholstered seats were clean and comfortable; there were curtains on the windows, AC and heat, and a TV and toilet. We found that the schedules were reliable. Although they may be unreliable in other places, here we were impressed by the fact that the schedule for the shuttle inside the park was synchronized to get travelers to the gate just a few minutes before the coach's departure at 2:30 p.m.

As the bus started out on the gravelly road, which eventually turned to asphalt, many people started to nod off. The two-hour ride gave me time to ponder why some people grab the window seat and then proceed to sleep the whole time. I can't even comprehend sleeping a moment during a ride through this stark, windswept, tantalizing country.

We stopped midway back to Puerto Natales to use the restrooms and get snacks. We ran into six of our warming hut (Los Perros) friends as well as the weird guy from Lake Tahoe, so we had a mini-reunion. They all agreed that going forward and over John Garner Pass had been a wonderful experience, but two of them said that they had been blown over on the ascent. I was not even feeling envious of them; I sensed that Ralph and I were coming back.

6 • Onward to Argentina

Journal

Thursday, March 19, 2009. Puerto Natales to El Calafate. We arrived back at Puerto Natales at 4:30 p.m. yesterday and checked in at the Casa Cecilia. We retrieved our "in town" nicer clothes that they had stored in a cupboard for us. Casa Cecilia is one of several budget places to stay in town. It's a level of accommodations that doesn't fit with star ratings systems and so you can find a mixed bag. The bathroom was modern, the bedroom is okay, but the bed was annoying. It was noisy, the flimsy sheet wouldn't stay tucked in, and the comforter weighed a ton. But it was a bed!

We had only a short time before dark last night in which to walk around, but because the town is small and we were staying only a couple of blocks from the commercial section and the lake, we saw the highlights. The view across the lake was picture-postcard beautiful: the water at our feet, black-necked swans, shorebirds and ducks near the shore, and a range of mountains across the strait.

Up early this morning after a restless night worrying about whether or not the alarm would work; we had to get to the bus station before eight. On top of that, the wind rattling the windows was worrisome. I tried telling myself that they had withstood far worse, but I continued to wonder if this would be the time they would be blown in.

RALPH HAS A cold and a temperature, so he feels lousy. He's driving me crazy with his sniffing and I am already feeling grumpy because I hadn't slept well.

We're now en route to El Calafate (pronounced "L Cal-a-fa-te"). We left the bus station at 8:00 a.m. and by 9:15 a.m., we had reached the border between Chile and Argentina where we had to go through Chilean immigration. Unlike the border crossing between Peru and Bolivia that we made several years back, the Chilean/Argentine immigration offices sit miles apart rather than mere yards apart.

CONSIDERING THE HISTORY of conflict between Chile and Argentina—particularly the disputes over the border—I wasn't sure how a border crossing would go. Shortly before Ralph and I left for this trip, we were pursuing anything we could get our hands on so that we'd have a clearer understanding of what to expect of Patagonia.

One of the things we found was a movie entitled *Mi Mejor Enemigo* (My Major Enemy) that takes place during a border dispute between Chile and Argentina in the 1970s. It was worth seeing not only because of the drama—the small group of Chilean soldiers learned about their enemy's humanity—but also because of the irony—they couldn't figure out where the disputed border was because it all looked the same.

I enjoyed seeing the countryside—the *pampas,* the Patagonia grasslands, seemed to stretch to the horizon. The grasses constantly bend from the wind—a visible reminder of the noisy and pervasive force that has been said to literally drive men mad.

How the governments of countries treat each other is not always how the citizens of those countries feel about each other, so we weren't sure how the peoples of Chile and Argentina get along—did they harbor ill feelings towards one another, or was it ancient history? Not knowing, I have just avoided mentioning one country to the people of the other.

Once again the details of our bus ride may be disappointing to those who were hoping to read about horrible bus trips in Latin America. No vicarious thrill of riding with a crazed driver taking riders on a harrowing journey on mountain roads with hairpin turns. No tales of fellow passengers lashing wooden crates atop the bus and letting their chickens run about the bus. No, none of that; the motor coach was all very civilized with clean, upholstered, reclining seats; an overhead shelf (the sort where we had inadvertently left our rain jackets earlier); adjustable curtains at the windows; and a Plexiglas sealed-off compartment for the driver.

The highways were more than decent—where completed— even superior to those in many parts of the U.S. It seemed that an ongoing major investment had been made in highway construction in these parts; it was going on everywhere. Their method of building highways was much different than ours; they're constructed a section at a time of concrete slabs rather than with long strips of rolling asphalt. I wish I had a better understanding of the economics of providing full employment because it certainly seemed like their public works projects kept a lot of people off the dole.

We came to a "T" intersection and an outpost that we passed yesterday, but this time we were on a different branch of the road. The bus rolled to a stop near a restaurant and gift shop, but we weren't stopping for food; we were here to go through Chilean immigration. The 40+ passengers filed off of the bus and went into the office.

As I was waiting, I wondered idly about what seemed to be a large gap in the security measures. We were supposed to get off, but there was no search of the bus to be sure no one had stayed aboard. However, the processing went quickly and I was able to head for the restroom (The bus has a toilet, but they're usually awkward to use.) When entering, I had my usual anxieties about foreign restrooms.

The first question on my mind was "Would there be toilet paper?" There was, but rather than in the stalls, it was in a large dispenser just inside the bathroom door. Woe to the person who failed to grab some before entering the stall! The second question was "Where do I put the used toilet paper?" As in many countries south of the border, the custom appeared to be that you should put the paper in the provided wastebasket rather than flush it down the toilet.

When we reached Argentina's immigration, we climbed out, passports in hand and once again formed a queue. Those first in line were able to enter the small building's lobby and a second small group managed to get into an anteroom, but the majority of us were stuck outdoors where the wind was blowing like mad and flinging sand into our faces.

I eventually took refuge behind a wall where the sun's warmth could be enjoyed and I was protected from the winds. Slowly but surely, several other women joined me. When Ralph reached the anteroom, I rejoined him. I was even a bit pushy; I suggested to others that they squeeze in tighter to let those outdoors have some protection.

On one side of the lobby was the immigration officer sitting at his cage with two other employees watching over his shoulder. As each newcomer approached, he would shuffle through the pages of the passport, look at the papers we had filled out giving our destination, and make the required stamps. He also checked our names against the bus's manifest to see that we were legal. It seemed odd that the names were not also checked against a "wanted" list, but I doubt that many criminals would try getting across the border this way.

On the other side of the lobby was a similar cage, this one with a small sign above it reading "Customs." The customs office was not busy; no one waited in line to see them—instead, the officers were playing Ping-Pong.

We reached El Calafate, where we planned to stay for two nights while we took day trips to Argentina's Los Glaciares National Park. It was in a beautiful setting on Lago Argentina, but the landscape was arid and wind-swept. Outside of town the vegetation was dry and low growing, but with habitation came modification and there were roses and stately poplars in the center of town and landscaped yards. The houses on the hillsides sat on their plots like those on the outskirts of Las Vegas—no fences, sort of forlorn.

El Calafate takes its name from the calafate plant; calafate is also the symbol of Patagonia. The calafate plant (*Berberis buxifolia*) is an evergreen shrub with edible berries (somewhat like blueberries) that are used to make jam. You'll not find it difficult to find a jar in town. There's a saying that eating the calafate berry guarantees that you will return to Patagonia; I wish that we had eaten several spoonfuls on our morning's croissants.

When we reached El Calafate we were hungry, so our first stop was for lunch. La Cocina served a wonderful salad with carrots, apples, and grapes. All this fresh produce was especially welcome after the heavy meat, potatoes, bread, and canned everything else we'd been having for the last week and a half.

We continued on to our lodging. The room was quite reasonably priced (110 Argentine pesos/US$37 per night). Nothing fancy—plain white walls, motel décor— but it was clean and had an updated bathroom with attractive tile, a bidet, and a great shower.

Later we ventured out again. The town's population was only about 8,000, so was small and easily walkable. The small commercial district came as kind of a surprise. We expected a city with a frontier feel—instead we could have been in a small version of Santa Fe, New Mexico or Truckee, California. Liberator, the main street and major route through town, was lined with trendy restaurants, art and souvenir shops, outdoor adventure stores, and tour guide companies.

The shops in town offered a variety of interesting goods and services, and I admired the workmanship of the silver and turquoise jewelry, leather clothing, and tooled belts with ornate buckles. There were, of course, the usual shops selling souvenirs: machine-made ceramic salt and pepper shakers, T-shirts, and postcards that one finds in any touristy town.

We were curious about the beverage *mate* (pronounced "MAH-tay"), but never got around to trying it. It's a caffeinated drink that you'll see enjoyed in much of South America. Mate is the national drink of Argentina and commonly drunk in Chile. It has many things in common with tea; the taste has been described as a cross between green tea and coffee, with hints of tobacco and oak. Like tea, it can be purchased in bags, but it's best prepared by steeping the leaves (*yerba mate*) in hot water. And finally, it is traditionally prepared and served with much ceremony.

We saw displays of the container (also called *mate*) in which it is served in all of the marketplaces. These came in multiple versions—from the traditional calabash gourd, sometimes coated with silver or leather, to those made of wood or clay. Some were left plain; others were personalized with silver initials or decorated with other motifs.

To drink mate, you use a *bombilla* (a special straw), which can be made of various metals such as stainless steel or the more pricey silver. The *bombilla* differs from a regular straw because the end that is in the beverage has a flared end with small holes that filter out any larger particles of the yerba mate leaves. After we returned home, I decided to learn more about it.

The Mate ceremony

Mate is a beverage consumed throughout much of South America. It's prepared by steeping the leaves of the yerba mate in hot water (not boiling). Although the method and best way of preparing mate varies from region to region and can be fiercely debated, the goal is the same—to prepare a delicious beverage of consistent concentration and flavor and to avoid as much of the particulate matter as possible.

Unless the preparation is carefully done, the heaviest particles of the mate will sink to the bottom of the container, and the finest particles will float. To avoid this, so that one doesn't get a mouthful of dusty residue when taking the first sip, there is an intricate procedure for wetting the mate, shaking the contents, tilting the container in a particular manner—all differing by tradition. This is done in order to keep the finest particles away from the filtering end of the bomba/bombilla (the metal straw).

Typically the process is to fill the mate container with leaves almost to the top and add the hot water. How the bomba/bombilla is placed in the container also varies from place to place: some people put it into the dry herb, some put it into the brewed mate.

Although mate is often consumed by individuals on their own, traditionally it is drunk in a celebratory setting, such as at family gatherings or with friends. Once the mate is ready for drinking, the cebador (the server) drinks the brewed tea to ensure that it is not too hot or too cold, that it is free of particulate matter, and that it tastes good. Once satisfied, the cebador refills the gourd and passes it to the first guest. This continues around the circle until the mate becomes lavado (flavor "washed out"). When all have finished, they thank their host.

In Argentina it's not uncommon to see people on to street carrying a mate cup and a thermos with hot water. Wikipedia states that "In some parts of Argentina, gas stations sponsored by yerba mate producers provide free hot water to travelers, specifically for the purpose of drinking during the journey. There are disposable mate sets with a plastic mate and bombilla, and sets with a thermos flask and stacking containers for the yerba and sugar inside a fitted case."

Although most urban Chileans don't drink mate, many rural Chileans do—in particular those of Chiloé and Magallanes and other southern regions[9].

Journal

NO MATTER WHETHER we were in a shop or restaurant, we heard a curious mix in the piped-in music—one moment it was The Doors singing "Come on Baby Light My Fire," then some Argentine tango and gaucho music, then blues and jazz, a bit of Beatles, and then more contemporary stuff thrown into the mix. Something for everybody?

Friday, March 20, 2009. Day trip from El Calafate to Glaciar Perito Moreno. Most tourists headed for the glacier, or elsewhere in Argentina's Los Glaciares National Park stay in El Calafate and arrange their tours from there.

Where we were staying was several blocks away from the main street, but only about a ten minute walk to most anything we needed. While walking to and fro, we passed a bakery that had the most amazing pastries on display. We stopped there for breakfast and had fresh orange juice, a flaky filled pastry, and a hot beverage. Then we continued on to the central bus station, which was a short distance uphill on the opposite side of Liberator.

It was a several-hour bus ride to Los Glaciares to see Glaciar Perito Moreno. I was surprised at how high the entrance fee was (60 pesos, which was about US$16 at the time, but it varies), but the highway within the park was new—with segments still under construction—and the visitor center was being enhanced, so it appeared that a lot of money was being put into the park and that the fee was for a worthy cause.

Parque Nacional Los Glaciares

Los Glaciares National Park is 1.5 million acres, which is about two-thirds the size of the U.S.'s Yellowstone National Park. Most of this World Heritage region is very rugged and inaccessible to visitors. However, there are two incredible areas that visitors can reach—the Glaciar Perito Moreno and Mount Fitz Roy near El Chaltén.

The Glaciar Perito Moreno was named after the Argentine scientist and explorer Francisco "Perito" Moreno and is justifiably famous; it's a spectacular natural wonder. A glacier slowly moves down a valley due to gravity acting on its increasing accumulation of snow and ice. Climate change is causing most of the world's glaciers to shrink, but Perito Moreno is one of the few that is not receding. Scientists consider it to be stable—growing and receding in balance.

The sheer size of the glacier is staggering—a wall of blue ice 14,760 feet (4,500 m) across and rising 197 feet (60 m) above the water.

Journal

WHEN WE ARRIVED at the first parking lot in the park, we were told that we could spend one hour at that location, and we could either take the boat ride (for an additional fee) to see the glacier, or hang out. We opted to take the boat and it headed out the short distance to the glacier. It was pretty impressive to be sitting at the foot of a glacier with it towering above us!

At the end of our hour, we all returned to the bus and continued on to a complex with several buildings, including an attractive new restaurant that offered a variety of salads, sandwiches, and hot plates. The restrooms were spiffy and clean; a visitor center and a gift shop were under construction.

From the far side of that parking lot, we took the walkway down the hillside to a series of balconies for different views of the glacier. The access was impressive—down brand-new grated steel steps and walkways that had replaced the asphalt pavement that formerly led visitors to the viewpoints of the glacier. As impressive as the glacier was from the boat, the view from the walkways was even more amazing. From our new perspective, looking down at the glacier, we could see not only the face of the glacier, but also the vast ice fields and mountains behind it.

Also incredibly beautiful and at least as thrilling was watching chunks of ice fall into the water. You'd see the ice fall, then see the splash, and then hear what sounded like the retort of a rifle. Then, after a brief delay, came a surge of water like a miniature tsunami. Most chunks were small, but we saw one piece that looked like it was the size of a refrigerator. It was very hard to tear ourselves away—who knew when a corner or even larger section of the glacier might fall!

Saturday, March 21, 2009. Day trip from El Calafate to El Chaltén. We headed north to El Chaltén; a six-hour round-trip bus ride. Only by a stroke of luck did we not miss our bus ride. Last weekend, while we were still in Chile, Daylight Savings Time ended (it's the reverse of what happens in the U.S. and Europe) and we got to have an extra hour of sleep—which of course we loved.

It was now a week later and just as we were about used to that change, we crossed the border into Argentina where the time zone changed and we lost the hour. It hadn't occurred to us that there was a difference; if we hadn't noticed a difference between the time on our watches and the clock at a restaurant where we ate the first night, we'd have missed out because it was dark when we had to get up and head for the bus terminal. I found out later that Argentina has had an on-again/off-again participation in Daylight Savings Time; they started in December, 2007, and ended March 16, 2008. They used it in 2009, but currently do not.

On the way to El Chaltén, the bus stopped midway at La Leona Roadhouse where the passengers piled out and headed for the café and restrooms. Little did we know that this remote outpost had played an important part in the region's rich history. Perhaps the most well-known renegades who came through here during the period of the Old West were the infamous Butch Cassidy and the Sundance Kid.

The Old West at La Leona Roadhouse

While traveling on Argentina's National Route No. 40, tour busses and other travelers often make a stop at La Leona Roadhouse & Country Lodge. The roadhouse is about 62 miles (110 km.) from El Calafate—halfway to El Chaltén.

This is the heart of the pampas, mostly open grassland, where the wind and climate combine to make settlements sparse, and permanent residences only for the hearty. Sheep browse, gauchos work at rounding them up, and fixing fences. The skies are big.

Water makes all the difference in a dry land. No surprise, then, that along the River La Leona sits an old establishment known as La Leona Roadhouse. Because of its unique history, it has been named "Historical and Cultural Patrimony" by the Province of Santa Cruz.

When today's tourists file into the cozy building and line up at the counter to order a cup of coffee, an empanada, or dessert, few have the time to consider the stories this site has to tell because their bus will soon be leaving.

However, the black-and-white photographs, some

faded or crinkled with time, are hung on the weathered wooden walls, and in between enjoying their food, visiting the restroom, or buying a souvenir, there's an opportunity for visitors to meet some of the infamous guests from earlier times. Those who want to stay over will find comfortable accommodations.

In 1877, Argentine explorer and academic Francisco Pascacio Moreno (usually referred to as Perito Moreno) made a surveying expedition to the Province of Santa Cruz. He explored numerous rivers, including the one that flows next to La Leona Roadhouse.

There, Moreno was attacked and badly injured by a female puma—*leona* in Patagonian slang—and that gave the name to the river and subsequently the roadhouse.

As you'll read later in Chapter 15, Moreno's exploration of Argentina also included a visit to the vicinity of the present-day village of El Chaltén, where he first saw and named the majestic peak that we know today as Mount Fitz Roy.

In 1894, the adobe brick La Leona Roadhouse was built by the Jensens, a family of Danish immigrants.

In 1905, three famous outlaws, Butch Cassidy, Sundance Kid and his wife Ethel Place, hid out at La Leona for almost a month. They had recently robbed the Bank of London and Tarapacá in Río Gallegos; it wasn't until after they departed that Mr. Jensen was shown their photos by the police and he identified them.

It's not only the notorious who have come to this remote region; it's also been a base camp for mountain climbers. Fitz Roy peak was first climbed by the French-Argentine expedition composed of Lionel Terray, Guido Magnone, Lieutenant Francisco Ibañez, Louis Depasse and Jacques Poincenot on February 2, 1952. On the way to basecamp, the expert French alpinist Poincenot drowned during a river crossing. Terray and Magnone went on to gain the summit; Casimiro Ferrari, on January 13, 1974, was the first to conquer the Torre. (Both peaks are in Los

Glaciares National Park.) Over the ensuing years there were several more owners.

In 1910, the Petersen family and Alfred Brodersen took ownership. They enlarged the hotel to four rooms, and added a saloon and general store. Later came Jul and Feliza Christensen, Saldia and the Westerlund family, and now Patricia and Laura Kargauer.

Today's La Leona Roadhouse still uses some of the original adobe buildings. The old bar and general store is now the teahouse and gift store. The Country Lodge has guest rooms in their updated, but historic building (with breakfast included) and a camping area and is open year round. Nearby, overlooking Lake Viedma, is Estancia La Estela, a guest house owned by the same family as La Leona.

Journal resumes

EL CHALTÉN IS the gateway to climbing and hiking in the Fitz Roy area. Now that the highway is nearly complete, it's seeing more and more tourists and has many hostels and restaurants to accommodate them. Still it is not as trendy as El Calafate.

Most of the houses in town are very simple in design—a rectangular box with a sloped roof. Interspersed are dozens of hosterías, youth hostels or albergues for all the backpackers and other tourists headed to Torres del Paine, Fitz Roy, or the Perito Moreno glacier. The town is extremely windy. I guess it usually is. Don't know how they stand it! Hard to walk. See one house that was originally in a rectangular shape—with its corners at 90 degrees—that has shifted into the shape of a parallelogram—all because of the constant wind.

WE HAD ABOUT five and a half hours to play with, so we took a hike into the hills behind town to *Torre Mirador*. Though it was a bit of a climb, it was quite manageable. It took about an hour and twenty minutes. At the mirador, we sat for a while, hoping for some clearing of the fog. It never reached optimal conditions, but I didn't care because the views from the bus had been spectacular.

Ralph napped, then we both scrambled up a nearby hill-side a bit further to be able to see the Rio Fitz Roy better. We took an alternate trail back. Although it took longer, it had more interesting views of the river and back toward the mountains.

When we arrived back in El Calafate it was almost nine. We strolled along Liberator reading menus and sign boards. The restaurants accommodated tourists by offering a more extensive menu than you would find in more remote towns, yet there were numerous places to find inexpensive fare. While walking about town to decide where to eat and comparing prices, we became aware that many restaurants charge a *cubiertos* (cover charge), or "tax," which goes from 2.50 pesos up.

If we'd wanted a huge platter of meat, we'd have gone into one of the restaurants that serve barbecue and offer *parrilladas* (a platter of mixed grilled meats). They were hard to miss; you looked in a storefront window and saw a skewered lamb stretched out over a huge indoor grill. Lamb is considered the traditional Patagonian meat and it will be grilled for several hours over the open fire. Ask about portion size before you order, because often the platter will be enough for several people. A Frommer's review recommended *Mi Viejo* (My Old Man) for its barbecue and noted that they also serve salmon, trout, and hare. Another El Calafate favorite was *La Vaca Atada* (The Tethered Cow); you'd know it by the cut-out cows standing outside. For us, it was late to have a large meal, so we settled for pizza and salad.

Some guidebooks have reported that game, especially gua-naco, wild boar, and introduced deer, is popular in restaurant cuisine. However, since the guanaco is a protected animal in both Chile and Argentina, it is unlikely to appear commonly as restaurant fare.

RALPH THINKS THE *place we are staying is too far from the heart of town and doesn't like its remoteness. We have to go through some dark streets, cut through some rows of shrubs with dark recesses, and cross a small stream on stepping stones. It doesn't bother me; I feel safe, and I like our motel because it is modest, but comfortable, quiet, clean, and inexpensive.*

SUNDAY, MARCH 22, 2009. El Calafate to Buenos Aires flight. We were able to sleep in, for once, because we had no bus to catch, and our flight wasn't until mid-afternoon. We had breakfast at the same bakery where we ate the last two mornings. We will miss this ritual of pastries and croissants with coffee and tea. Never did we figure out why the hot beverages were accompanied by a small glass of sparkling water—to refresh the palate? To jazz up the drink?

I purposely left behind my red down jacket at our hotel. I was surprised at how hard that was to do. I've always felt that it was too bright (bought it on sale), but it was like giving up an old friend. I couldn't help remembering our long history together—all the places we had traveled. I had a new jacket at home that I purchased because it was lighter. I hoped it would be at least as warm as the old one; that was the plan.

"I saw the maid find it and she was obviously pleased to get it," Ralph told me later. After that I felt better; it must get very cold here in the winter.

We bought some ceramic pieces as souvenirs in one of the local shops. We were not able to bring our backpacks onboard as carry-on bags for our flight to Buenos Aires, so we hoped that the fragile items would make it home intact in our checked duffel bag (they did). We noticed that many shops charge more for using credit cards (up to 20%) than paying with cash so we used cash for smaller purchases. We also noted that some establishments record your passport info on credit card invoices.

Before heading for the airport, we ate a light lunch of empanadas, fries, and beer. We said goodbye to the ever-present street dogs that were gathered en masse—perhaps eighteen or so. The ratio was seventeen males to the one female who was in heat. There were a few growls and snaps among the pack members, but they seem to settle their disputes quickly.

Most of the dogs weren't well groomed, but they weren't starving either. Although some of the dogs had owners, many strays seemed to survive as communal pets. They seldom barked. They mostly lay around when nothing was happening, only stirring themselves to follow someone when they thought they might get a handout.

Leave taking went on schedule. Security seemed standard in terms of how long it took and how thorough the inspections. I reflected again on the differences we had seen during the trip between their security system and ours: such as whenever we arranged a bus ride, we had to give our passport numbers. And outside of El Calafate, there is a *policia* station where the buses (but not the taxis) had to stop and give head counts.

Puerto Natales sky

7 • On the Streets of Buenos Aires, Argentina

Journal

Sunday, March 22, 2009 (continued). Flight El Calafate to Buenos Aires. When we boarded the LAN flight at the small, new airport in El Calafate, we found that there were already many passengers on board—presumably returning from Ushuaia. We enjoyed our three-hour flight to Buenos Aires.

When we arrived at the local airport (Jorge Newbery "AEP") in Buenos Aires, we quickly found a taxi. The man calling the taxis forward loaded our packs into the cab's trunk before we could say a word and then was quite insistent that we give him a tip. However, we couldn't find any small change, so I guess he remained annoyed.

It was only a 15-minute ride and a 20-peso (then US$7) taxi fare to our hotel, the Costa Rica, in the Palermo District.[10] The street, by the same name, looked pretty good at first; we drove by many trendy shops and outdoor cafes. However, when we reached the block where our hotel was, we saw lots of graffiti and I began to wonder what I had arranged, sight unseen, online. The buildings that lined the street were old and past their prime.

Once inside, however, we were pleased. The staff was welcoming. There'd been extensive remodeling and the lobby, small bar, and reception area were clean and contemporary. Our room, which was up two flights of stairs, was starkly decorated. The walls were white, the floor concrete, and the only wall decoration was an abstract painting in bright reds and oranges. The sink and shower room were up-to-date.

After unpacking we were ready to venture out and interact with the *porteños* ("people of the port"/the people of Buenos Aires). We stopped in our hotel lobby and the owner, Yann, gave us a map and very helpful recommendations on where to eat and what to see during the three days we would be in the "Paris of South America."

Following his recommendations, we walked about five long blocks to look at a pair of restaurants. Yann had told us that the same person owned both, but that there were some differences in the menus and atmosphere.

At the first of the two, we found a crowd vying to enter their names on the waiting list. Reservations would have been helpful, of course, but we hadn't known which restaurant to choose sight unseen. As we inched our way forward, I wanted to hide my feet—more precisely, my shoes. We were in Buenos Aires, tango capital of the world, and I was standing in line for dinner wearing hiking boots. I had other shoes back at the hotel, but I couldn't have walked that far in them.

The men were wearing slacks and well-pressed striped dress shirts; the women were wearing sleeveless dresses and strappy sandals or rattan slides. Ralph's shirt wasn't in much better shape than my shoes; it was clean, but a bit frayed at the edges. I felt way too embarrassed by our appearance and we decided to go elsewhere.

"Elsewhere" was the sister restaurant just down the street. When we arrived, the hostess was courteous to us, and wrote our name on the waiting list and suggested we check back in 20 minutes. I figured she had taken one look at us and decided to keep us waiting indefinitely. But, no, when we checked back later, a table was ready.

I squared my shoulders, pulled in my stomach and tried to project an image of confidence as I followed the waiter to our table. The restaurant was full except for the three small square tables placed side by side where the waiter seated us. When he pulled the tables a few inches apart from each other. I was still being somewhat paranoid and wondered if he was trying to isolate us from later arrivals. Soon, however, the server brought us the menu and filled our water glasses and I began to relax.

Another couple arrived and was given one of the two remaining tables—with the empty one between us. They nodded to us in greeting. They spoke Spanish to each other and the waiter and ordered quickly; it obviously was not their first visit.

I ordered the short ribs. The waiter said, "Do you want an *order?*"

"An order?" I wasn't sure what he meant, but responded, "Yes, an order."

"It's very large," he said, "you might want to order the half portion." I relied on his judgment and ordered the smaller portion. Ralph ordered confit of duck.

Our neighbors' food came. We glanced to see what they had on their plates. Both had ordered sausage. They smiled at us and indicated that we should try some. Before we could even respond, they'd each cut off an inch of the meat and put it on our plates. It was the perfect blend of crunchy casing, spicy interior.

While waiting for our food, I looked around at the other tables and noticed that most diners had bread and appetizers. Just about the time I had decided that we were being ignored, our food arrived. My "half" portion of ribs was three meaty pieces, each about ten inches long. Ralph's serving of duck confit was also more than generous—two thighs and two legs. And that wasn't the end of the food! More than a dozen side dishes were placed on our table: small bowls containing mashed potatoes, lentils, ratatouille, garlic cloves, hearts of palm in Thousand Island dressing, potato salad, olives, pickled artichokes, mushrooms, vegetables, applesauce and so forth. Our bottle of wine—a blend of cabernet, Malbec, and merlot was also quite good.

After we had eaten the main course, we were stuffed, but when the waiter brought a flan with *dulce de leche* (sweet caramel) and a fancy concoction with whipped cream piled high to a couple seated behind us, I turned to admire the desserts. The friendly pair laughed and said, "The first time we came here, we made the same mistake you did—we each ordered an entrée. This time we shared one so that we could have dessert."

We started talking about our various experiences in Argentina and Chile and as our conversation progressed to other travels, we learned that they were from Tours, France—more precisely they lived just off the major pilgrimage trail from LePuy, France that they had hiked as we had. After conversing for a while, we had to say goodbye.

I had to rate our evening as a great success—shoes or no shoes.

We returned to the hotel exhausted and stuffed. Slept well with the air-conditioner (which was needed as it was 80 degrees in the afternoon).

Monday, March 23, 2009. Buenos Aires. After croissants, tea, and orange juice (US$4), we set out to explore. We knew that we were both completely uninformed about the city of Buenos Aires. We knew that it is the capital and largest city of Argentina, but I hadn't realized that it is an autonomous federal district (like Washington, D.C.). It's distinct from greater Buenos Aires, which is a province. The city has a population of approximately three million, but greater Buenos Aires—the city and the surrounding provinces—has a population of about 13 million.

Yann had suggested we take the #152 bus across the city as a means of seeing the various districts, which we did. Luckily he had told us that exact change would be required for public transit, otherwise we would have had to go searching for some before boarding. Apparently residents and visitors alike bemoan the fact that it's hard to get change from almost any denomination of currency.

The bus was hot and crowded and took forever. We went through quite a range of neighborhoods—middle class, ritzy, then under the tracks, to the slums. By the time we got to the end of the line, to the district known as *La Boca* (the mouth), on the waterfront, we were the only passengers still on the bus. When the driver started to pull into the terminal, he glanced in the rear view mirror and seemed startled that there was still anyone on the bus.

Buenos Aires is on the southern shore of the Río de la Plata. Our first stop was to see an old iron bridge that's now an historic monument and not in use. Alongside the bridge small boats were using poles to carry passengers across the river. This is not a tourist attraction, but a work-a-day transportation option. The guidebooks, however, warn readers not to venture across the river.

We walked a few blocks along the waterfront and reached La Boca. Although the area is a major tourist attraction, it was not terribly crowded and we found ourselves fascinated by its colorful buildings surrounding the central plaza and streets. Many of the shops and dwellings were of corrugated metal and painted in vivid shades of pink, turquoise and yellow. Some say that this tradition has evolved from earlier times when dock workers and residents would use whatever paints came their way from the ships.

Artisans' wares were set out on long tables. Although I normally buy few souvenirs, I couldn't resist picking up a couple of ceramic cups with "Buenos Aires" and tango dancers painted on the side. I hoped they would survive the journey home.

The central plaza was surrounded by several restaurants, many with outdoor seating. Tango dancers performed in the street and in open spaces next to the restaurants. They flirted with the tourists, and for a fee, you could put on a feather boa or a rakish fedora and dance with one of the professional dancers.

As we wandered along, we noticed the life-sized dolls leaning out of the second-story windows. I imagine that any real dolls in the area are much more discreet.

Next we took a taxi to lunch. We had been told to do so and small wonder; you have to travel through a scary part of town. People had taken up residence on the sidewalks—furniture and all. There was laundry hung street-side and people were rummaging in boxes and cans for who knows what.

The restaurant, El Obrero, had been in the same family for three generations. After taking in the metal bars on the windows and the patched plaster on the front of the building, I knew we weren't going to find fancy table service. What we found was an old-world, unaffected atmosphere. The many choices were listed on a chalk board. The prices were very reasonable and the portions were generous. Soon after we arrived, the restaurant filled quickly with locals and tourists, and so we congratulated ourselves for not having to wait. I ate too much again.

Afterward, one of the elderly waiters called a cab and was very insistent that we wait for the right one. This was the second time that we had been instructed only to take one from a particular fleet: black cars with gold lettering indicating that they were summoned by radio dispatch. We waited out front for about twenty minutes. Another patron came out and told us, "You don't want to go walking around in this area." The area seemed fairly quiet and benign—rather like a warehouse district, but I noticed four men standing nearby who seemed to have nothing occupying their time.

The taxi arrived; we hopped in and drove through some more rundown blocks. People had set up house not only in, but also outside of some of the buildings. A man sitting on a chair on the sidewalk might not seem unusual, but a woman lying in bed partially covered with a blanket seemed odd!

The driver took us to San Telmo. The old marketplace, which ordinarily has stalls with everything from veggies to collectibles, stamps to old-fashioned crank telephones, was fairly empty. Most vendors and shoppers seemed to have left for the day. We walked around the square dodging the tables, chairs, and umbrellas of the numerous outdoor cafes and stopped to watch some tango performances. Like all the other tourists, I suppose, I enjoyed watching the women in their six-inch high heels and tight, black dresses and the man in stripped suit and black patent leather shoes doing the sensuous dance.

Finally exhausted, we took the bus back to the hotel.

Tuesday, March 24, 2009. Buenos Aires. It was a bad night. I suffered from diarrhea and had to get up multiple times. Ordinarily, I wouldn't have minded quite as much that the bathroom door was not a solid one, but this one had a gap of about two feet at both top and bottom. Nor would I normally have minded quite so much that the toilet did not refill and flush well, but in this case it was embarrassing.

I felt quite wrung out in the morning and wanted to take a taxi to sightsee, but Ralph asked directions and was told how to take the subway (SBTE). I got annoyed with him for not taking my illness more seriously and then annoyed with myself for not being more insistent about taking the taxi. As it turned out, the walk to the station was tiring, but the subway itself was fine.

Because we were tourists, we thought we should follow some of the recommendations in our guidebook, so we did. We went to the capitol building. I didn't find our visit particularly thrilling, but I did enjoy seeing the balcony where Eva Perón had once stood. I could almost see her there, standing before her audience, casting her spell as she spoke. I've never seen Eva in person and so I am undoubtedly holding a romanticized version of her from the movie with Madonna, and from the live performances I've seen of *Evita*.

We took a taxi out to the Recoleta District to see the La Recoleta Cemetery where Eva is buried. The cemetery is huge—with 4,800 aboveground vaults and tombs. It is so costly to be buried there that it is said to be the most expensive real estate in Buenos Aires. The architecture is eclectic: Neo-Classic, Art Deco, and Art Nouveau. Tombs are shaped like pyramids, castles, and temples.

Even with the map an aide handed us and following the street names posted on each lane's corners, it took some searching to find where Eva Perón is buried. She is in a mausoleum that is labeled "Familia Duarte." Duarte was her father's name.

Eva Perón

It is much easier to find Eva Perón's place of burial now than it was for many years. After she died of cancer on July 26, 1952, her embalmed body was placed on public display. Then she was moved to safe-keeping during the lengthy embalming process and while a monument was begun. However, before the monument was completed, her husband, President Juan Perón, was overthrown in a military coup. He fled the country, and Eva's body disappeared. In 1971, her body was found in a crypt in Milan, under an assumed name, and returned to Juan Perón who was then living in Spain with his third wife, Isabel. In 1973, Juan Perón returned to Buenos Aires to become president for a third time, Isabel was elected vice-president, and Eva was left behind in Spain. Then when Juan died in 1974, Isabel succeeded him, and she had Eva's body brought back to Argentina and displayed next to Juan Perón's. Subsequently, Eva's body was buried where it rests now—in the Duarte family tomb.

A tour of La Recoleta Cemetery will give you even more tales to share—the tale of Rufina Cambaceres (1883-1902), for example. Cambaceres, it seems, was buried alive. The 19-year-old was at home, dressing for a social event, but then found seemingly dead by her mother. She was pronounced dead—by some say three doctors—and placed in a coffin.

The legend varies, but most agree that Rufina regained consciousness and woke up screaming and clawing at her coffin. Some say that the coffin had moved, days after Rufina was placed in it. The coffin was opened, but in the interim, she had had a heart attack and died. Rufina is buried at No. 35 and many believe that her ghost can still be heard screaming at night.

Journal

WEDNESDAY, MARCH 25, 2009. Final day in Buenos Aires and return flight home. After a full night's sleep, I finally had some energy. It was also a bit cooler (70s) so maybe that helped. After breakfast, we packed, then left our luggage behind the hotel's counter and went out. I was uncertain if I was up for a day of walking, but we took it slowly and all went well.

We walked to the *Museo Evita* (Evita Museum), which is devoted to researching, collecting, and presenting information about Eva Perón. The museum is in a mansion constructed in the early 1900s for the Carabassa family and which became *Hogar de Transito #2* (Temporary Home) in 1948. On July 18 of that year, Evita inaugurated El Hogar with these words, "The Temporary Home shelters those in need and those who have no home ... for as long as necessary until work and a home can be found...."

It is said that Evita offered the women and children "an open door, a place set for them at the table, a clean bed," as well as "consolation and motivation, encouragement and hope, faith and self-confidence."[11]

The museum was fascinating—videos of Perón speaking to her supporters, mannequins dressed in some of the expensive clothing that brought her criticism from her dissenters, depictions of the many shelters to care for both young and elderly, and hospitals for any in need. The museum tells the story of Evita in a positive light, but ignores the fact that there are still some remaining questions about whether or not the Perons lived too high on the hog and whether or not any of the huge amounts of money raised by her foundation went into secret Swiss bank accounts. Eva Peron, or *Evita* as she came to be called, remains an extremely controversial figure.

After our visit, we had lunch outdoors in the museum's restaurant. By late afternoon, we were tired from our wandering but we still had some time to kill before heading for the airport; we returned to the hotel. They had been very accommodating by keeping our luggage while we out exploring, and then by letting us sit in the lobby and read until our taxi for the airport arrived. Hotel Costa Rica was definitely a good choice.

Our flights home were long, but uneventful—just the way we like them!

WE HAD TRIED to use up our pesos before we left the city, so we wouldn't have to take another loss at the exchange bureau of the airport. We reserved pesos (the equivalent of US$18) for the required departure tax (similar tax would have been demanded if we had left from Chile).

There's an office where foreign visitors can get refunds of the *impuesto al valor agregado* (IVA; value-added tax) on some of their purchases of Argentine products upon their departure from the country. The IVA is close to 20% of the purchase price.

However, you have to have made your purchases at a shop that participates in the program (generally high-end shops), and we didn't make enough purchases to qualify. (If you do make significant purchases at participating shops, save your invoices and other paperwork and be prepared to go through another line at the airport!)

Dogs of Puerto Montt

8 • Intervening Time

A chieving success requires more than wishful thinking. Although both Ralph and I were okay with our decision to turn back near the John Garner Pass because of uncertainty about the weather—wind and rain—we both subconsciously must have thought we wanted to give it another try because we soon were talking about a return in 2010, as a foregone conclusion.

However, before setting everything into motion, I think we both wanted to know that we were better prepared—more accurately, that *I* was better prepared. We wanted to try again, but we wanted to be successful and that would require more than wishful thinking.

For me, this required I focus on two major tasks. My first step was to start gathering more information about the trail so that I would be considering facts rather than dwelling on fears. My second step was to broaden my physical training.

We were hardly home from the trip when I emailed the hikers that we had met that rainy, cold March night at Los Perros camp asking if they would be willing to answer some questions about their Patagonian experiences (and telling them that I was working on a book). Although I'll never know for certain, it seemed that Ralph and I were the only ones who turned back at that point and that all of the others we had met continued on and over the pass.

Henry Leinen was the first person I heard back from; Henry, who was in his fifties, had traveled to Torres del

Paine with two friends. When we met them at Los Perros camp, they were spending their second night while waiting for better conditions for crossing over John Garner Pass.

He wrote, "Approaching the pass from camp Perros was not difficult. While still in the trees—one-third of the walk is in trees—you will have to walk through root infested bogs. This problem could be alleviated by trail maintenance and installing drainage.

"Once out of the trees I made a very easy ascent to the pass. At the pass, I was confronted by the famous wind warned of on the local maps. The trail descending went straight down (no switchbacks) and made slipping prevalent. The scary wood ladders seen in advertisements have been replaced with very strong metal ladders akin to those used on ladder trucks of fire departments. I would rate the trip strenuous and wet."

Henry added, "Even though it is a federal park, do not compare it with U.S. Also, do not bring meat or vegetables to the border. Buy them once you cross because they will be seized by the other country. Also, the maps available on the Internet did not accurately reflect the trail profile. Stay away from the salami down there. Everyone who ate it got sick." (We had salami there and were fine.)

Rob Hodges and his wife, Kate Ellis, were both in their mid-thirties and hailed from Austin, Texas. They came to Torres del Paine to hike the Circuit during a 15-month travel adventure. By the time they reached the park, they had already spent considerable time in South America.

Rob, a freelance travel writer, said, "We didn't specifically train for our hiking in Patagonia, but we had done a ton of trekking in South America during our previous seven months in the continent. We did a lot of high-altitude trekking in Peru and some mountaineering in Bolivia. But then we spent a month drinking wine, eating rich food and staying up late in Argentina and Uruguay prior to visiting Patagonia, so I think we cancelled out any 'training' we had done.

"My wife had never done a proper backpacking trip (i.e., backcountry trekking and camping with all your gear and food) prior to visiting Torres del Paine. We had a `crash course' trip of 3 days/2 nights in Fitz Roy just a few days before coming to Torres del Paine. My longest backpacking trip before it was just four or five days, though I had had several of that length and felt very prepared. For Kate, it was a true baptism by fire.

"The pass and glacier were intense and mind-blowing for both the gale-force winds and the beauty. The scale of Glacier Grey was just so massive! Our pictures do not do it justice at all. And during the wind at the top of the pass, I felt like one of those poor reporters they send out into hurricanes just to show how miserable the conditions are. There were times we had to dig in and brace with our trekking poles just to stand up."

Then Rob added a comment about an animal sighting that gave me another reason (not that I needed one!) to return to Torres del Paine. "We saw a puma up-close! Kate was cooking our breakfast at Campamento Serón, and I was in the tent breaking down camp.

"All of a sudden, she yelled, 'Oh my god, a puma!'

"My first reaction was to wonder what she was looking at that she thought was a puma because they are so incredibly rare. But when I jumped out of the tent, I saw a full-size puma just 30 feet away! It was inside the campground, walking along the back fenced-in area. It paused to look at us briefly before slowly slinking away just like a sleek little house cat. It went straight for a hole in the fence, which indicated that it was very familiar with the area. We think it must have come into the field in the camp in order to catch some of the rabbits we had seen the night before.

"We managed to grab our cameras and get off a few shots of the puma, but the quality is not good. By the time we were shooting, the puma was on a ridge about 50 feet or more away. But we watched him for a few minutes, and he paused and looked at us several times. It was very surreal.

"We, especially Kate, were really nervous about climbing the [Garner] Pass, especially since our previous day had been so tough and there had also been blizzard conditions on the pass the day before. (We arrived at Los Perros the night that everyone had been stranded there due to the blizzard.) But it ended up being a breeze! We had phenomenal weather, and the climb really didn't seem that tough for either of us. We had much harder climbs in Peru, Bolivia, and China (not to mention the Grand Canyon and Yosemite!)."

Deborah and her husband wrote from Germany, had this to say about Garner Pass, "We were both blown over by the wind. Very difficult—not just [because of] the wind, but [also because] the descent was extremely steep and slippery."

I contacted Rose Tomey, the woman who had lightened my mood the morning we decided to turn back. Rose, who is a medical writer living in the San Francisco Bay Area, wrote, "I've been thinking about the pass. For me, the article that I was going to write about the pass was about all the fear built-up around it (especially after sitting around for a couple days). When I actually did it, I wished I hadn't heard anything as the dreaded pass wasn't anything I couldn't easily/reasonably handle as long as I had reasonable humility.

"People made it sound like we were all going to be climbing a completely vertical (and haunted) mountainside while hungry birds pecked at us and unrelenting hailstorms clouded our vision. Meanwhile, food would run out and we would be lucky to finish with even one boot on.

"This was not exactly the case.

"In short, I felt that if someone says something's difficult, what does that really mean? One size/fear simply doesn't fit all. A person can always conjure up a worse scenario in his or her imagination than really exists. I felt it was more of psychological/spiritual test than anything and it wasn't as big a deal as I felt encouraged to believe. Then again, I'm 30-something, in good to very good shape, and enjoy difficulty (though I don't like truly scary things).

"I found it much more of an exciting adventure than anything. I would easily do it again. I will say it was windy at the top, but I thought that was incredibly cool. In fact, one of my contact lenses got blown off! Fortunately, I had a spare. Yes, it was steeper on the downhill than most trails I've been on, but with humility and a reasonable pace it wasn't anything I couldn't handle.

"There were a couple ladders…those were a bit daunting and I wouldn't really want to do those again. I'm not really afraid of heights but I don't like to overly test fate either. Probably more psychological than anything, but I didn't really find it that much fun. I just somehow distracted my mind from the fact that I was going down the ladders (a few 100 feet down?) and somehow made it (thank you, God). That was one of the scarier things I've encountered in my hiking days, but it looked like everyone safely made it across."

Facing the fears

AFTER GETTING COMMENTS back from those that we had met and who had continued on to complete the Circuit, it was time for me to process the added information. What we had seen and experienced in Torres del Paine was so wonderful that I was dying to return and make it completely around the Circuit. That of course required making it over John Garner Pass and down the other side toward Grey Glacier.

There were several challenges, but I figured that one of the biggest ones was my fear. I had to face that obstacle by focusing on the facts and minimizing my emotional responses.

The facts were:
- the weather is totally unpredictable and constantly changing;
- the winds are notoriously fierce— particularly going over John Garner pass;
- the trail down from John Garner Pass is steep and difficult and gets very muddy and slippery particularly

if it has been, or is, wet or icy;
- and my body is not getting any younger.

Although when I looked at the list of obstacles, they seemed overwhelming, I decided that I would look at them one at a time and see if indeed they were insurmountable. After all, I've always been inspired by the quote by the Chinese philosopher, Lao-tzu, "A journey of a thousand miles begins with a single step." And that's how I've dealt with other major hikes that we've done: the various routes of the Camino de Santiago, the Pacific Crest Trail, and climbing Mt. Kilimanjaro. It's also how I've worked through other big projects in my life—such as writing and publishing books.

First, I realized that there's not much we could do about the weather. However, recognizing that we would pack for severe conditions (bringing our 4-season tent, for example) was reassuring. Beyond that, we could allow more time to sit and wait for better conditions.

Likewise, I have no control over the wind patterns, but we can likely handle whatever comes either by finding a window of time that works or by turning back as we did previously. I have a tendency to see obstacles as an all-or-nothing proposition when in truth, sometimes it's fine to continue going forward and make a final determination of risk vs. safety when you are closer to the perceived threat.

It is reassuring to know that Ralph will turn back when I ask. We have already talked about how we will head up from Los Perros toward the pass and turn around if necessary. The expression, "There are *old* climbers and *bold* climbers, but not many *old, bold* climbers" (an ancient climbing proverb) comes to mind.

Our next challenge, assuming that we made it over the pass, would be facing what is rumored to be the worst trail in the park and a slippery descent to the glacier. I almost always use hiking poles, so that was not an issue, but on top of that, I decided I would prepare myself to slide down on my butt if necessary. (I later found out that it was totally impractical to do much of this because of the distance in-volved, but it reassured me at the time. It was much like my plan when I climbed Mt. Whitney on my very first backpacking trip in 1989—in that case I had told myself that I would crawl through the narrow, windy sections if necessary—also highly impractical!)

Then I had to realistically assess my physical condition, and when you are 68 years old, that's something of a chal-lenge because sometimes joints hurt and sometimes they don't. At the time I was most concerned about my knees. I was finding that even if they weren't hurting when we were on backpacking trips, they often became sore and stiff when we had a long stretch of downhill hill hiking to do. I had more work to do on increasing my confidence level. I wanted to be ready for the steep inclines I imagined we would face.

Some of our commonly-held fears—such as of spiders or snakes—have undoubtedly been passed down in our genes from ancestors that wanted to survive. Perhaps you are terrified—as many, if not most people are—of public speaking. Quite possibly you are anxious or tense when you hear of terrorists' threats. If you have ever been afraid of anything—whether a real or imagined—you have surely felt the paralyzing effects.

As a long-distance hiker and backpacker, most of my fears over the years have involved physical challenges—bears, rattlesnakes, steep slopes, roaring streams or rivers to cross, forest fires, lightning.... Each time that I have had to face one of these potentially risky situations, I've had to deal with my fear in order to move ahead.

One Christmas I decided to put all of my journal notes from our Pacific Crest Trail hikes—2,350 miles worth—into book form as a present to Ralph. One of the things that struck me as I was consolidating my entries was the num-ber of times that I had worried about upcoming trips and the obstacles we might face. Not only did I fret during the trip itself, but also I worried for months before the event that I might drown, fall, get bitten, or in some other way get injured or die.

As I realized that time after time I had worried, I also realized that *none* of the things that I had ever worried about had come to pass. How much wasted energy! While it is true that I've had to shoo away a couple of bears, I've had to ford rivers that were scary, and I've had to maneuver around a few rattlesnakes, I've *never* been injured.

After I went through this series of reality checks, Ralph and I talked about some more solutions. Because he hikes with me regularly, he knows that the knee pain that I experience is not in my head. He has watched me try various strategies: zigzagging down a trail, sort of crouching, searching for solid footing rather than loose rock, holding onto the branches of shrubs, and even going backward when the I-band has gotten so tight I couldn't proceed without severe pain.

Ralph asked, "Why don't we practice going down increasingly steeper hills around here with a different technique. You can try shifting more weight onto your hiking poles; you know, 'Trust your poles,' as they said on Mt. Kilimanjaro."

I said okay, but I had my reservations. The problem is I *don't* trust my poles and I don't want to shift my center of gravity forward because I am afraid of falling forward, or in a heap, and breaking something. I'm going to start the downhill practice this week. I'm also planning to strengthen my knees by incorporating some of the stairways near us in my walks. We have public stairways between streets that have several hundred steps.

To paraphrase the saying, "It's crazy to keep doing things the same way and to expect different results," so I knew that I had to gain more confidence and skills for dealing with heavy wind and steep terrain.

From this realization had come a plan—to bring the *live in the moment* philosophy more deeply into my life. I didn't expect to instantly transform into a heedless risk taker, but I did plan to pay more attention to the reality and less to the paralyzing fears. This could be done by gathering information about the threat, preparing for contingencies, and having confidence in my ability to make a good decision about whether to proceed or to turn back when faced with obstacles.

Having the fears is one thing, I'll probably never be without them, but giving them too much power robs us of living our best life!

Six weeks, non-stop togetherness

I'm lucky. My husband is easy to travel with, and I'm fairly easy—which translates to he rarely complains, and I'm free to. We met on a Sierra Club car camping trip that was a series of everything that could go wrong, goes wrong, but dealing with the mishaps and chaos just provided us with the opportunity to see each other without pretenses (no makeup, slept-in clothes). We both always chose dishwashing as our daily chore because we knew the dishes would be washed properly, we'd have warm water once a day, and our fingernails would get clean.

We embarked on that trip to Baja in two cars, returned in one (after arranging for another person to drive the other car back). We were pretty much committed to each other at that point. At one point, another member of the Sierra group said to me, "Ralph is a man who you'd be safe traveling with anywhere in the world." How prophetic was that! We were married a year and a half later.

My backpacking adventures began in the summer six months after that, when we decided to take a 60-mile trip into the Sierras and climb Mt. Whitney. Over the last 24 years we have taken dozens of backpacking trips, long car camping trips to the tip of Baja California, adventure trips to Copper Canyon (Mexico), Peru, Bolivia, Tanzania, and long-distance hiking trips in Europe. Travel, therefore, has been a significant part of our relationship since the beginning. In 2001, we took our longest hike and vacation ever— a 6-week pilgrimage. We were hiking 12-15 miles a day to complete 450 miles on the Camino de Santiago, an ancient pilgrimage trail in northern Spain. This meant almost constant time together. What we realized was that we have evolved, over time, our own way of creating needed personal space. Although we are essentially together, we respect each other's desire to have time alone. Although some of the time we walk and talk together, much of the time we walk separately. We're usually close, but not side by side.

I am the one who needs more time for contemplation, and if I really want to be able to reflect on my surroundings, or thoughts, I'll ask Ralph to walk perhaps 100 feet, or even 100 yards behind me—because when he walks just behind me I find his footsteps distracting, like I have to think about someone passing me.

Often I walk a bit behind him, which allows me to walk along in more of a daze, knowing that someone ahead is sort of shielding me. Ralph satisfies his need for personal space in a non-physical way. Although it doesn't distract him when I am right on his heels, or when I'm right ahead of him, he appreciates the fact that I don't demand constant conversation. He's a quiet person. He finds my normal amount of talking to be enjoyable, and he enjoys my company, but he doesn't want to be required to converse non-stop.

Another aspect of our different personalities is how we deal with pacing as it is important to walk at your own pace. It is uncomfortable to be pressured to walk faster, or required to walk slower, to match someone else's rate of walking. I generally am the slower walker, but I don't want to walk alone all day. My competitive spirit is really tried when I can't keep up and I get very self-critical if I can't keep up.

Our solutions have evolved over time. Ralph walks at his own rate, but stops frequently (giving himself a break) to wait for me. If I have to make a stop to adjust my backpack, or adjust a shoelace, he waits for me. When he needs to stop to put on his jacket or remove a rock from his shoe, I continue on ahead knowing that he will soon catch up with me, and that I saved him from one of those "wait for me" stops.

Another way that we give ourselves some independence, even when we are together, is when we read, when I write in my journal, and when we take photographs. With each of these activities, we are able to escape into our own little world for peace and quiet. We both love to read, and look forward to a quiet time in the evening for putting aside other thoughts or chores and getting back to a favorite book.

Finally, on our trip we did often encounter, or stay overnight at the lodgings with, other people. And though these were not situations where we individually met and talked with old friends, we were able to have those interactions with someone else, and thereby express our own personalities.

Navimag ferry at Puerto Montt

9 • Return to Patagonia via Ferry

Journal

Monday & Tuesday, February 22-23, 2010. San Francisco to Puerto Montt and Puerto Varas, Chile. I was somewhat nervous about heading for Torres del Paine and trying the Circuit again, but mostly I was just excited about going to the park again. We booked a late-night flight because we wanted to arrive in Santiago mid-morning. Our transfer at Dallas/Ft. Worth was easy because both flights were on American, but soon things went awry.

We had barely rolled back from the gate when the captain came on the intercom and told us we were overweight. Did I hear right—only 200 pounds? The delay, he announced, would be "just a few minutes."

We sat there trying to be good sports, as minutes turned into two hours and until they removed a pallet of junk and completed the follow-up inspection and paperwork. Goodbye connection in Santiago—where we had expected we'd have one and a half hours to get to the LAN Airlines' gate for our final flight that would take us to Puerto Montt.

Once in the air, I decided that I would try taking a sleeping pill (a first) on the flight because I rarely can sleep when flying and am therefore usually exhausted by the time we arrive anywhere. The directions on the prescription Ambien said to take one when you had a minimum of eight to nine hours of uninterrupted time. So I took one just as dinner was served. I made it through the chicken and salad, and then, according to Ralph who watched with some trepidation, I zonked out.

He told me later, "You went from 'normal' to 'weird' in about 15 minutes. You kept stabbing your salad dressing packet with the plastic knife and couldn't open it. You couldn't figure out how to open the pat of butter. When you started talking about how the airplane was like riding a bus, I pushed the call button for the flight attendant. I thought you were having a bad reaction to the pill and maybe they'd know what to do."

I don't remember any of this, but I do know that I slept for most of the flight and woke up refreshed. (Later, when I reread the directions, I saw that they included the warning that taking the pill with, or just after, a meal delays the pill's effects.)

The first task when arriving at Santiago's airport was getting through immigration. This went smoothly for us because we still had our certificates showing we'd paid the entry fee last year. (As long as your passport is still valid, you don't have to pay another entry fee.)

Then we had to pick up our checked bag and go upstairs to the LAN sales counter to get our boarding passes for a new flight and recheck our bag. Amazingly, there was a new flight available with minimal delay and they booked us on that—at least we were making progress. We made it through security and boarding with no further glitches.

I was pleased that I had remembered that the best seats on the Santiago to Puerto Montt flight are on the starboard (right) side as you face the cockpit so that you can see more of the volcanoes, mountains, and lakes of Chile. Just like on the buses, there were people who took the window seats and then pulled down the shades and slept. I can't fathom why they would have paid an expensive fare to take this amazingly beautiful flight along the spine of the Andes and then slept through it.

I was impressed with the spanking-new airport in Puerto Montt, and I was really happy that Andres, who runs the hostel where we were going to stay in Puerto Varas, was still waiting for us in spite of our delayed arrival. The twenty-minute drive to the resort town Puerto Varas (aka the *City of Roses*) gave just a glimpse of the scenic beauty of the region. Later, when we went for a stroll, we saw that Puerto Varas sits on the edge of huge

Lake Llanquihue. (Llanquihue is correctly pronounced "yan-key-huay," but you can get away with "Yankee-Way.") Across the lake is the snow-capped Volcán Osorno, a conical-shaped mountain that looks like Japan's Mt. Fuji. Volcán Osorno is part of Vicente Pérez Rosales National Park, the oldest national park in Chile. It was no wonder the town was filled with tourists during the summer season, and I was grateful Ralph had made reservations for the hostel.

We were intrigued with the German-influenced architecture. Many of the homes and businesses dating from the early 1900s were of that design: lots of clapboard sidings, decorative shutters, and shingled roofs.

The weather was great—even with gusty winds picking up in late afternoon. Though the beachfront and downtown areas were busy, we had little difficulty finding a satisfying place to dine.

The Casa Azul, where we were to spend the next couple of days, was not luxurious, but at US$35 for a private room with bath and US$3.50 each for breakfast, we didn't expect 500-thread count bedding. The bed was comfortable, the sheets stayed tucked in (which is not always the case in inexpensive rooms), and we had a warm comforter and extra blankets. The only downside was the lack of privacy. Though we were at the end of a hall, the free, shared computer was just outside our door so people were there, or sitting in the hall, to use the Wi-Fi or computer much of the time. However, we both slept well that night and for once I didn't have any jet lag.

Wednesday, February 24, 2010. Puerto Varas. Exploring Chile's Lake District by car, day #1. This morning we walked to the downtown to pick up a rental car from an office near the beach. Ralph had arranged the rental before we left the U.S.; rental cars in Chile are easily obtained in major cities, but not in smaller towns. The paperwork went smoothly, but when the car was brought around, I noticed that the driver's side mirror was dangling, so we asked for another car. That caused a delay, but the service people were so friendly and apologetic that we couldn't be annoyed.

We started out going clockwise to drive around Lake Llanquihue on *Ruta* (Route) 5. Almost immediately, we came to a tollbooth on the highway. We'd observed on the way in from the airport that tolls are usually paid when you leave the freeway so that traffic doesn't come to a standstill every few miles. I know that there are many toll roads on the east coast of the United States, but there aren't many where we live on the west coast, so I was surprised to find them here. When we turned onto secondary roads, tolls no longer were collected. I'm sure that Ralph, who was driving, was relieved that they drive on the right side of the road.

We were in the heart of the Lake District, which includes parts of both Chile and Argentina. There are 20 large, fresh water lakes in the Lake District and fishing for salmon or trout in this part of Patagonia attracts sportsmen from throughout the world. We didn't have time to drive to San Carlos de Bariloche or any other resort areas in Nahuel Huapi National Park, the oldest[12] Argentine national park, but I was excited about being on our own in Chile with the means of exploring wherever we wanted.

We stopped first in the small hamlet of Frutillar, established in the late 1800s, and walked along the main street, which closely parallels one of Llanquihue's sandy beaches. The entire town looked spic and span—no doubt its German and Austrian heritage—with signs offering *kuchen* or *strudel* hanging in many a shop window. *Kuchen* (pronounced "KOO-hen") is German for pie, *kuchen de quesillo* is a kind of cheesecake, and *strudel* (say "ess-TROO-dayl") in Chile as in the U.S. is an apple pie pastry.

Brightly colored flowers grew everywhere—in gardens, hanging pots, and planters. Every other building seemed to be a cottage, cabin, or timbered chalet displaying a sign that read *Disponible* (available). We, not wanting a beachside holiday, drove on.

As we drove along the highway through Puerto Octay, we noticed a quaint, weathered church down the hill near still another lake. We parked the car, walked down the steep dirt and gravel road to take a closer look and to find a place for lunch.

The listings in our guidebook were outdated and none of the restaurants mentioned were open. We located a café on our own, climbed its worn stairs to the second floor and, without benefit of menu, managed to place an order for food. We ordered the "menu of the day" and looked forward to trying the regional fare even though we didn't know what we would get. Even though it was freshly prepared, I was disappointed with the results: the fish was fried and the accompanying vegetables were overcooked.

We drove on toward Volcán Osorno, the volcano we'd been admiring from across the lake, and came to a gravel and dirt road with heavy construction underway. There was very little traffic on this far side of the lake, but it seemed to us that the road improvement projects—straightening the curves, paving and widening the road—were going to make travel easier and thereby bring tourist dollars to the area.

We reached the turnoff and started to climb the mountain. The highway engineers apparently had decided that straight up was the way to go; unfortunately our rental was unused to the demands of a road that ascended at such a rapid clip. We watched the temperature gauge rise steadily as the road climbed. Finally we had to roll down the windows and turn the heater on full blast so that the car's engine wouldn't overheat. This seemed to help because the gauge then held steady.

Turning on the heater so that the car won't overheat may seem counter-intuitive, but it's a trick that we both learned long ago. In the "good old days" when on Highway 5 traveling south into the Los Angeles basin, one would often see multiple cars pulled onto the shoulder of the road. The long, steep grade climbing the so-called "Grapevine" was too much for many cars: engines would overheat, the radiator water would turn to steam, and there was little recourse but to wait on the side of the road, in the baking sun, until the water cooled.

Turning on the car's heater draws some of the heat out of the engine, and thereby cools it. Even though newer cars are generally lighter and have more efficient cooling systems, it still can make a difference.

When we reached the end of the road, we found a cluster of buildings including a restaurant, gift shop, and an aerial lift. Visitors could take the lift to two higher elevations. There were also guided tours available as well as hiking trails for those who wanted to climb the mountain on their own. One of the trails was on loose cinder, another followed a paved road— both would have been totally exposed to the sun because they were above timberline.

Climbing to Volcán Osorno peak entails a full day's hike, starting before sunrise. Climbers continuing beyond the volcanic rock to the 8,701-foot (2,653 m) summit have to ascend through glaciated ice on the upper slopes wearing crampons, ice axe, and ropes. They must either go with a guide or be certified mountaineers carrying the proper gear.

None of this was in our plans, so after a couple of photos, we drove back down the mountain. Now we had another challenge—would the steep grade burn out the brakes? Luckily, all went well.

Far down the mountainside, there was another trail, this one through the forest and running on a relatively level course, and offering a two-hour hike. We were quite surprised as we neared the trailhead to see a trio of foxes running across the road. Ralph pulled to a stop on the shoulder of the road; I hopped out and ran back to take some photos. Considering the proximity to a trail and the willingness of one of the foxes to pose, I suspect these fellows were looking for a handout from passersby.

When we had started our drive mid-morning, there were few people up and about, but as we completed our circuit and neared Puerto Salas, we were astonished to see hundreds of people on the narrow beaches. There were wall-to-wall sunbathers and beach umbrellas on the sandy strips. Inside a roped-off area were many swimmers and it must have been pleasantly warm because it was not just kids who were enjoying the water.

The clerk at our hotel recommended a restaurant for diner that was only a short drive east of Puerto Varas. The place was packed with vacationing families as well as local residents. I didn't find it thrilling because most of the items on the menu were what we call "comfort food"—breaded, baked, or fried. I ordered grilled salmon thinking it would be a healthy option, but it was served smothered in a cream sauce with a few tiny shrimp. Rice (white) cost extra. We did indulge in dessert—by sharing a slice of meringue filled with cream and raspberries. It was the best part of my meal.

Thursday, February 25, 2010. Exploring Chile's Lake District by car, day #2. Today when we set out we had no particular destination in mind, but we still had the rental car so we decided to drive counterclockwise as far as Ensenada, then on the highway to Cochamo, an even smaller town on a fjord. I wanted to see an old wooden church that was shown in the guidebook and an eco-adventure lodge, Campo Adventura. We'd read that they offer single and multi-day guided horseback rides, hikes, kayaking and rafting adventures.

When we reached the Cochamo, we parked on the side of the highway and walked down the unpaved main road to the church and then on to the waterfront. There were rows of cages for raising farmed salmon and a few boats tied up on the pier. The views across the fjord were enchanting—the calm water before us, the clear blue sky above, and the snow-capped peaks of the Andes in the distance. Although few people were on the streets during our visit, intrepid hikers, equestrians, and others leave from here to enter the rainforest of Cochamo Valley[13] and La Junta area.

We spent some time walking along the roads of the town, admiring the small, shingled houses and looking for someplace to eat. There were signs for food, but nothing grabbed us. After we returned to the car, we made a half-hearted attempt to find Campo Adventura,[14] but were unsuccessful. I didn't want to stay there, I was just curious to see what their main lodge looked like. It turns out that they have two rustic lodges, and you can make reservations online or at their travel office, Outsider, back in Puerto Varas.

We drove back along the lake and river, then at Ensenada turned toward Petrohué, which is on another lake, Todos Los Santos. Along the way we entered another section of Vicente

Pérez Rosales National Park. We found signs indicating Saltos del Petrohué. Suddenly my reverie, brought on by the leisurely drive, was broken by Ralph's pulling into a parking lot, and I felt irritated. I didn't like the fact that we were leaving a lightly traveled road and going into a parking lot crammed with cars.

"Why do we want to stop *here?*" I shot at Ralph.

"You'll see," he said as we climbed out of the car. I lagged behind him as he led the way to the entrance station and pulled out his wallet to pay the 12 pesos (US$2.50) entrance fee. We followed the crowd, me still in a snit, but a short way along the trail, I found out why everyone and his brother was there: *saltos* means "jumps" and the Saltos del Petrohué, on the *Rio* (river) Petrohué, is a turbulent river that sends its water rushing, churning, blasting through the volcanic rock, and splashing and pouring over short drops.

We walked out on a set of sturdy planks over the rocks just above the monstrous river to several different viewpoints. We watched as jet boats came up the river, edged as close as they could to the thundering falls, and then drifted back—allowing their passengers to take photos—then approached again. It must have been quite a ride—though the boats were only a short time below the falls, it looked exhilarating.

The setting was gorgeous and in the distant background, we could see the Volcán Osorno, which is one of the sources of the water for Lake Todos Los Santos and the river.

After we explored the short network of trails, we hopped back in the car and drove another six miles, now on dirt and gravel roadway, to the end of the road and Petrohué. Petrohué, at the western end of Lake Todos los Santos, is more of a settlement than a town. It boasts a fine old hotel, aptly named Hotel Petrohué, and camping nearby. There were few people on the small beach, and but no one was swimming in the river or lake.

Although there was not a lot of activity when we were there, this is a popular stop for tourists visiting the chain of lakes, viewing the nearby mountain peaks, by boat and bus. There's a jetty where passengers board a boat to take them across the lake to the small settlement of Peulla. From Peulla, they can continue on to the Argentine border at Pérez Rosales and then to San Carlos de Bariloche. (Good map of the area: visitchile.cl/regiondeloslagos.htm)[15]

When we returned to Puerto Varas, we stopped for gas before turning in our rental car. We saw that the fuel prices were about one-and-a-half times higher than the average U.S. price, yet cheaper than in most of Western Europe.

We returned to the restaurant where we'd eaten the first night for dinner. My fettuccine with seafood and cream sauce was excellent—the mussels were succulent. We shared a bottle of Torres del Diablo, a cabernet, which we've added to our "favorites" list. For dessert I had vanilla ice cream atop a brownie. I'm usually hesitant to order cake in Latin America because I've often found it too dry. Not this time, the chocolate was moist and rich—perfect.

Our weather had been good—two solid days of sun. Even though it was a bit hotter than I would have preferred, we weren't complaining. The driver had said during our drive to Puerto Varas that they had had much more rain than usual.

Friday, February 26, 2010. Return to Puerto Montt and on to the Navimag ferry for cruise. We woke to overcast skies. Last night two guys sat outside our door talking quietly, but every sound traveled through the pine paneled walls. Ralph finally asked them to converse elsewhere. I felt bad at asking, but sleeping had been impossible.

Ralph had tried to reach Navimag (the car ferry that we will soon be taking) all week. We decided to get to Puerto Montt's waterfront early because we hadn't been able to reach anyone by phone. When we arrived at 9:20, we found that we couldn't board until 2:30 that afternoon; we spent the intervening time walking around the dock area.

Puerto Montt has two major sections—the waterfront and the main residential and commercial districts. Since most people arrive and leave by boat, and because the larger part of the town is some distance away and up a hill, most tourists spend their time on the waterfront.

Luckily this relatively small area near the dock where we would board the ship is an interesting one—and considered one of the best places in Chile to get a bargain on the products sold. The shops and booths of Feria Artesanal Angelmo that line the access road to the waterfront have good prices and bargaining is expected. We found a wide variety of goods for sale: plumbing materials; hand-dyed and hand-woven wool or alpaca sweaters and hats; straw baskets; leather ponchos and boots; art, as well as souvenir trinkets.

At the end of the road stands the weathered wooden building, partly on stilts above the estuary, which houses the *pescados y mariscos* (fish and seafood), meat and produce market that supplies residents and visitors with reasonably-priced, fresh products. Most businesses accept U.S. dollars, although the items might be priced in pesos. Bargaining is worth a try, although your success may depend on whether you can communicate adequately in Spanish or even Mapudungun, the language of the indigenous Mapuchu peoples.

We explored the ground floor of the marketplace, which was relatively quiet because no passenger ships were docked and because early bargain shoppers had come and gone. Vendors were rearranging the rows of fish on the crushed ice inside the glass display cases. Others were swabbing the concrete floors with mop and bucket. We wandered and admired the stands without anyone paying much attention.

The upper level was a different story—it was filled with tiny restaurants, one after another, primarily serving seafood. Most restaurants were just big enough to hold about four tables and a tiny kitchen. As we walked along the corridor trying to choose where to eat, we could look into the kitchens at the bubbling pots sending up enticing aromas and see a plateful of the luncheon specials. Those women who weren't busy serving customers were industriously prying mussels or clams open with a knife, or chopping onions or tomatoes for the soup. You can get a bowl of soup or a more filling lunch with *curanto* (meat, potatoes, seafood stew) for a very reasonable price.

It was nearing noon and we must have looked like good prospects for a hot lunch. As we walked along the wooden slats, each woman in turn called out, "Hay comida," (There is dinner.)

"¿Quiere salmon?" (Do you want salmon?)

"¿Buenos tardes, quiere comer?" (Good afternoon, do you wish to eat?)

After going through the entire labyrinth, we went back to one we had passed earlier that had appetizing sausage on display in the store-front window. We squeezed into the small benches at one of the tables.

"I also like this choice because it has the most people in it," added Ralph.

"They could all be family for all we know," I replied.

Maybe yes, maybe no, but all were Chilean. At one table was a family of four—dad, mom, and two children under six. At the second table, another family. A man of about forty occupied the third table—slumped over, asleep. After a while, a woman of similar age came in and tried to wake him by shaking him. No response. She spoke briefly to him, still no response. She left. Everyone quietly watched and wondered what would happen next. The woman at table #1 chuckled just as I had.

We were served our lunch—potatoes, sausage, soup—and a small vial of Pisco Sour as a treat. All of a sudden, I saw the slumped-over man start to fall. It happened in slow motion. I knew what was going to happen, but I couldn't do anything to stop it. He slowly rolled out of his seat and landed on his head with a loud "thud." Everyone jumped. The shop owner from next door came in, and with the help of the restaurant owner, hauled the passed-out man outside and propped him up on a bench where he could lean against the wall. I had the feeling that this was not a rare occurrence. Eventually, passed-out man gained consciousness and staggered on his way. Whether he was drunk, coming off a fishing trip or just the town drunk we'll never know.

The waterfront was a fun place for taking photos. There were lots of small boats—originally brightly colored, but now with faded and peeling paint. These are fishing boats, not pleasure boats, and well used. Dock workers were struggling with heavy carts and dollies loaded with boxes and crates headed for our ship's hold.

By the time we returned to the Navimag's waiting room, the chairs, many of which had spent their younger days as airline seats in the economy section, were filled with the hundreds of passengers. Animated conversations in German, French, and English had transformed the warehouse-type room into a friendly space.

As departure time approached, the Navimag staff came out to welcome us—first in Spanish, then English. Then a short list of names was called and when "Alcorn" was announced we were invited to follow one of the personnel onboard. Although I knew we were going to have a private room—I had insisted to Ralph that we have our own bathroom so I could throw up when seasick in the privacy of my own place, I didn't realize that this made us part of the "AAA team."

We were escorted to our room, invited to tour our group's private dining room, and given a complimentary bottle of wine. I was happy to have my own room rather than sleeping in a room with multiple bunks, but I knew that we were going to have a different experience than if we mixed with all of the passengers.

Not that our cabin was fancy. Unlike the deluxe rooms on cruise ships, which provide private balconies accessed by glass doors, Navimag's AAA rooms do not have an outside wall of windows. Nor were there a TV, bar, hand-held hair dryer or fancy lotions. On one wall were our two bunks; on the other was a set of drawers and wardrobe closet. I gave bonus points for the fact that the small bathroom had a curtain to keep the shower spray from soaking the rest of the room.

After we unpacked, we toured the rest of the ship. The Navimag is not only a passenger ferry for walk-on travelers like us, but also a car and transport ferry. We watched the maneuvers of the truck drivers as they were guided into their places on the lower decks; it was impressive how well orchestrated the procedures were and how tightly all the vehicles were packed. After that lengthy process, the crew released us from the dock and our four-day voyage began. We came out of Reloncaví Estuary, entered the more open Ancud Gulf and by sunset had entered Corcovado Gulf. By the time we went to dinner, we had already seen two dolphins and a whale.

Our small dining room was comfortable: carpeted, furnished with four round tables, each set for four couples. Our server was Felipe. He was a student in his 20s—very polite and non-intrusive. We eventually managed to pry some more information out of him; he was trying to decide whether he wants a career working in an emergency room or as a paramedic.

We were served soup, salmon, green rice (flavored by parsley), an iceberg lettuce salad typical of the 1950s, and melon for dessert. I had expected a mediocre meal, hurried wait staff, and much less cushy surroundings, so I was pleasantly surprised by the upscale food and service.

When we returned to our cabin, I noted that we did not have terrycloth towels twisted into elephant, rabbit, or stingray shapes placed on turned-down bedding like we'd have on a Carnival cruise. It was less fancy, but more exciting. With some effort, I managed to open the porthole. However, the wind coming in was so strong that everything loose in the room blew around and so leaving the "window" open would have made a mess. At least the knowledge that I could open a window kept me from feeling claustrophobic.

Saturday, February 27, 2010. Navimag ferry, day #2. When we explored the common areas of the interior yesterday, we had discovered that most of the passengers ate self-serve in a cafeteria and learned that they paid extra for their wine. We have mixed feelings about being in the superior accommodations—of course it's wonderful to have the extra service and better quality food, but it also makes us feel apart from the other passengers, in particular the more adventurous travelers.

Midday, Ralph and I wandered into the cafeteria completely unaware that an announcement had been made earlier requesting that everyone come to that room. The director read from a multi-page letter that a 9.5 magnitude earthquake had hit Chile at 3:34 that morning, centered in Concepción and not far from

Santiago. We sat there, like everyone else, sort of in shellshock. 9.5! It was beyond comprehension.

It was announced that ninety-five percent of the homes in Concepción (Chile's second largest city, 62 km. from the epicenter) had been destroyed and that people had fled to the streets to be out of danger; there had already been more than forty aftershocks. We heard conflicting reports of damage at the Santiago airport, but learned that it had been shut down. Phone and Internet services were non-functional (whether down or overloaded we didn't know.) After the messages had been read in both Spanish and English, the notice was posted on the wall and several people went over to read its contents for themselves.

In the afternoon, as we passed a small settlement on one of the nearby tiny islands, many people grabbed their cell phones for the few minutes of phone reception that allowed them to make some contacts.

AT DINNER, WE realize that one of the couples in our small group lives in Concepción. When they made phone calls earlier, they reached one son, but not their second one—who had been traveling and was due back home. It can't be much fun to be stuck on this ship when all you want to do is find out if your home, your community, and your family are okay. The husband keeps up his good-natured banter with the rest of the group, but his wife is subdued and barely speaks. I can't blame her; I'd be beside myself.

OTHER THAN MEALTIMES, most of our day was spent roaming the ferry, inside and out. At sunrise we were going through the Moraleda Channel, one of the deepest on the route, and at sunset we sailed into the Pacific around the Gulf of Penas. I imagine everyone was a bit curious how it would be in the open waters of the ocean, compared to the more protected channels we'd been in. I was worried about seasickness and continued with my pills, but it was pretty much a non-event. Although we were about 12 hours in the open, most of that time we were sleeping. Luckily the seas have been very light—

three- to five-foot waves at most; other passengers said that they had been on the ship when the waves were in the 20-25 foot category.

Sunday, February 28, 2010. Navimag ferry, day #3. We received no more official word about the earthquake or the expected tsunamis. News was passed from one person to the next and we learned that the rating had been officially recorded as 8.8. There had been tsunami warnings along the coast of Chile, in Hawaii, and as far away as Australia. The damage to Santiago International Airport was minor—an outbuilding and a highway overpass that brought traffic to the airport. Another one of the couples in our dining room was trying to figure out if their scheduled flight home from Santiago would be cancelled or not. As time went on, we learned that the airport stayed closed to commercial travel for a few days, but was open for emergency aid.

Considering that the earthquake was 8.8 and the one in Haiti earlier this year was a 7.0 (making the Chilean one almost 1,000 times stronger than the one in Haiti), the discrepancy between the numbers of fatalities is amazing. While Haiti's government initially said that 150,000 had died in the January 12th earthquake, in February, they raised that number to at least 230,000. In Chile, the earthquake and the tsunami together left approximately 450 dead.

As the ferry made its way through the archipelago, we saw hundreds of tiny, mostly barren and uninhabited islands. There were also islands covered with scrub or Cypress and Lengas forests down to water's edge. Zillions of waterways. Ribbons of waterfalls drifting to the sea. We saw few other boats, but we passed the Capitán Leonidas, a rusted, sunken Greek cargo ship.

The Capitán Leonidas, built in Bremen, Germany in 1937, has been in the channel since it ran aground in 1968, on the partially-submerged islet known as Bajo Cotopaxi in the Strait of Magellan. Running aground in the Strait of Magellan was not unprecedented; in fact the freighter Santa Leonor had been wrecked and abandoned in March of that same year. What was unusual was what happened afterward.

After delivering its cargo of sugar, the captain of the Leonidas carried out a scheme whereby he would run the ship aground, then claim the sugar had dissolved in the water, and then collect the insurance on both vessel and cargo. The plan backfired—the ship didn't sink. The Greek captain went to prison.

After that the Chilean navy used her for target practice, further damaging the ship, but still not sinking it. Although the official story tells us only that it is now used as a lighthouse and as a navigation point for sailors, some say there's also a ghost onboard.[16,17]

Lunch was enormous! We didn't eat it all, but we were served empanadas stuffed with steak and potatoes, as well as salad, soup, wine, pineapple ice cream and cookies. I'm so glad we refrained from stuffing ourselves—my pants are already way too tight.

In the afternoon, the ship reached the tiny town of Puerto Eden and most people took the tenders over to reach the small village. It cost US$20, which was reasonable enough, but we hadn't heard any compelling reason to leave the ship, so we stayed put. We amused ourselves by watching everyone else make their brief visit. They were required to wear their life jackets the whole time they were on the boats *and* the island. They had a choice of two walking routes through town and then uphill to a sheltered overlook. It was pretty easy to follow their progress because their orange vests could be spotted a mile away.

After the island call, we went into another waterway to see a huge glacier. Ralph said that, like the Glaciar Perito Merino that we saw last year in Los Glaciares National Park, Glaciar Pío XI is part of the Southern Patagonia Ice Field. Pío XI (also known as the Brüggen Glacier) is approximately 40 miles long and one of the few glaciers in the world that continues growing.

I was amazed at how close the ship was able to go and how long we stayed near it. Because we had been told that how close we'd be able to get to the glacier depended on the weather and seas, I think we were all holding our breath in anticipation.

It was quite beautiful; the water at the base of the glacier was so still that we could see the reflection of the glacier in it. There were lots of chunks of ice floating in the water and our friendly crew went out in their rafts and collected ice chunks for our piña coladas and afterward, we all posed for photos holding large chunks.

That evening's conversation over dinner made me glad that we hadn't bothered to go to the island. Even though it would have been nice to get off the boat and walk around with the others, the consensus was that there wasn't much to see and there were no shops to visit.

After dinner, there was a bingo game and then some sort of party. I'd wanted to go, but we had stayed up late the night before watching a video in the dining room and we were too tired to stay up. Even though we weren't getting any exercise except for our quick ten laps around the deck, standing for hours on end to watch the passing scenery was tiring.

Monday, March 1, 2010. The Navimag Ferry reaches Puerto Natales. Ralph thought the ship would arrive at Puerto Natales this morning, but at breakfast we learned that it would not arrive until 2:00 in the afternoon. That threw a cog in the works for the next couple of days because we had planned to catch the bus to Torres del Paine at 2:30 p.m.

We tried everything we could to make our connection. We packed early and obtained permission to wait by the staircase down to the main deck so that we could leave the ship with the first batch of people as soon as we docked. But it became clearer minute by minute that there was no way we were catching our bus. The docking process seemed to take forever—small boats pulled alongside us and crew would catch a rope and help pull the ship into position. Then the ship would power slowly back and forth to get close to the dock without ramming it.

It was after three o'clock when we finally were able to disembark. We moved quickly out to the street, but then couldn't find an unoccupied cab. Ralph and I had a disagreement. He continued to walk towards the hostel where we were going to leave our extra bag with our town clothes; I continued to harp on the fact that we were walking away from the center of town and we'd never find a cab at that rate. I was hoping against hope that the bus would be running late and that we could catch it.

Because Puerto Natales is a small town and our hostel was only six blocks from the pier, we reached the Casa Cecilia quickly. When I had communicated with Rob Hodges (previously mentioned on p. 90) regarding the trip he and his wife took last year, he had highly recommended the Erratic Rock Hostel. It's inexpensive and known for giving detailed information about the various hikes in Torres del Paine and elsewhere. But we had enjoyed staying at Casa Cecilia last year, so we returned. Because we had arrived without a reservation, we were lucky that they had a vacancy and that we had a place to sleep. (US$50 for room with bath, and breakfast)

The owners assured us that it wasn't a problem that we had missed the bus; we could catch one in the morning. We spent the remainder of the afternoon walking around town, which seemed to have more shops, restaurants, and hostels than last year. Overall, the town seemed cleaner. We had a pricey dinner—steak for Ralph and seafood stew for me.

When we came back to Casa Cecilia, we struck up a conversation with another woman staying there. She and her husband had just completed the trail that we were going to do. They had encountered perfect weather, but she had heard that the pass had been closed because of snow the week before they were there. She echoed all the other reports about going downhill from Garner Pass—that it is long and very steep.

She also mentioned that Camp Italiano, which gets hikers from two different routes, was too crowded and had only one toilet, making it very unsanitary. We'd like to bypass this camp, but to go further in one day is probably too much.

Finally I had access to a computer and was able to e-mail everyone that we were okay.

10 • Torres del Paine — Circuit or Bust!

Tuesday, March 2, 2010. Puerto Natales to Torres del Paine by bus; hike to Campamento Serón. We set the alarm for 6:30 a.m. and quickly ate breakfast because our bus was scheduled to arrive at 7:15 a.m. But it didn't. Once again I sat anxiously wondering if our plans were going to be thrown off, but the hostel's owner made a call to the bus company and reported to us that the bus was making the rounds of the various hostels picking people up, and would definitely come by Casa Cecilia as well. At 8:00 a.m., it did.

Then we were underway on the bus Gomez. Bus Gomez is not a chickens-in-the-aisle, crates-on-the-roof kind of operation. It's a first-class bus with reclining upholstered seats, woven-cloth curtains that can be pulled open or shut, and a toilet at the rear. The roughly two-hour ride to Torres del Paine is a traveler's bargain. We were traveling under sunny skies with distant views of snow-capped mountains and brilliantly-white glaciers. Closer were the wheat-colored grassland and the tough brush blowing in the wind. Photogenic guanacos and rhea appeared with such regularity that it was almost as if we looking at a backdrop in a movie studio.

The process of entering Torres del Paine had been simplified since last year. While we were on the bus, we were given a form to fill out with our name and passport information—which made our registration at the entrance station at Laguna Amarga go quickly. Once we arrived, Ralph paid the entrance fee and I ran to use the restroom. I had started out in the wrong direction and so wasted some time getting there.

Still, it looked to me like filling the shuttle would take a bit of time, so I didn't rush. When I came out, the bus driver was waving to me to hurry up, and Ralph was standing in the bus's aisle looking rather stressed. He'd told the driver that I wasn't on board.

"I think your running for the bathroom when we are boarding a bus/airplane, etc. is one of your defining characteristics," he said. This was not meant as a compliment!

"It's no different than when I was a teenager and had to keep running to the bathroom when I was waiting nervously for a date to show up," I replied. "I can remember being in the bathroom and worrying that my date would arrive and hear the toilet flush."

There were more guanacos and rheas alongside the road as we entered the park, but the rocky dirt road was too bumpy to allow any photos. The Torres range was out in all its glory.

We got off at Refugio Torre, filled our water bottles, and got on the trail for the Circuit at 10:45 a.m. We were back on schedule and excited that things had finally fallen into place.

The first couple of hours were sunny, even hot. I discovered that I had left my favorite sun hat behind. Ralph had a bandanna he could spare, so I ended up wearing that, Babushka-style, tied under my chin. Then it began to sprinkle. Ralph stopped promptly to put on his rain gear, but I tried to ignore it. Who wants to stop and unpack and put on raingear when it's only a little wet?

The drizzle continued to the point where I had to stop, and luckily I did because the rain increased and the wind picked up. I put on my Packa, an all-in-one pack cover and rain jacket combination that we were using for the first time. Mine worked well except for the clammy feeling on my arms. I've sort of given up on our old system—separate pack cover and rain jacket—because the pack cover hasn't done its job so my pack always gets wet.

Finally during the last hour of the hike, the sun came out, my pants dried, and we arrived at Campamento Serón. Part of the change in precipitation is due to location. Just like large mountains often create their own weather, where you are in Torres del Paine matters. You can be in the open and dry one moment, and then on the wet side of the glacier with wind blowing moisture the next.

RALPH AND I are pleased with ourselves for our earlier than expected arrival at camp. The suggested time for the hike is four hours and it took us only a half-hour more—and that includes the time spent unpacking and packing raingear.

It is comforting to be returning to a place where we've been before and not have to figure out how everything works. Although the host from last year, Felipe, is no longer here (he is working elsewhere in the park), the new host is friendly too. We order dinner for seven o'clock.

Not much has changed from last year, except for the fact that none of the rental tents are set up. The grayed, wooden outbuilding, which formerly looked like someone might be sleeping there occasionally, has been converted to a storage shed for tools and wood.

There is one big change, however, and that is the state of the kitchen. Felipe, sweet as he was, was not the most organized or tidy person. On his watch, dishes, washed and unwashed, were strewn everywhere. This year's host carries a cloth around with him and wipes up spills before they dry.

BY THE TIME night had fallen, about a dozen tents had been set up in the grassy clearing.

Wednesday, March 3, 2010. Campamento Serón to campground at Refugio Dickson. After our breakfast in the refugio at Serón: cornflakes, scrambled eggs, bread and jam, we were underway about eight-thirty.

The hike itself started with some good climbs and subsequent short downhills—trickier when dry. At a couple of points, the trail became a suggestion of a path. There were footsteps to follow in the rock, but I was acutely aware that missing one of the indentations would be bad. I didn't allow myself to look down for more than a second; I didn't want to consider how serious a fall would be down the mountainside. The longer I hesitated, the more nervous I became, so I forced myself to take a deep breath, look only at where I wanted to go, and go for it. Sometimes I felt that I must have been supported by some other force; more than once I felt that my steps were only on air—sort of like when you're driving and the road is too narrow and you mentally shrink your car like you pull in your stomach.

My bunions were acting up—sometimes sending little jabs of pain, other times making me limp. I was sure it was brought on by wearing boots instead of trail runners, but I felt I needed the additional support of the boots, so it was a trade-off. It was just hard to enjoy the hiking when my feet hurt.

I'd forgotten about the swampy stretch near the end of the day—the empty paint cans that we saw last year were still sitting by some boards and the so-called "bridge" was still unfinished. There were no planks to walk on; we had to make our way across using the 4 x 4s along the edge. Maybe the whole bridge project had been halted because the bridge, even when completed, wouldn't go nearly far enough. After we made our way across the structure, we still had to walk in the squishy mud for many yards. At this point, I was glad I had on boots—bunions or not.

We did notice that the trail had been improved in one way; it was now extremely well marked with posts or bright-pink plastic streamers. Less adventure, but more reassuring.

The final descent to Campamento Dickson was as challenging as I remembered. The only difference was that I was determined to make it down the side of the steep moraine by myself. One minute we were walking along the top of a cliff and then suddenly we had to drop 200 feet down on a dirt trail with loose rock and nothing to hold onto. It didn't seem to bother the majority of hikers—who being much younger seemed to have no problem with their knees and could almost run down—but I had to focus on every step and plan every turn.

Even though Ralph would have taken my pack down like he did last year if I had asked, this time I was determined to do it myself, and standing up. Ralph helped this time, too, but by talking me down it.

His instructions of, "Just go as far as that root, it's stable," and "Trust your poles," were reassuring.

"Why isn't this little stretch mentioned in the guidebooks?" I asked. "It's worrisome that the guidebook authors talk a lot about the difficulty of the John Garner Pass ahead of us, but don't say anything about this part of the trail."

Granted it was comparatively short, but still not everyone in their sixties and seventies would be able to handle these descents. I had to stop and catch my breath. I felt drained, but I was elated. Maybe I *was* better prepared for the tests to come!

We got to Dickson about quarter to five. Most of the time the weather was fantastic—clear blue skies and amazing views of the peaks and glaciers. It was such a contrast to last year's rain, wind, and fog—and lengthier time of the trail.

Dinner at Refugio Dickson was okay (though disappointing compared to last year's fish): soup, mashed potatoes, meat with gravy, canned peaches, and weak pineapple juice. It was worth the cost of admission, however, because it gave us an hour's respite from the mosquitoes. When we went back to our tent, we watched the Canadian couple camped near us battling the mosquitoes. I offered them some of our DEET, which the young woman gratefully accepted.

"I carried DEET for months all over Central and South American and didn't use it, so I finally got rid of it," she said.

Later, when I walked over to brush my teeth, I walked by a fellow standing alongside his picnic table. He had his stove going full blast and he was holding it out in front of him trying to burn up some of the irritating bugs.

Thursday, March 4, 2010. Dickson to Los Perros camp (8:30 a.m. - 2:20 p.m.) Today was our third hiking day. It was just above freezing when we got up. Even though I was very cold, I didn't want to bother digging out my gloves. We wanted to be out early on the trail, which was important because we always took more time than the CONAF map suggested.

We had set the alarm for 6:50 a.m. in order have breakfast early and to get an earlier start. I thought charging US$10 for a small bowl of cornflakes with hot milk, toasted hamburger buns with butter and jam, and tea or coffee with milk was a rip-off. I know it meant saved time and effort for us in the morning, that we'd have less to carry, and that they had to have it brought in, but still….

WE HAVE MIXED feelings about our new air mattresses. They are comfy because we don't feel the hard surface or any rocks under us. However, there's a problem with the length of the mattresses. Since they are only ¾-length, my legs or head, or both, are suspended in air. If I overinflate it, I feel like I am on a surfboard. I have to stack up a mound of clothes and put my feet on my empty backpack to create a level surface. Then during the night everything shifts around and has to be reconstructed in the dark.

In addition, if we are on even the slightest slope, they slip out from under us like a greased pig slips out of a farmer's hands. Luckily our four-season tent has double-wall construction and most of it doesn't get wet inside from condensation. That's good, because the mattress and I end up against the tent wall each night and if the sides were wet, I'd get soaked.

I suppose in time we will learn how to stay atop our mattresses, and in position. Otherwise, when we take our next trip with our regular backpacking tent that is a single wall construction—rather than the four-season—we will have problems with the greater amount of condensation.

WHAT A CONTRAST weather-wise to last year. We put our raingear at the top of our packs in case we needed it, but we walked through the forest with broken sunlight, then overcast skies, all day. No wind. It seemed to both of us that there were new footbridges and many more markers, so it was easy to find the way. And, because the ground was dry, the trail was much easier to hike. The steep climbs remained, but they were short. The moraine, which gave us so much grief last year, was a breeze (actually the air was practically still!). This was a very good day.

When we first arrived at Perros, we were surprised to see several bright orange tents set up. Ralph was a bit out of sorts about it because they were in the very place where we were last year and he had hoped to set up there again. Because the tents were all in a group, and of the same color, we assumed that it was a guided trip or an expedition of some sort.

What was most impressive about them was that each was not only securely staked, but also was surrounded by at least a dozen large rocks weighing down the tent fly. They were prepared for serious winds. After I snooped around a bit more, I found out that the tents were empty—they were the campground's rental tents.

The map said this would be a four-and-a-half-hour day, and 8.7 km. We decided that seemed accurate. Although it took us six hours, we stopped multiple times for snacks, peeing, lunch, and photos, so we weren't too far off the mark.

Ralph put up the tent and we unpacked. I sat alone inside the green metal warming shelter and watched a sparrow that had hopped in looking for spilled crumbs. The scene was so different from last year's. It was more interesting when the hut was crowded with campers cooking meals or sitting by the stove and with wet clothes draped on lines strung from rafter to rafter.

This would be the first meal we'd cooked for ourselves on this trip. As I was writing this, camp was showing more activity as more people showed up. There was a three-some from Switzerland: a blond guy who doesn't speak much English, his wife, who is more outgoing and with whom we exchange greetings, and an older woman who we presume is the mother of one of the two younger ones. We had been leapfrogging them for a couple of days. .

There were two twenty-year-old girls from Punta Arenas who just finished a three-month season working at Refugio Grey (which was still ahead of us) and who were now doing the Circuit before they headed home. Men staff the three refugios that we'd stayed near so far and we noticed that their spirits brightened when the girls checked in. Most of the women that we saw on the trail didn't wear makeup, but these young women did and the fact that they are young, cute, and friendly had not gone unnoticed. There was also a solo middle-aged guy.

The Canadian couple we'd met in the last camp made a brief stop, looked around, but since it was early afternoon, decided to continue on. We'll never know if they went only a short distance so they could avoid the camping fee or if they went on over the pass. It made me sad to realize that we would probably never catch up with or see them again.

I was still expecting to see the two Swiss guys we'd seen each of the last two nights. It may have been wishful thinking, but I usually felt that there was a better chance that we could get help on the trail if we'd previously established some contact with other hikers.

TOMORROW WILL BE the big day; we will try to go over Paso John Garner. This is what we've been thinking about for almost two years (and what I've been worried about much of that time!). I am trying to stay in the present and not worry about the future.

FRIDAY, MARCH 5, 2010. Los Perros to Campamento Paso. 7.44 miles (12 km.). it took us two hours to get underway this morning because we cooked breakfast. We wished we could have been speedier, but we were not willing to give up our hot cereal and beverages, so we were stuck.

We started out about eight o'clock, which was earlier than most people in camp. We wanted to be among those first out because we wanted the reassurance of knowing that someone was behind us in case we needed help. The CONAF map said it would take six hours, but Ralph wisely had estimated fifty percent more time.

The start of the trail was worrisome; it began with a very steep climb up footholds that had been dug or worn into the hillside. I just about threw in the towel in right then; I couldn't imagine going through such strenuous terrain for miles. Luckily, we only had to maneuver through a short section of tree roots and then it leveled out. Next was a long, swampy area, still through the spindly Lengua trees, where the challenge was to find firm ground for each footstep. Of course mishaps were bound to occur; I managed to step into a soggy spot and the mud went just short of the top of my boots, but my hiking pole went in about fifteen inches. Finally, we reached some exposed rocky areas, which then alternated with the forest, and the footing was better.

Eventually we were above timberline and began to climb through rock to the pass. Luckily the way was easy to find—with orange-tipped stakes, or orange paint on a rock, or flags. By the time we reached the top, about a 2,100-foot climb, almost everyone else from Los Perros had passed us and was sitting within the shelter of large rocks having lunch; it was noon.

As everyone else was doing, we took photos of the summit and looked at the collection of socks, scarves, and other "offerings" that had been left in a makeshift monument. A second pile of rocks had a string of faded Tibetan prayer flags attached.

I thought of a comment that Rob Hodges had sent me, "The wind on top [of Garner Pass] was hellacious, making it really difficult to stand." We had no wind at all.

As we'd made the climb, the sky had looked like rain was likely, but other than a few sprinkles, we had lucked out. There was enough sun to highlight Glaciar Grey below us. It was impossible to take in the scope of the ice field at one time and impossible to photograph in a way that showed how immense it is. It's part of the Southern Patagonian ice field (as is Argentina's Fitz Roy), which is the third largest ice cap in the world (about the same size as Hawaii or Wales).

We worked so hard for this victory—yet for me at least, the most difficult part was still ahead. The trail started down fairly gradually through the granite, and then started to switchback through the rock. Eventually we reached forest again—and continued down relentlessly for about 2,600 feet.

Everyone passed us, many without poles, but apparently with stronger knees. If it hadn't been for the trees and the wooden and metal railings along the way, there's no way I could have done the hundreds of steps.

In the process I shed a few tears, more from frustration at my slower-than-average pace than anything. My knees got stiffer as time went by, and my bunions hurt at times, but all in all, I did well. Thank god Ralph had the patience to go as slowly as I needed to go.

Not far from the end of the hike, we had a *very* difficult bridge crossing (for me anyway). It was simply two logs with flattened tops, about eight feet above the water and some huge rocks, spanning the river. A fall would have meant something broken to be sure. I managed to do it carrying my own backpack. It was a big victory for me—even Ralph said so, which was perhaps an even bigger victory. Once safely on the other side, I turned to see Ralph's expression, lost my balance and almost fell over backward.

THE CAMPGROUND, CAMP Paso, is a dump. We are in a nice enough setting, but there is toilet paper everywhere you look. I can hardly blame people for using the shrubs as a toilet however, because the one provided is even more disgusting.

The building that houses the toilet is bigger than a regular out-house—perhaps 10 feet square. The concrete floor has a hole in it (into which one "goes") and mounted on the wall behind the hole is a regular toilet tank complete with pull chain for flushing. I have no idea if the flushing part works, or how effective it is, because I am so thoroughly disgusted by the mound of used toilet paper that has been thrown against the wall nearest the door that I am leaving.

WE GOT TO camp before 5:00 p.m., so the nine hours Ralph had estimated was correct. It was a very long, tiring day, but we made it over the pass! It was now 8:00 p.m. and it was pouring rain. I shudder to think about what it would be like to be on the pass right then; was it possible that someone was looking out for me?

Saturday, March 6, 2010. Camp Paso to campground at Refugio Grey. A remarkable day! Since it rained the day yesterday, I had wondered what this day would bring, but it was perfect weather-wise, not too hot or cold. We hiked 8:30 a.m. - 3:00 p.m. (six and a half hours for what the CONAF map listed as a four-hour hike, but we were making our usual stops for snacks and photos.)

The morning was spent cautiously continuing our way downhill through forested areas. Then we came to the first deep gorge—with ladders. We had to make our way down the slope, cross the river by walking on one set of flattened logs that led to a huge rock that we could grab onto and then onto another set of logs. Once across, we had to climb up the other side of the gorge using a steep set of ladders connected to one another.

As we approached the first one, I thought of what the experienced mountain climber from Lake Tahoe that we met last year had commented, "I don't know your skills, but the ladders could be quite challenging." I remembered Rose's comments when I interviewed her last winter, "I don't ever want to have to use the ladders again." That, too, had been food for thought. Next to my fears about making it over the pass, using the ladders had been my biggest concern about the hike. At the same time, there was no way that I was going to turn back and go over the pass in the opposite direction. Somehow at those moments, I acquired a fatalistic approach.

When we approached we found the ladders were made of two- or three-inch diameter pipes each about eight feet long and bolted to the next ladder. Huge cables anchored the whole works to rocks above. It looked doable.

It *could* have been different—in fact in the past it *had* been different. Remnants of several old, rotted wooden ladders were visible across the ravine—barely clinging to the slopes. Having to use one of those abandoned relics would have been a different story altogether. Although it didn't feel at all risky while we were there, if it had been raining it would have been rather unpleasant. And it could have been a treacherous crossing if there had been more water flowing in the creek. As it turned out, it was a piece of cake; I felt like I was home free!

Further downhill, we came to Campamento Los Guardas, which is also a free campground (like Paso). It was in a beautiful wooded setting backed up against a hillside of large rocks. Although I didn't check the inside of the outhouse, at first glance Los Guardas seemed cleaner—there wasn't toilet paper in every nook and cranny.

A young Chilean who was doing some maintenance at the camp gestured toward a sign, *Mirador*, so we did a brief detour that took us out of the woods and to an overlook of Grey Glacier; it turned out to be a magnificent place for lunch.

Continuing downhill, we started meeting day hikers coming uphill from Refugio Grey and, coincidentally, the trail became a very easy track—no roots, rocks, or climbs—just a nice, almost manicured, dirt path. It was wonderfully welcome not to have to watch each and every footstep.

Yet there was a part of me that felt some chagrin that the day hikers would not get a real sampling of what we had en- countered. I wished that they'd had to struggle along with me so that they would appreciate and acknowledge my hard work and bravery. Of course it shouldn't have mattered one iota to me what they thought, but my ego wanted my every accom- plishment to be noticed.

We checked in at Campamento Grey to pay our camping fees and arrange for dinner. The refugio at Refugio Grey is much nicer than the ones at Serón and Dickson. It was newer, had restrooms with showers that had normal water flow and temperatures, and I wouldn't have been afraid to sleep in the bunk beds because it seemed so clean.

At 4:00 p.m., the ferry from across the lake at Hostería Lago Grey (a four-star accommodation not to be confused with where we were at Campamento Grey) arrived to collect the day visitors. After they left, it was quieter in the campground, but because Refugio Grey is both the terminus of one of the legs of the popular "W" route as well as one of the stops on the Circuit, there were dozens of tents set up in the beachside campground.

I took my journal and paperback inside the refugio to read. We skimmed the hikers' logbook and noticed that many people had mentioned enjoying "Gato." It took a while to figure out why they were writing about a cat, but then Ralph saw boxes of *Gato* brand wine on a shelf and bought us some to drink.

I felt like I was in a dream—warm, cozy, and safe. I sat there relishing the fact that I was once again sitting in a chair with a back to it, in clean clothes, and warm and dry. As I sipped my wine, I enjoyed listening to the kitchen staff joking back and forth as they set the tables. I took pleasure in watching their antics when they stopped their chores from time to time to dance along with the upbeat Latin music. A delicious sense of well-being came to me as I recalled the thrill of successfully navigating the ladders.

Sunday, March 7, 2010. Campamento Lago Grey to Italiano. Trekking day #6 was a long one, 9 a.m. – 6 p.m. We had the usual breakfast of cornflakes, hot milk, and hamburger buns, with a bonus of watered-down juice and a slice of cheese. The cost of the meal still irked me, but I did like eating inside where it was warm.

The trail section from Lago Grey to Paine Grande was rated "moderate." Still, considering how easy yesterday's final section had been, I figured it would be fairly easy. It wasn't—there were lots of ups and downs and we were mostly going through forest.

It was one of the prettiest sections—mosses and plants growing from fallen trees and lots of purple and white varieties of foxglove. In a couple of places the trail takes one climbing through rocky outcroppings where a slip would send you sliding down a hillside to the lake—that is unless the thorny shrubs below tore you up and stopped you first.

I had to readjust my thinking—snob that I can be. The "W" hikers and the day hikers weren't going to have it easy; they were getting a good workout and a fair sampling of the variety of the terrain.

As we were coming through a valley before the turnoff to Paine Grande, it became very windy and we saw three condors soaring above the nearest ridge and occasionally lighting on the highest rocks. They were close enough that we could see the flashes of white on their wings. My camera isn't capable of taking National Geographic-type photos, but at least I was able to capture a few images of these magnificent birds.

We reached the turnoff to Paine Grande at early afternoon, but we stopped only long enough for a couple of photos of the cabins. Although there was also a campground, it was relatively early in the day and our plans were to go farther. I was disappointed that we couldn't go into the lodge and have lunch and get to a computer for emails, but all that was somewhat off our trail. When Ralph told me that some of the rooms featured hot tubs I was even more curious, but we weren't tired and so I didn't complain about continuing on.

It's a weird, but real, phenomenon that long-distance hikers seemed to have a built-in resistance to leaving the appointed trail. We would walk 20 miles to get to the next destination, but refuse to detour 500 feet to see some unscheduled curiosity.

The trail's rating changed to "easy," but it certainly wouldn't allow wheelchair access. Along the edge of Lago Skottsberg, the wind, which had been mild, became increasingly brisk. As we watched, the waves grew noticeably higher and then turned to whitecaps. Miniature water spouts danced across the water. Exhilarating and refreshing!

Several stretches of the trail had to be crossed using logs or planks that earlier hikers had dropped across the boggy soil. Other places required rock hopping in order to avoid the mud. We were happier when we were in the forested area because we were sheltered from the wind.

We heard a mighty roar ahead, which meant that we were approaching either a whole lot of wind or water. We came out of the trees to a bridge. On the other side of the river was our day's destination, Campamento Italiano; on our side of the bridge was a hand-lettered sign reading "No mas dos personas" (no more than two people). At least the bridge had sides—after a fashion! There were steel cables to hang onto and there was also chicken wire strung along the side so that we couldn't fall off.

As I walked across the wooden-planked swinging bridge, it bounced with every step and my thoughts turned to the scene in the *Bridge of the River Kwai*, which I guess was the first time I'd heard that soldiers crossing a bridge have to stop walking in cadence so that the resonance doesn't break the bridge.

The Italiano campground, which was used by "W" hikers on their way up the highly-regarded Valle del Francés as well as the Circuit hikers, was filled cheek to jowl with tents. We found a flat place and while Ralph set up the tent, I went looking for the toilets. Signs directed me downhill, across a couple of log-spanned creeks, about two-tenths of a mile.

There were two doors to the building with the restrooms that served the camp. One of the doors had been nailed shut. The second door had a sign that read, "Closed for repair." Great, probably 80 people were camped in a small area that had a sign posted saying "Capacity 40" and there was no working toilet!

MONDAY, MARCH 8, 2010. *Italiano to Los Cuernos. 3:00 a.m. Trekking day seven of our Circuit hike is starting too early. I am lying in our cozy tent, the roar of the river drowning out any snoring or movement that might be made by the dozens of other campers nearby. Ralph is sound asleep and I am hoping my small headlamp won't wake him. There is an even higher-pitched roar—the wind. Although the trees with their thin trunks bend and sway, they still buffer us from the wind's force. A softer, scratchy sound is made by the small golden leaves that are being blown and blasted from the trees this fall morning.*

At least I think we are protected—falling branches are always a possibility, but is a risk most of us ignore. There was one exception to this laissez-faire attitude last night—a red-jacketed man, camped a hundred yards up from us, shimmied up a tall tree to knock down and break off the limbs that were hanging over his bright orange tent.

5:00 A.M. I fell back into a sound sleep, but was re-awakened by a huge crashing sound that echoed down the mouth of the canyon. It must have been a refrigerator-sized chunk of ice falling from one of the glaciers higher up the valley. A second shot. I wondered if the tremendous new icebergs could make the river rise a measurable amount for even a few seconds. I suppose it would be infinitesimal—so huge is the canyon and the volume of the river. I marveled that such a huge object dropped into the glacier's pool was of no more consequence than that of a tiny one.

We packed up our gear, but left some of the heavier equipment behind as we set out on our side trip from Camp Italiano into the French Valley. We planned to go as far up the valley as we could before we had to turn around; we wanted to be back to the camp by two o'clock. I fretted (some would say complained) on the way up that we didn't have enough time to get to the best part of the valley. I assumed that coming back downhill would take at least as long as going up. The climb was mainly through forest, sometimes clambering over the rocks.

When we reached the first *mirador*, we caught up with a young man from Nebraska, who we'd seen previously several times. He said we were at the best viewpoint before Británico. That was a consolation because even though it had never been our intention to go all the way to Campamento Británico (another couple of hours further into the canyon), we didn't want to stop just short of some other major attraction.

So we had our lunch and I let myself enjoy my surroundings rather than worry about the time. We watched the waterfalls blowing as the wind blew furiously. I hated to leave the spot. There was no way that my camera could capture the scale, the scope, the ethereal beauty of our surroundings, but I had to try to bring home some images to bring up memories in the future.

Going downhill was no big deal after all, even with the rain blowing off the mountains. We actually got back to Italiano a half-hour earlier than we'd expected. After picking up our tent and sleeping bags, we were back on the Circuit and continued on toward our next stop at Refugio Cuernos.

It started easily enough—and then the wind picked up. The furious wind picked up water from the mountainside and drove it sideways. Some of the time we were protected by trees or rocks as we made our way downhill, and then we would get blasted as we crossed an open area.

The trail skirted a large lake, Lago Nordenskjöld. Like Lago Skottsberg, it was covered with whitecaps and its shores were being hammered with high waves. We found ourselves on a rocky beach, the wind blowing surf spray at us. The sun and spray combined to form a rainbow in the foreground. We loved it—the exhilaration of dodging in and out of forested areas and the fierce wind!

We passed a Yosemite-class waterfall; what was most remarkable was that half the time the water was flying upwards because of the wind's updraft. In time, it all became tamer. The water crossings were not difficult and the last half-hour was relatively painless; there was less chance of being blown over.

Los Cuernos has a range of accommodations: a campground, cottage, and rooms in the main lodge. Putting up the tent was a bit difficult: even though the sites were in the forest, we still had to struggle with sudden gusts that blasted through the trees.

Tent staked down, dinner reservations made, showered, clothes washed and hung to dry, it was time to kick back and enjoy a beer. The dining room was set up with five rows of varnished wooden picnic tables and their benches.

We took a seat near the wall of windows that overlooked the lake. The walls creaked and the windows shook, but I tried to reassure myself with the thought that this wasn't the first time the wind had been this strong.

Javier, a young Chilean from Punta Arenas, delivered our beer.

"Is this the normal—the wind?" I asked him.

"Yes, today's it's only 130 km. (78 mph), but it could easily be 180 or 200."

When dinnertime came, the 40 guests gathered—most finding seating with others speaking their own languages. So, there were the German tables, the Latin American tables, and the English speakers' table. Javier managed to deliver the dinner plates, bring the beverages, and find time to briefly chat with everyone.

Behind the scenes, the chef, wearing the traditional tall white chef's hat, was filling our plates with the best meal on the Circuit so far: pan-fried white fish and risotto, homemade rolls, and a dessert of rice pudding with a peach in juice. There was even a strawberry and orange slice on a skewer. We were definitely emerging from the wilderness into the front country and that didn't feel all bad. What a wild day!

Tuesday, March 9, 2010. Los Cuernos to Los Torres. 6.82 miles (11 km.) Day eight of our Circuit hike. After breakfast at the refuge—cornflakes and scrambled eggs, and homemade biscuits (instead of hamburger buns), we were on our way.

The trail took us over two minor summits. When we came to a stream crossing, I debated where to wade through because I knew I couldn't make it across using the rocks placed for more sure-footed hikers. A man, who I judged to be a local because of his bronzed torso and unhurried manner, was sitting on some large rocks on the other side of the water. Without a moment's hesitation, he came back across the stream and gave me a hand so that I could stay balanced on the bridge of rocks. I was very happy to have my shoes stay dry.

Lago Nordenskjöld was so still, without a ripple on its surface, that no one would have believed that the wind had whipped it to boiling yesterday. The day became hot and I wished that I had my sunhat. I think I left it behind in storage in Puerto Natales. I've made do with a bandanna the whole trip, but it was not very comfortable when the temperature rose.

The last section of the trail was quite different from what we had seen to that point. There were small patches of brilliant-green grass—where vernal pools had sat earlier in the season—surrounded largely by barren landscape. There were many dark rocks, but there seemed to be very little soil to support plant life.

I WALK SLOWLY—EVEN more slowly than usual—because I hate to see our hike coming to an end. I love this park; everywhere you look is photo-worthy, and everything changes constantly. A shift in the wind, the sun is out and hot, clouds come over and it darkens and cools. Wisps of clouds come drifting like tendrils of smoke or dark ominous ones spill out. It is a perfect hiking day.

WE ARRIVED BACK at the campground of Los Torres, where we started the Circuit. The hot shower felt wonderful even though the showerhead dribbled out a pathetically weak stream. I washed lots of clothes, as did Ralph, and hung them on lines he strung. The wind had picked up; it was not as severe as yesterday, but fairly gusty and the clothes whipped around and got tangled on the clothesline.

My reverie was interrupted periodically because I had to get up and untangle the laundry, but I liked the fact that things dried quickly. It was not as if we needed to wash everything we owned, but the urge to have our clothes fresh and clean was irresistible.

I moved indoors to sit at a small table in the Refugio Torre— such a far cry from the primitive accommodations at Serón and Dickson. We were once again in the "front country," complete with a handicap-accessible washroom.

The bar was furnished with hand-hewn wooden tables and chairs. The chair seats and backs were, we decided, made of guanaco hides. The wood-burning stove had cords of wood stacked neatly beside it, but a fire wasn't needed because the sun streamed in the west-facing windows and that provided plenty of warmth. Outside the wall of windows were masses of daisy-like flowers with foliage that looked like chamomile.

The towers of Los Torres were straight ahead; the next day at sunrise would be our last opportunity to catch them at their best for photos.

I was glad, and sort of amazed, that we had finished the Circuit, and very happy that my worst fears—having to slide downhill for a couple of miles on the seat of my pants on the descent from Garner Pass, or slipping to my death onto Grey Glacier, didn't come to pass. In fact, none of the worries that I entertained from time to time came to pass—no falls, near drowning, or frostbite.

I faced a lot of fears on this one, not only the pass and the ladders, but also the many long downhill stretches and the stream and river crossings that are hard for me. Although I was okay with the fact that the trip was winding down, I also envied the many we've met who were going to be traveling for months more.

My daydreaming ended when a platter of glassware loudly crashed to the floor in the dining room. Preparation for the 7:00 p.m. dinner seating was underway. The cacophony of sounds was amusing: kitchen help chopping onions, food sizzling in a frying pan, metal pots being pulled out.

Dinner was soup, chicken and rice, bread, and the rest of our bottle of Casillero de Diablo Cabernet, which I gave judged "fair." We sat with Mary and John, brother and sister, and their guide. They appeared to be about the same age we were and they were also avid backpackers. Mary said that she had written a guidebook and was working on a new one about Eastern Washington where she lived and hiked regularly.

They had just arrived in the park and were ready to start; I was envious. Mary was the more talkative of the two, but still a bit guarded. It seemed strange—most hikers we talked to about the trail were more open, but perhaps I was just starved for conversation after being away for the past week. Or perhaps she felt threatened by the fact that we did it on our own and they had a guide. Truth be told, if we hadn't made it this year, I would have pressed to hire a guide and come back a third time.

The evening was not over. Things had changed by the time we headed back to the campground—the wind had picked up again. The wooden plank bridge across the rocky gully that we crossed to get from the campground to the refugio had been blown over. As we approached, we watched the unsupported mid-section of our tent flatten repeatedly from the strong gusts.

Ralph figured that everything would be okay if we crawled inside because our weight would keep the tent in place; I was a little dubious. We started setting up "our home" for the night—blowing up the air mattresses, unrolling the sleeping bags, arranging our clothes. The sounds that accompanied the blasts of wind were deafening. I knew I'd not be able to sleep with all that noise and started to look for my earplugs. I still wasn't convinced the tent would be okay.

I climbed back out to go to the nearby restroom and noticed on the way that many people had moved their tents so that they were in the lee of the shower/bathhouse.

"Several people have moved their tents over by the bathrooms. Are you sure that the tent can hold up in this wind?" I asked Ralph when I came back.

"I'm sure," he answered, "It's been used on lots of mountains and it's designed to withstand 95-mph winds."

Apparently the next gust was 96 mph because suddenly there was a loud cracking. The support pole, one of the two, had snapped. I moved over against the place where the broken pole was to help hold the tent upright. Ralph climbed out to inspect the damage. The sleeve that the pole went through was torn, but by sitting against the side, I could keep the tent erect.

While Ralph headed over to the lodge to see if we could find a place to spend the night indoors, I hurriedly repacked our backpacks and then sat in the tent waiting for him to return. Whenever the tent shuddered from another blast, I had visions of being speared by the broken tent pole, but mostly I wondered how we would sleep in the noisy tent.

"No places available," Ralph said when he returned. We decided to move the tent, so we collapsed both poles and then carried the groundsheet and the tent, still filled with all of our gear, about fifty feet and set it down behind a sheltering patch of shrubs. Ralph located his Swiss Army knife, cut a couple of holes in the tent so that he could string a rope around the tent pole and then tied the rope around a shrub so that we could have some headroom and be able to crawl in and out.

About two minutes later, the wind died down and ended for the night.

Wednesday, March 10, 2010. Bus to Puerto Natales. In the morning we walked to Hostería Los Torres, a decidedly more upscale lodge than the Refugio Los Torres, to look in the gift shop and use the computer while we waited for the shuttle to take us out of the park. We shared a huge lunch: a large pile of French fries topped with hard-boiled eggs, chorizo, chicken, steak and tomatoes. The dish was 7500 pesos, my soda was 2800 (US$5.60), which must be in the running for the most I have ever spent on a diet cola.

From the shuttle, we transferred to a bus and began our ride back to Puerto Natales. It started uneventfully, but when the driver began making and receiving phone calls, I found it worrisome. After all, our several tons of vehicle and its contents were barreling down the highway with a distracted operator.

The back and forth calls continued. After some time, we found out why. One minute we were zipping along on the main road; then without warning, the driver slowed and pulled onto the shoulder. He slowly crept forward to make a U-turn in the two-lane highway. Luckily, there was very little traffic.

We still had no explanation. He drove back, turned onto a different paved road, and then the reason for our detour became obvious—another bus was sitting on the shoulder of the road, driver's legs sticking out from underneath, the passengers standing on the edge of the highway next to the broken-down bus. We picked up the stranded passengers and their luggage and made our way back to the major highway. Most of the new passengers had to sit in the aisle for the remaining hour of the ride.

After we arrived at Puerto Natales' hillside bus station, we walked the few blocks to Casa Cecilia. We reclaimed our stored bag, walked around town trying to find a handicraft store where we'd seen masks for sale earlier. I was hoping to add one to my collection. Our hunt was unsuccessful, so we quit and went for pizza for dinner. This time we had a double bed and bath. Slept well. Wonderful to be in a real bed once again.

Thursday, March 11, 2010. Bus from Puerto Natales to El Calafate. Up this morning at 6:45 thanks to the annoying sound of our alarm cutting through the dark. We had our simple breakfast in the Cecilia's cheerful yellow dining room and then sat to wait for the bus, which was due at 8:30 a.m.

As usual I had to run to pee just as the bus was about to leave. Ralph said he was going to write a book entitled, *My Wife is in the Bathroom*. Each page would show the title translated into a different language, and he could show the appropriate page to the bus driver or another employee so that he wouldn't have to worry so much about me missing our departure.

We were going a different route this time, exiting Chile and entering Argentina on Highway R40. The customs office in Argentina looked new and it was pleasant to wait inside instead of outside in the cold wind like last year's border crossing. Soon we were driving past a ski area. Its lifts were closed until winter, but the fields of daisies were very pretty.

We went through Rio Turbio, a fair-sized industrial town. Although it has had its ups and downs as a coal mining area, it still has the country's largest coal deposits. Most recently, with significant economic support from the government, it was seeing a rise in production. If the coal-fired power plant under construction is completed, it will revitalize this remote area, but as Greenpeace and others have stated, at a very high environmental cost. I wonder, since coal is the most highly polluting of the fossil fuels and a significant factor in global warming, what impact the project will have on the Patagonian ice fields, which are only a couple hundred miles from Rio Turbio.

From the bus we could see a huge facility with obsolete buses, steel beams, and other metals piled high. City planners had tried to brighten the town—implementing a campaign to paint the walls and roofs of the homes and stores with bright yellow pigment.

The bus climbed the hill very slowly out of Rio Turbio. It was still 152 miles (245 km.) to El Calafate—a long ride.

Ralph had decided to find us a hotel in El Calafate that was a bit closer to the main street than the one we stayed in last year, and so he booked us in Che Lagarto Hostel.[18] A very enthusiastic young staff greeted us; there were no "white hairs" in evidence. We had dinner the same place we first ate last year. I ordered the salmon with salsa on pasta. It was good, but not great. We did another search for a mask, but came up empty-handed.

Friday, March 12, 2010. Morning flight El Calafate to Buenos Aires. With an hour and a half to kill before heading for the nearby airport, we looked around the local gift shops again. We found a mask that looked as if it had been made from a large coconut shell, but I couldn't be sure. After we purchased it, I began to wonder if it would be confiscated when we went through the agricultural inspection station back in the U.S. (It wasn't.)

When we got to the small airport we were stunned to find a long, slow-moving line for check-in. We had arrived an hour before departure, but appeared to be the last to get in line. As it turned out, the plane was delayed about fifteen minutes and we made our flight.

When we arrived in Buenos Aires, we headed by taxi for the Hotel Costa Rica where we had enjoyed staying last year. I looked forward to staying in somewhat familiar surroundings.

The manager, Yann, was just as friendly as he had been previously and gave us an animated talk of places to eat and to see. We went for a walk and stopped at an outdoor café that had a sign posted reading "two-for-one happy-hour margaritas." So we ordered an appetizer plate of bread and cheese and salami, and two margaritas. When the bill came, we saw that we had been charged for two margaritas and asked why. Turned out that we each had to order two margaritas in order to get our second ones free. Rather than protest, we each ordered a second one!

We suspect that they poured more generously than we are used to. We rarely get drunk, but after our margaritas, we were both a bit tipsy and then too full for dinner. We ended up skipping dinner, weaving our way back to the hotel and falling into bed.

Saturday, March 13, 2010. Buenos Aires, day two. Ralph went down to the hotel lobby early to get his coffee and to get coins for the bus rides. We needed enough change to get us back and forth to La Boca district. The hotel didn't have enough, so Ralph went out searching for a shop where he could get some. Only one place was open nearby—a small market selling groceries and liquor. Ralph tried to buy a soda for me. When it came time to pay, the owner denied him the purchase because it would have required giving back too much change. Lesson finally learned: use bills whenever possible, rather than paying the exact amount with part bills and part change, so that you can accumulate coins.

We walked the several blocks to the street where we caught the #152 bus to La Boca, at the end of the line. Because it was the weekend, there were tons more vendors, open shops, and tour buses than we had seen last year. It was fun watching all the activity. We had our pictures taken; we stuck our heads through the openings in a wooden board painted with tango dancers. Fun!!! Then we walked along the river in the revitalized section.

Sunday, March 14, 2010. Buenos Aires, day three. This was a big day in San Telmo; we went to the *Feria de San Telmo* (the San Telmo fair). This is a very popular event in one of the oldest and most architecturally beautiful neighborhoods of Buenos Aires. It runs from 10 a.m. to 4 p.m. every Sunday. What sets it apart from other flea markets, art shows, festivals, or farmer's markets is the quality and variety of the items available. Antiques and art are displayed in full measure. Rather than cheap cellphones, think old, wood, wall crank-style telephones. Instead of Teflon-lined sauté pans think copper bowls. You'll find alpaca sweaters, but you'll also find clothing designed by young, new designers.

It was pretty overwhelming to take in all that there was to see, so we soon joined hundreds of others who were seated at tables around the plaza and ordered beer. That allowed us to people-watch, which was at least as interesting as looking through the vendors' booths.

A trio of musicians announced its arrival by playing New Orleans-style jazz as they made their way down the cobblestone street. They progressed along one side of the square, holding a hat out for propinas as they progressed. The tango dancers invited passers-by to pose with them for a price. Since we had arrived early, we had been able to make our way around fairly easily, but as we sat at the small table sipping our drinks to make them last, we watched with amazement as the number of people coming into the area became a sea of humanity.

Then I had a stroke of luck. I needed to find a restroom, so I went inside the bar to ask. The bartender directed me upstairs and I followed his instructions. When I came out, however, one of the employees gestured for me to follow her as she went to a row of windows and balconies. From there, I had a birds-eye view of the entire scene without the elbows and hips of the mob blocking my view. It also was a great vantage point for taking some photos unobserved. I indulged myself for a little while and then rejoined Ralph so that we could make our way back to the hotel.

When I told Yann that it was my birthday, he insisted on treating us to a drink from the bar and then made our reservation for a nearby restaurant, Lo de Jesus, a restaurant of the classic style. It was comfortable weather for dining al fresco at the small tables lining the sidewalk. The servings were ample, the beef filets tender and succulent, and the Syrah the perfect accompaniment.

Monday, March 15, 2010. Buenos Aires to home. Because I had booked a late-evening flight home, we had to check out of the hotel before it was time to leave for the airport, but they kindly allowed us to leave our bags behind the counter while we wandered the streets of the city.

Our explorations took us first to the Museum of Latin American Art of Buenos Aires (MALBA) at Av Figueroa Alcorta 3415. The handsome, modern building with its three-story high airy atrium has a relatively small, but highly regarded collection of contemporary art. The permanent collection is predominantly 20th century work and includes *Retrato de Ramón Gómez de la Serna* (Portrait of Ramón Gómez de la Serna) by Diego Rivera and *Autorretrato con chango y loro* (Self-portrait with Monkey and Parrot) by Frida Kahlo. (Note: Admission is free on Wednesdays.)

Afterward, we decided we wanted a quiet end to our visit, so we crossed to the nearby Japanese gardens. The Buenos Aires Japanese Gardens have a lake in the center, which is surrounded by the featured flowers, shrubs, and trees. Some of the plants, such as the azalea, are from Japan. The silk floss tree, with its thorny trunk and bold white and pink flower, is native to South America. We spent most of our time either studying the bonsai collection or watching the antics of the numerous koi.

When we were too tired to wander any more, we returned to our hotel to sit in the lounge reading our books until the taxi came to start us on our return trip home.

Reflections

THE URGE TO return and complete the backpacking Circuit in Torres del Paine was irresistible. There was never any doubt in my mind that we would go back and try again after our aborted attempt in 2009. In fact, by the time we went back in 2010, I was so determined to successfully get over the John Garner Pass and down the other side to see Grey Glaciar that I vowed that I would hire a guide and try at least one more time if that attempt had failed.

As you've seen throughout this book, during *good* weather the Circuit hiking in Torres del Paine is generally rated as moderate—except over the pass where it becomes challenging. The trail can be a slog and therefore slower than anticipated, but nothing a good hiker can't enjoy. During *inclement* weather, however, attempting to go over the pass could become a disaster.

Over the many years that Ralph and I have backpacked together, there have been very few times when we stopped short of our destination. We usually have completed our hikes due to the fact that we've tackled reasonable routes, planned well, and have been determined to see it through come hell or high water (and we've seen a fair amount of both!). The few times we've not reached our destination, it has been due to injury or floods.

Every hike, and every day of a hike, there is something to celebrate—the scenery, the people we meet, the wildlife, but not every moment of a hike is fun and much of it is just hard work. It's inevitable that a hiker will have favorite hikes. The Circuit hike of Torres del Paine is on my list of top 10 long distance trails completed. In fact, it is such a superb hike that I would go back and hike it again and again if time, money, and health allowed.

Glaciar Grey

11 • Visitor Information

When to go, documents, transportation, street smarts, and health

When to go

Of FOREMOST IMPORTANCE in the early stages of planning is when to go. When you think about what months or season to hike or backpack in a particular place, like most people, you undoubtedly consider the weather. Who wants to go someplace, unless they are interested in winter sports, where it's going to be constantly raining or snowing—or excessively hot and humid for that matter? Because the seasons are the opposite of ours, South America's summer is December to March. Patagonia's major tourist season is November through March; November and March are "shoulder seasons."

Documents

THE GOOD NEWS is that visas are not required of U.S. citizens or Europeans for stays of less than 90 days. You *will* pay a visa reciprocity fee when you go into Chile or Argentina of about US$130—what the U.S. charges those countries for visas. U.S. citizens will need their passports going and returning. (Note that neighboring Brazil *does* require a visa, which should be obtained in advance.)

International air transportation

ALTHOUGH SOME PEOPLE drive or take the bus to Patagonia from the U.S., most fly because of both time and distance considerations. International flights to and from the capital cities of Santiago, Chile and Buenos Aires, Argentina are frequent. Keep in mind that most flights from the United States will involve a domestic layover.

Chile by air

THE MOST COMMON entry point for overseas visitors to Chile is the international airport, Arturo Merino Benitez Airport (SCL), in Santiago. There are airports in other towns, but Santiago is the main hub for flights throughout the country. (When making reservations, be aware that there is more than one city named Santiago in the world.) Arturo Merino Benítez is only about fifteen minutes from downtown Santiago on urban highways.

LAN is Chile's flagship airline. One of the great things about flying with LAN is their comparatively liberal flight change policies. On their website, they state that passengers can cancel reservations without penalty and get a refund if they make the request within 24 hours of making the reservation *and* the original purchase was made seven or more days before the first departure date. Of course, if you change to a date or flight with higher fees, there would be an additional charge for the flight. Keep in mind that prices vary on a daily basis and are usually more expensive on weekends and holidays than on weekdays. If you are using oneworld® frequent flier miles, investigate whether or not LAN still permits unlimited stopovers free of charge. LAN's flexibility may, in part, be due to the unpredictability of Chile's weather—a reminder to allow flexibility in your travel plans.

Besides LAN, Sky Airline, and Aerolineas del Sur fly from Arturo Merino Benitez (SCL). Aerolineas del Sur (which is based in Buenos Aires) has a limited Chilean presence, but does offer flights between Santiago and BA.

Buenos Aires by air

ARGENTINA'S CAPITAL CITY has two *international* airports. The Ministro Pistarini Argentina (Spanish: Aeropuerto Internacional de Ezeiza Ministro Pistarini), frequently called the Ezeiza Airport (EZE) is used for traveling to Europe, North America and other continents.

The Jorge Newbery AeroPark Airport (AEP) (Spanish: Aeroparque Jorge Newbery) is closer to downtown Buenos Aires (about a 15-minute taxi ride), but is mainly for *domestic* flights and flights to other Latin American countries. Aerolineas Argentinas is Argentina's flagship airline.

Technicalities

AS IN CHILE, official visas are not required for short-term tourist visits to Argentina. As mentioned in Chapter 1, there is a fee when entering Chile from the United States and several other countries. This is also true of flights from the U.S. into Buenos Aires' Ezeiza (EZE) airport, so if we had taken our flights in reverse, flying into Buenos Aires and out of Santiago, we would have paid the reciprocity fees there.

In December 2009, the Argentine Government started charging an "Airport Entry Fee" for citizens of certain countries. The fee paid by travelers is dependent on their nationality. For example, visitors from the United States are charged US$140, Australia US$100, and Canada US$70. The general rule is that these are reciprocal charges, in line with the costs incurred by Argentinean citizens travelling to these countries for similar purposes.

The Airport Entry Fee allows unlimited entries to Argentina for a period of 10 years for U.S. citizens. Citizens of other countries may find different requirements—Australians, for example, must pay the fee each time they arrive at the Buenos Aires international airport.

Visitors flying out of the airports in Buenos Aires (Ezeiza or Jorge Newbery) must also pay a US$29 departure tax, *if* it was not already included in the ticket price.

Domestic air transportation

FLIGHTS BETWEEN CITIES and towns within Chile and within Argentina, as well as flights between the two countries, are much less frequent. Chile's airlines handling most domestic flights are LAN and Sky Airline.

Chile: When planning your domestic flights with LAN, consider reserving your tickets before entering the country. Flight coupons are recommended. These can be obtained online at the same time you book your flight from the U.S. to Chile.

Argentina: Domestic flights and flights to other Latin American countries, to and from Buenos Aires, are usually from the Jorge Newbery AeroPark Airport (AEP). Aerolineas Argentinas serves the major tourist destinations within the country and also has limited international flights (currently does not serve the U.S.) www.aerolineas.com.ar

International travel by bus (coach)

IF YOU ARE already in South America, it is often most reasonable to travel by bus—both because of the lower fares and the extensive network of buses. You will, of course, want to consider the duration of the trips and the time you have available.

Compare for example, the options of flying or taking a bus from Mendoza, Argentina to Santiago, Chile. The flight would cost about US$625; the bus/coach fare would be about US$40 (2011 prices). You can fly in just over an hour (plus the time allowance for checking in) or you take a comfortable bus ride of about eight hours.

If you were strapped for time, you might choose the flight, but if you wanted to tour the vineyards of the region, you'd probably opt for the beautiful ride on the RN 7.

Tom Coroneos describes his ride from Santiago. "Died and went to heaven. Lovely Mendoza, after a stunning bus ride..... The Andes separating these two regions [Santiago and Mendoza] are incredible... [the highway] heavily traveled during the day...maybe 40 hairpin turns, maybe 3,000 meters high at volcanic pass, and still Mt. Aconcagua looks down from 7,000 meters.

"[Mendoza] in the central Chilean valley, is rich with agriculture, and watered by the Andes. [It} offered rich vineyards and a lovely inexpensive hostel, which featured a group BBQ and great wines." (You wouldn't want to count on taking this highway during the winter season—June through August—because snow and ice frequently cause lengthy road closures in the mountains.)

Chile also has buses arriving daily from Arequipa, Peru; and from Bolivia. The roads vary in quality; do not expect freeway conditions to prevail. Buses from São Paulo, Brazil arrive on Mondays and Thursdays. If you are prone to altitude sickness, keep in mind that some of these high altitude crossings can be up to 13,000 ft. (4,000 m).

Domestic travel by bus

CHILE'S BUS SYSTEM is extensive, relatively inexpensive, and comfortable. Particularly if you are traveling long distances, always inquire if the bus is non-stop to your destination. Otherwise, you may be stopping every few miles at a new station. Turbus and Pullman are major players.

Santiago's local transportation

THERE ARE SEVERAL means of getting around Santiago. Their *Metro* (subway, underground) is the largest system in South America, transporting more than two million riders each day. It is widely regarded as efficient, clean, safe, and cheap. The fare varies depending on time of day (more expensive and crowded during commute hours) and you can either buy a single-use fare or the multi-use "BIP" card. There are also *Micro* buses to pick up the slack. To use this system, you must buy a BIP card, which you can do at stations and many stores. In addition, there are *colectivos* (collectives)—cars or vans that follow a set route.

Taxis, of course, are available. When you arrive at Santiago's airport, you can prepay a set price taxi ride to your accommodations. You'll want to do this at one of the counters *inside* the terminal because once you leave the secured area, you are going to be approached by taxi drivers who may or may not be honest. Santiago's Universidad de Santiago subway station has a bus terminal housing several bus companies that provide transportation beyond the city.

A metro map can be found at: metrosantiago.cl[19] and the city bus info at transantiago.cl[20]

Buenos Aires' local transportation

IN BUENOS AIRES, you also have options of public transportation—subway, bus, and taxi. The *subte* (subway) has several lines carrying people throughout the city. Payment is by coin or multi-trip pass. The city buses, sometimes called *colectivos* there, are similar to what we normally find in the U.S. The fare depends on the distance you travel or how many zones you pass through. A typical ride would be about 80-100 centavos (about 30-35 cents U.S.)

In either country, when you want to take a taxi from your hotel, ask the front desk to make the arrangements. The hotel's employees can tell you what the usual fare is to your destination. If you are at a restaurant, follow the same precaution. Taxis are required to post a fare schedule in their front window and to have the meter within sight. If you're going to an out-of-town destination, settle the amount of the fare *before* you get in the cab. *Propinas* (tips) are not usually given to taxi drivers, but some travelers round up to the nearest dollar or give small change.

Although hitchhiking in South America is not uncommon among adventurous young tourists and residents, it's not practical for those with limited time. On major highways such as the Pan-American, it's almost impossible. On secondary roads it is legal, but the more remote the location, the longer the wait for a hitch.

Continuing on to Patagonia

THERE ARE FOUR towns you need to remember as key points (hubs) for accessing key destinations in Patagonia (besides the gateway points of Santiago and Buenos Aires).

Punta Arenas, Chile. Punta Arenas is Chile's largest city in the southernmost part of Chile and would be considered its hub.

Puerto Natales, Chile. North of Punta Arenas is Puerto Natales, which is considered the gateway town to Torres del Paine.

El Calafate, Argentina. North of Torres del Paine and Puerto Natales is El Calafate, which would be considered the Argentine transportation hub.

Ushuaia, Argentina. Ushuaia is a major tourist destination and jumping off point to Antarctica, and is served by several airlines. Visitors traveling on to other sites from "the end of the world" will need to continue via air or boat.

Routes according to destination

To REACH TORRES del Paine is a multi-step process:

A: From *Chile,* fly Santiago to Punta Arenas; from *Argentina,* fly from Buenos Aires, Ushuaia, or Río Gallegos to Punta Arenas.

B: Punta Arenas to Puerto Natales. According to the fslodges.com faqs, there are buses leaving Punta Arenas every one to two hours for Puerto Natales, starting around 7 a.m. Catch *Buses Fernández* at Armando Sanhueza 745, or *Bus Pacheco* at Avenida Colón 900, or *Bus Sur* at José Menéndez 565. The trip is approximately three hours. www.busesfernandez.com/en/ www.bus-sur.cl or www.busespacheco.com/rutas.htm

C: Puerto Natales to Torres del Paine (through the Laguna Amarga entrance station) According to *Fantástico Sur* website,[7] buses depart twice daily for the park during the high season (Oct. 15 - Mar. 15) at 7:30 a.m. and 14:30 p.m. (which we from the United States call 2:30 p.m.). During the off-season (Mar 15 - Oct 15), buses are scheduled only for the 7:30 a.m. departure. The ride to the park's Laguna Amarga entrance station is approximately two and one-quarter hours. *Buses Gomez* leave from at Arturo Prat 234; *Buses JB* from Arturo Prat 244; and *Buses Turismo Maria Jose* from Bulnes 386. www.busesgomez.com/horarios.htm

Alternate: A second, recently improved route from Puerto Natales to Torres del Paine via the Milodon Cave is described in detail on p. 191, but as of 2012, there is no scheduled bus service, only tours.

To reach Los Glaciares (Glacier National Park) *by bus* is a multi-step process:

A: Travel to Punta Arenas and on to Puerto Natales as you would for Torres del Paine (see previous page).

B: Puerto Natales to El Calafate. There is currently no bus *station* in Puerto Natales, but there are a few bus companies, each operating out of their own offices, that are near the center of town.

C: El Calafate to Los Glaciares. There are several options for travel. The Terminal de Ómnibus (bus terminal) has several companies operating out of it.[21]

Alternate: There are several routes by which you can fly directly to El Calafate eliminating steps A-C above. There is regular service from within Argentina—including flights from Buenos Aires, Río Gallegos, and Ushuaia. (You can also reach El Calafate from Santiago, but this is not recommended because of the convoluted routing: Santiago to Buenos Aires, to Ushuaia, to El Calafate. The total flight time can range from 13-20 hours.)

Return flights to Santiago or Buenos Aires

FLIGHTS FROM PUNTA Arenas to Santiago are scheduled two to three times per day.

Flights from El Calafate to Buenos Aires will range from about US$150-350 depending on the day. There's usually only one flight a day; weekend and weekday flight times vary.

Flights from Punta Arenas to Buenos Aires, because you are routed through Santiago, cost about US$450.

Navimag ferry system

THE NAVIMAG FERRY that we took from the Lake District port city of Puerto Montt through the Patagonian Fjords was a four-day, three-night trip to Puerto Natales. Prices vary according to season and accommodations. See navimag.com[22]

Your starting point, Puerto Montt, while in the Chilean Lake District, is more of a transportation hub than a tourist town. If you were going to be in the region for a few days before your scenic ferry trip, you'd probably find more of interest if you stayed in the vicinity of nearby Puerto Varas.

There are several levels of accommodation (seven at this time) on the ferry. The deluxe level (AAA) had many perks. Our small group was escorted onto the ferry first, given a tour, and had a separate dining room with a dedicated server (as opposed to eating in the cafeteria).

The AAA-level staterooms were not anything like you would normally find on cruise ships, but we had a porthole that opened, adequate bunk beds, and our own bathroom. The least expensive level by far is the Level C, which has 22 people in the room, dormitory style.[22]

Other ferry companies offer more extensive glacier cruises: continuing through Chile's Inside Passage and the Beagle Channel, around Cape Horn, passing through glacial valleys such as Laguna San Rafael, and all the way to the Argentinian portion of Tierra del Fuego.

Money and valuables

ALTHOUGH WE KNEW we would be able to use our credit cards in Santiago and Buenos Aires and occasionally at other accommodations, we initially carried Chilean pesos (CLP) that we had obtained at our bank back home. We didn't bring much U.S. currency. We knew we would be able to use it in major cities, but not always in places off the beaten track.

We expected to pay in Chilean pesos for our reciprocity fee, campgrounds and meals, and buses. We planned to replenish our supply of cash during the trip a couple of times at local ATMs. At the time of our visit, the rate of exchange was about 1,000 Chilean pesos (CLP) to US$1.50, and about 4.25 Argentine pesos (ARS) to US$1.

We saw exchange bureaus in three gateway towns near Torres del Paine: Punta Arenas, Puerto Natales and El Calafate, and their rates were often better than in banks. We avoided changing currency in hotels and airports because of the unfavorable exchange rates. We would never do an exchange on the street—both because it could be counterfeit and because displaying cash in public is risky.

Because we were backpacking, I had no need for a handbag and rarely carry one when traveling anyway. I wore a money belt hidden away. Keep some smaller denomination bills handy (perhaps in a zipped pocket) for minor purchases. Keep larger denomination bills in the money belt. Some people have a "throw away" wallet to satisfy criminals.

I make a small chart of the currency exchange so that I don't confuse, for example, a 10,000-peso bill for a 1,000. In Chile, all of the bills are the same size, but they are different colors and designs.

Be aware that many stores and shops in Chile do not accept the currency of Argentina and vice versa! On the Torres del Paine Circuit, we found that some refugios took dollars, Euros, credit cards and pesos and others did not (details in Chapter 12).

Street smarts

LEAVE EXPENSIVE JEWELRY home; carry electronic gear judiciously. For my personal safety when traveling, I leave my engagement ring at home and wear a plain wedding band and simple earrings. (I've also read advice to leave laptops and other electronic devices at home to avoid attracting thieves.)

More than once during our trip I was warned not to carry a camera for the same reason. I chose to take it with me, but I kept it tucked away when I wasn't using it. Even though I ignored warnings not to carry my camera in public, I was careful of my subject matter. I learned this lesson many years ago while in Mexico City. While in the airport, I was captivated by what I thought would be an artistic shot of several officers sitting in a row getting their shoes polished at shoeshine stands. I raised my camera to take a photo and it ended with my film being confiscated. So, don't take photos of military installations, ships or other vehicles, or personnel without permission. Unless you want to risk getting hassled (or arrested) for taking photos, first ask "okay?" and then point to your camera and at what you want to photograph.

We don't bring much in the way of electronic devices when traveling, but since we did plan to bring cameras and a cell phone, we had to have various adaptors and recharging units. Because the electricity is 240 volts, you need the round two-prong adaptor for Chile (three if ground required), and two-round or two-diagonal adaptor for Argentina. Remember that you need a voltage converter, not just a plug adaptor if your appliance requires 110 volts. (Our camera battery charger will convert 240, but our cell phone charger will not.)

Telephones, Internet, Wi-Fi

PUBLIC PHONES ARE becoming as difficult to find in South America as they are in the U.S. because increasing numbers of people carry cell phones. You might consider leaving your cell phone at home and buying a cheap one from the local store so you can make emergency, hotel or flight information, or personal calls back home.

If you need a public phone, look for one inside a store or phone center. Prepaid cards for mobile phones and landlines are sold at most newspaper kiosks, supermarkets, gas stations, pharmacies and phone dealers. In remote areas including Torres del Paine, it will be only in the upscale tourist lodges of Torres del Paine where you will find telephones, Wi-Fi, and pay-by-the-minute Internet available.

Cell phones for Chile and Argentina are GSM, but as far as we could find out, cell phones don't work in the park. Phones work in Punta Arenas. ATT's GSM map shows coverage in Puerto Natales, and then nothing north of there until Cochrane, which is north of Bernardo O'Higgins National Park. There is some GSM coverage from Telefonica in Puerto Natales, Punta Arenas, Puerto Montt and larger cities. Service areas are expanding; check for updates at maps.mobileworldlive.com[23]

As in any travel, your home wireless carrier will impose roaming charges, which vary from tolerable to immense. Check with your carrier in advance. What we do is carry an unlocked multiband GSM phone we got from eBay, and get a SIM card for our travel destination. Sometimes we have bought it when we arrived there; sometimes we have ordered it in advance. Once you have the unlocked GSM phone, just Google (for example): Chile sim card and you will find various sites that will rent you a card in advance.

Cybercafes (Internet cafes) are available in most cities and in tourist spots. Small towns may have computer and Internet services available at public libraries or tourist offices. A program called *BiblioRedes*[24] has brought computers to libraries in more remote areas; you can use these computers and Internet free of charge. Some libraries have Internet satellite connections.

Increasingly Wi-Fi hotspots can be found in transportation centers such as metro stations and airports and at public buildings, shopping centers, and cafes. *Gratis* indicates it is free.

Emergencies

IN CASE OF emergency, you can call the *Chilean Carabineros* (Chilean national police) at 133 free from any phone; they are well regarded. The American Embassy is at Avenida

Andrés Bello 2800, Las Condes, Santiago. Hours 8:30 a.m.- 5 p.m. Phone: (56) (2) 232-2600. chile.usembassy.gov/
    In the city and the province (surrounding area) of Buenos Aires, Argentina, you can dial 911 for police. Within the city, dial 100 in case of fire or 107 for an ambulance.
    The U.S. Embassy Buenos Aires, American Citizen Services, is in the Palermo district at Av. Colombia 4300, C1425GMN Buenos Aires. While in Argentina, U.S. citizens can call (0-11) 5777-4354. Outside of working hours (8 a.m. to 5 p.m.) and on weekends call (0-11) 5777-4873.

Pre-trip medical

No one wants to become ill when traveling, so it's advisable to get whatever vaccinations your health provider has recommended ahead of time. Be sure to visit the Center for Disease Control and Prevention (CDC) for health advisories before leaving for a trip. They routinely advise that you see a health-care provider at least 4–6 weeks before your trip to allow time for your vaccines to take effect. Be sure that your *routine* immunizations for flu, chicken pox, polio, DPT (diphtheria/pertussis/tetanus), and MMR (measles/mumps/rubella) are up to date.[25]
    Although the following was accurate at the time it was written, conditions change, so study the map on the CDC site. As they suggest, "the level of risk for vaccine-preventable diseases can change at any time."

Vaccines for Chile

According to the CDC, *typhoid* vaccine is recommended for those visiting "temperate South America, especially if staying with friends or relatives or visiting smaller cities, villages, or rural areas where exposure might occur through food or water." The risk level of acquiring *Hepatitis A* is low in southern Chile.
    Hepatitis B is recommended for all unvaccinated U.S. children and adolescents (under 19 years of age) and for "at risk" individuals. The CDC says, "Unvaccinated persons

who have indications for hepatitis B vaccination independent of travel should be vaccinated (e.g., men who have sex with men, injection drug users, anyone who has recently had a sexually-transmitted disease or has had more than one sex partner in the previous 6 months)."

Although the chance of contracting typhoid, dengue, malaria, or rabies is not currently considered high in Chile's Patagonia, these are serious diseases. If you do plan to venture into other areas of South America where malaria is a risk, you and your health care provider need to determine if you need a prescription anti-malarial drug.

Both dengue fever and malaria are caused by mosquito bites, so follow these guidelines to avoid insect bites. Wear long-sleeved, repellent treated clothing, use repellent (DEET is the most effective), use treated mosquito netting, and stay indoors (in screened areas) at dawn and dusk where mosquitoes are prevalent.

Vaccines for Argentina

THE CDC GIVES the same recommendations before traveling in Argentina as it does for Chile except for Yellow Fever prevention. It is recommended that those traveling in the north and northeastern forested areas of Argentina are vaccinated. That does not pertain to Buenos Aires or Patagonia, but would include those traveling to Iguazu Falls.

In case of a medical emergency requiring an ambulance, you can call 131 (free), but the operator may not speak English fluently.[26] Details on our first-aid kit are in Chapter 13.

Staying healthy

IN GENERAL WE avoided tap water, and drank bottled water (or used our water purification tablets/pump.) Alternately bring a Steri-pen. Sometimes just the fact that the local flora and fauna is different is enough to cause intestinal upsets, so we took the standard precautions of avoiding ice cubes in beverages. You can get ice cubes made out of filtered water in most supermarkets.

We didn't take any particular precautions regarding the food we ate. When purchasing food at marketplaces, purchase from popular vendors where the food is kept hot (or refrigerated as appropriate) and the turnover is fast. A standard tip in restaurants is 10%.

We encountered many tasty-looking items in the Chilean marketplaces such as empanadas and sopaipillas. Fish and seafood is offered everywhere. Because Chile is a leading producer of farmed salmon, it is often on the menu. There is also local fish such as corvina (sea bass), congrio (conger eel), lenguado (flounder), albacora (swordfish), and yellow fin tuna.

Of course we had to have the national drink, the Pisco Sour. It's a brandy made from the skin of white grapes and it has a pleasant tartness similar to a margarita. Although we didn't visit the wine-growing regions of central Chile, we enjoyed three excellent and reasonably priced reds: Cabernet Sauvignon, Merlot, and Carmenere with our meals.

(A more complete listing of foods and beverages can be found in Vocabulary, p. 267.)

Besides these typical foods, you can find most staples that you'd find at home: rice, potatoes, meat, and bread. Central Chile and Argentina have temperate climates and vegetables and fruits are grown in abundance. In general, portion sizes increase the farther south you go.

Pre-trip physical training

IF YOU ARE attempting to do major hiking in Torres del Paine or elsewhere, part of your trip preparations will be assessing how fit you are and then either starting, or continuing, a training program so that you lessen the chance that you will be injured. Although I'm sure there are some individuals who can tackle this trip without much increase in training, Ralph and I are not among those so blessed (or young?).

When we went to Patagonia, Ralph was in his seventies and I was in my sixties. Even though we hike regularly when at home, our routine hikes aren't as strenuous or as lengthy as our backpacking days are. When we have a backpacking trip lined up where we will have to spend several days to several weeks carrying packs weighing twenty pounds or so, we ramp up our physical training.

Everyone starts from a different place when preparing for a major hike. Because of differing ages, levels of fitness, and goals, each person will need a different length of time to reach his or her optimum condition before a trip. Although we never seem to find the time to get as physically prepared as we should, we do we get more serious about our exercise program when our next big hike is only two or three months away.

I have found the most effective way of making that happen is to write the exercise and fitness appointments on the calendar just as you write in social and business engagements. We resume walking three times a week and one of the hikes is a long one.

What we have found most successful is to come up with a plan that gradually increases both the distance we hike and the amount of weight that we carry in our backpacks. As a rule of thumb, we increase one or the other each week by about ten percent. In the three months before our hike (luckily we were able to start this right after the Christmas holidays!) I was able to work up to carrying 18 pounds comfortably on an eight-to ten-mile hike, which was what we figured was adequate for the conditions we'd encounter in Torres del Paine.

It's also advisable to incorporate other types of physical conditioning and activities into your program—such as strength training (so you can lift your pack without strain) and yoga, Pilates, or Qigong (Chi Gong) for added flexibility. I found that attending a once-a-week Pilates class as well as meeting with a fitness trainer for an hourly session was quite beneficial.

Our home in the San Francisco Bay Area is at an elevation of only about 1,000 feet, but because most of the Circuit

Trail of Torres del Paine is only about 2,000 feet—and the highest pass is only about 4,000—elevation is not much of a consideration. Nevertheless, we do almost all of our training in the hills because that is what we will encounter (and also what we most enjoy!).

Customs

BEING AN OLDER couple, white and American did not seem to cause any great disturbances, but I have read reports that, although Chile's population is primarily non-white mestizos, there are occasionally situations with Chileans staring at foreigners, even name calling.

Not unlike most countries in the world, Chile's customs remain relatively traditional. Although teenagers and young adults wear anything from blue jeans to designer fashions, most women wear modest dresses or skirts and men wear long pants.

Spanish is the national language for both countries but many Chileans can speak and understand English. It's certainly worthwhile to learn a few expressions in Spanish. However, we found the Chileans to be a friendly people and accepting of our limited Spanish.

The border dispute in northern Chile, a territory which the country won after the War of the Pacific, is still controversial. Peru and especially Bolivia still claim northern parts of the country which has angered the Chileans. Similarly, there is no love lost between Chile and Argentina!

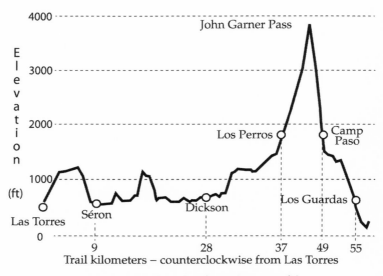

Part one, Circuit elevation profile

❖❖❖❖❖

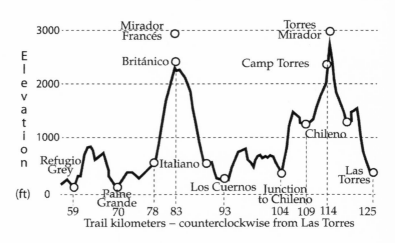

**Part two, Circuit profile including "W" – all elevations
are estimates from park map**

12 • Your Trek in Torres del Paine, "W" or the Circuit?

As mentioned previously, when planning of a trip to Patagonia, Torres del Paine in particular, one should be mindful of the seasons and weather. Although Torres del Paine is open year round, the major trekking season is November through March, with December through February being the busiest months. During the summer, temperatures generally range from 41 °F (5 °C) to 68 °F (20 °C). If you go outside of that time, you find few accommodations open and most roads closed. Major hiking is curtailed because the backcountry becomes like an ice sheet.

Even with the limitations, and the temperatures dropping to 28 °F (-2 °C) to 43 °F (6 °C), you can have a great vacation during the winter. The winds die down, the scenery is perhaps even more amazing with a layer of snow, and the crowds have gone. There are still many activities in the "off" season. Private tour companies can provide snowshoeing and climbing expeditions during the winter. The Explora Hotel, for example, offers horseback riding year round.

The wind, it's driving me crazy!

WHEN RALPH AND I started the research for our backpack trip in Patagonia—a place we knew little about except from the breathtaking photographs we had seen—we learned that it wasn't primarily rain or snow that people mentioned, it was all about the *wind*. From the early accounts of sailors and explorers come such graphic expressions as "fearsome, horrendous, and drives a man insane." Contemporary guidebooks tell us that the weather is unpredictable—and then they add, "if you don't like the weather, wait a couple of hours, and it will be different."

Ralph and I had faced harsh weather before: days of rain and snow on the Grand Randonnée (GR 65) pilgrimage route in France, unrelenting heat on the meseta (plain) of Spain's Camino de Santiago, even strong winds on the Pacific Crest Trail. Once, while backpacking on the Pacific Crest in Southern California's Mojave Desert, we encountered winds that we estimated in the 60-mph range. The gusts drove us forward, and then hit me from the side forcefully enough to throw me off balance. The next day, we had to leave the trail because of my back spasms.

Our friends Harv and Monica went to Patagonia on their honeymoon. Their sobering account of one of the nights during their circumnavigation of the National Parque Torres del Paine went this way, "We heard a sound like a train in the distance. The train came closer and closer. Finally, it sounded like the train was upon us. The winds howled and ripped at our tent, then just as suddenly, faded away."

In the movie, *Mi Mejor Enemigo,* which is set in Patagonia, one of the characters says in effect, "the wind, it's driving me crazy!" The fabled winds of Patagonia sounded like a beast of a totally different color.

I read of winds surpassing 100 miles per hour, with rain thrown in for good measure. We watched movies where sailors had lashed themselves to the deck so that the seas wouldn't push them overboard. On the news we have seen all that hurricanes, tornadoes, and cyclones in different parts of the world could bring.

I began to wonder, "How harsh might Patagonia's storms be?" Until I started doing the research and giving the matter some thought, I had imagined that our trip would be day after day of sparkling clear skies—with perhaps an occasional cloud for its dramatic photo opportunities—and minimal wind or rain. Doubt began to creep in—was I mentally and physically prepared for whatever weather Patagonia would throw at us? It was difficult to know while sitting at home—comfortable and warm—if I was tough enough.

The wind never stops?

WHILE NEARLY EVERYTHING I read about Patagonia mentioned the wind, to say that it never stops is an over-simplification. It tends to be windy in Patagonia October through May and then stop during the dark and cold winter months. Hikers should be prepared for fierce winds, but it's an exaggeration to say that the winds never stop. It's more accurate to say that their occurrence, duration and intensity are unpredictable.

Your hike in Torres del Paine

THE MAPS ON the next pages show the primary hiking routes in the park, the"W" route and the Circuit, as well as locations of hotels and other facilities. The chart at the start of this chapter shows the trail elevation profiles.

The Western leg of the"W" route ends at #7 on the map, Refugio Grey. The middle leg goes up the Valle del Francés, ending at #10. The eastern leg ends at #13, the Towers del Paine mirador.

If you want a more detailed map, the entire visitors map is available online at parquetorresdelpaine.cl/maps.html This is the official CONAF site for Torres del Paine. The site is slow to load, but once it comes up, there is a small outline map on the left side. Click on a segment and the corresponding map segment is zoomed in. This is the same as the map given out at the entrance station.

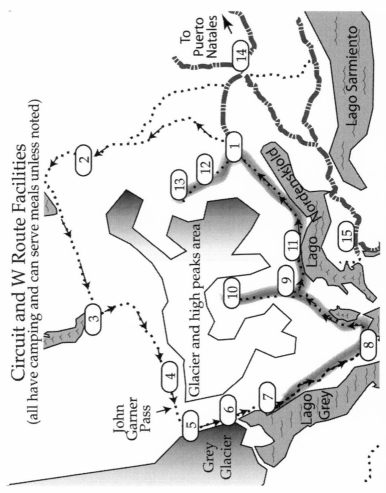

Circuit and "W" Route

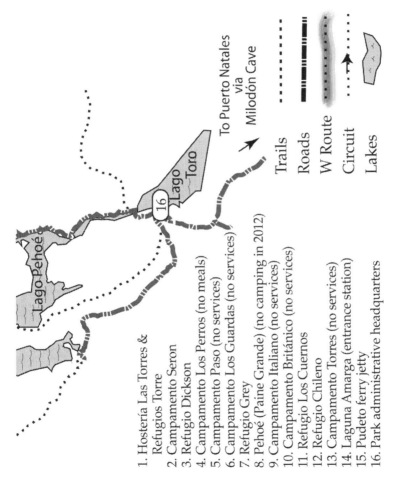

Circuit and "W" Route facilities

1. Hostería Las Torres &
   Refugios Torre
2. Campamento Seron
3. Refugio Dickson
4. Campamento Los Perros (no meals)
5. Campamento Paso (no services)
6. Campamento Los Guardas (no services)
7. Refugio Grey
8. Pehoé (Paine Grande) (no camping in 2012)
9. Campamento Italiano (no services)
10. Campamento Británico (no services)
11. Refugio Los Cuernos
12. Refugio Chileno
13. Campamento Torres (no services)
14. Laguna Amarga (entrance station)
15. Pudeto ferry jetty
16. Park administrative headquarters

Trails
Roads
W Route
Circuit
Lakes

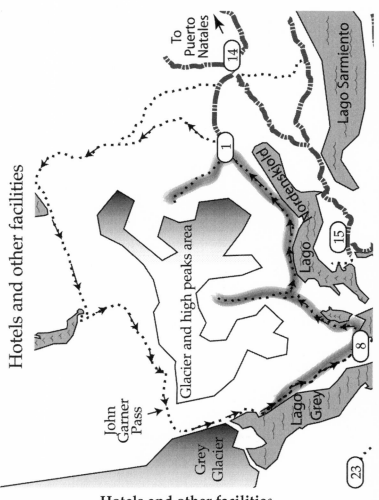

Hotels and other facilities

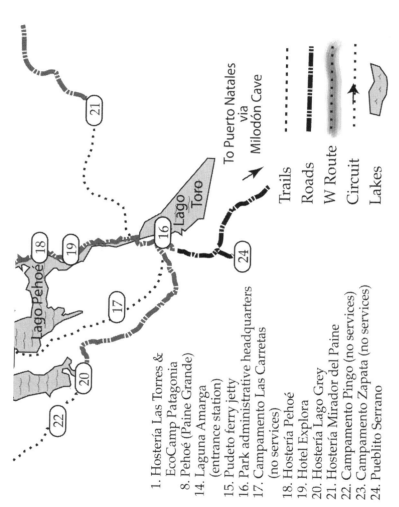

Trails
Roads
W Route
Circuit
Lakes

To Puerto Natales
via
Milodón Cave

Lago
Toro

Lago Pehoé

Hotels and other facilities

1. Hostería Las Torres &
   EcoCamp Patagonia
8. Pehoé (Paine Grande)
14. Laguna Amarga
    (entrance station)
15. Pudeto ferry jetty
16. Park administrative headquarters
17. Campamento Las Carretas
    (no services)
18. Hostería Pehoé
19. Hotel Explora
20. Hostería Lago Grey
21. Hostería Mirador del Paine
22. Campamento Pingo (no services)
23. Campamento Zapata (no services)
24. Pueblito Serrano

Alert: **Recent fire in Torres del Paine:**

IN LATE DECEMBER of 2011, a fire raged through the heart of Torres del Paine for several days burning more than 31,000 acres (48.5 sq. miles) of the 444,160 acres (694 sq. miles) park (about 7%). The fire started on the western leg of the "W" route near Grey Glacier. More than 400 visitors and employees were evacuated. Emergency personnel from both Chile and Argentina responded and requests were made to Australia and the United States for assistance.

On December 30, Vicente Nunez, Director of Chile's emergency agency, Onemi, said more than 11,000 hectares (27,000 acres) had been consumed and that efforts to contain the fire were hampered by strong winds, challenging terrain, and an abundance of combustible vegetation. Subsequently sources reported that President Sebastian Pinera had announced the park would remain shut throughout January, however, by January 4, the fire had been contained and much of the park and its trails were reopened. The trail near Glaciar Grey was, at least temporarily, rerouted. Torres del Paine, with its 100,000 visitors annually, is very important to Chile's tourist economy.

Some of the structures, accommodations, campgrounds, and hiking trails of the "W" and Circuit routes were affected, but have been reopened—including those at Grey, Valle del Francés, and Italiano. At the time of the writing of this book, the Pehoé (Paine Grande) campground was closed, and only time will tell how quickly it will be rebuilt.

Torres del Paine also suffered a disastrous fire in February 2005. The ten-day conflagration, which charred approximately 33,063 sq. acres (51 sq. miles), was started when the flames of a camping stove of a Czech tourist ignited nearby vegetation while he was camped in an unauthorized campsite in an area intended for grazing.

The "W" route and Circuit treks

THERE ARE MANY options for hiking in Torres del Paine depending on the amount of time that you have, your interests, and your abilities as well as trail and weather conditions. When you arrive at an entrance station of Torres del Paine, you will most likely receive a pamphlet (with the map) produced by CONAF (Corporacion Nacional Forestal) that gives the distances, times, and degree of difficulty of the most frequently-taken hikes within the park.

An estimated 50% of the hikers in Torres del Paine tackle the "W" route. When you look at the maps, you can easily see why it's called the "W"—it takes that shape. The three legs take you—starting from the left—up to Glaciar Grey; into the Valle del Francés; and to the Towers del Paine. Hikers or backpackers who have less time than needed to complete the entire "W" route often choose among the three legs; the hike to the Towers del Paine is the most popular.

The Circuit route is a major backpacking route that not only does a full 76.7 mile circuit around the Torres range, but also heads into the valleys that comprise the "W" route.

When reading the following lists of accommodations and suggested itineraries for both the "W" and Circuit routes, keep in mind the following:

There are two companies that run the refugios and campgrounds: Fantástico Sur (FS)[7] fantasticosur.com and Vertice Patagonia (VE).[27] verticepatagonia.com. (VE) calls some of their facilities Mountain Lodges, but we usually refer to them as refugios. (You'll find our list of destinations on p. 175-176, and our list of hotels on p. 192-193.)

You can buy breakfast and dinner at the Fantástico Sur refugios (FS). *Except* for Los Perros, the Vertice Patagonia (VE) locations also serve breakfast and dinner. For both these companies, full board includes a box lunch.

All camps have spots for tent camping, except for the one at Pehoé (Paine Grande), which was closed (we hope temporarily) in early 2012 because of fire damage. Camps with lodging require that the lodging be reserved in advance—if possible before you arrive in the park.

At the VE locations, there is camping equipment for rent including sleeping bags and mats. We also found that the *staffed* backcountry camps in Torres del Paine had rental tents. That means that *theoretically* you can make the Circuit without carrying your own tent: reducing your pack weight and allowing you to avoid having to set up/take down a tent. If you want to try this without the safety net of having your own shelter, *reserve at least a day or two in advance* to make sure tents are available and that you can reserve one at each camp.

Keep in mind that the distances between the VE locations are long, but combined with overnight stays at the lodges, this plan might work for strong hikers.

Cash (in pesos) was required in the backcountry to pay for tents, meals, snacks, etc. We found that it goes fast even though we carried most of our backpacking food. As of January 2012, figure on about 3,500 Chilean Pesos CHP (US$7) for camping per night. Meals at Vertice Patagonia (Grey, Dickson, and Paine Grande) for example, are currently 5,500 for breakfast, 7,500 for lunch, and 9,900 for dinner. This is about $11, $15, $20 U.S. dollars for one person.

The term "store" is generous; selections are limited to begin with and dwindle as the season progresses.

Point-to-point distances of the Circuit and "W" routes

Numbers refer to the points shown on the maps earlier in this chapter. All locations have camping unless noted. 10 kilometers = 6.2 miles

Start	Destination	Distance and time	Facilities at Destination
Refugios Torre #1	Campamento Serón #2	9 km 4 hrs	store, meals, tents
Campamento Serón #2	Refugio Dickson (VE) #3	19 km 6 hrs	dormitory, store, meals, tents
Refugio Dickson #3	Campamento Los Perros (VE) #4	9 km 4.5 hrs	store, tents
Campamento Los Perros #4	Campamento Paso #5	12 km 4.5 hrs	no services
Campamento Paso #5	Campamento Los Guardas #6	6 km 3 hrs	no services
Campamento Los Guardas #6	Refugio Grey (VE) #7	4 km 2 hrs	dorm, store, meals, tents
Refugio Grey #7	Pehoé (Refugio Paine Grande) (VE) #8	11 km 3.5 hrs	dorm, meals (camping closed by 2012 fire)
Pehoé (Refugio Paine Grande) #8	Camp Italiano #9	7.6 km 2 hrs	no services
Camp Italiano #9	Campamento Británico #10	5.5 km 2.5 hrs	no services
Camp Italiano #9	Refugio Los Cuernos (FS) #11	5.5 km 2.5 hrs	dorm, store, meals, tents
(Continued on next page)			

Point-to-point distances of the Circuit and "W" routes

Numbers refer to the points shown on the maps earlier in this chapter. All locations have camping unless noted. 10 kilometers = 6.2 miles

Start	Destination	Distance and time	Facilities at Destination
Refugio Los Cuernos #11	Hostería Las Torres & Refugios Torre (FS) #1	11 km 4 hrs	hotel, dorm, store, meals, tents
If you are going from Los Cuernos to Refugio Chileno there is a cutoff that takes a higher and shorter route; we don't have details on that route other than it is labeled "shortcut to Chileno".			
Hostería Las Torres & Refugios Torre #1	Refugio Chileno (FS) #12	3 km 2 hrs	dorm, meals, tents
The Las Torres location is strung out over a kilometer or so. Westernmost is Hostería Las Torres, closest to the trail to Chileno and the Towers. The campground is next, and then the Refugios Torre (Central and Norte). Easternmost, up out of sight behind a hill, is the EcoCamp.			
Refugio Chileno #12	Campamento Torres #13	5 km 1.5 hrs	no services
Camp Torres #13	Mirador Torres	1 km 1 hr	view of the towers
(Table continued from prior page)			

Warning: In Chile we sometimes encountered hot water faucets on the right/cold on the left. That also applies to some campground showers. In general, be prepared for everything from cold to scalding with changes possible moment to moment!

Tackling the "W" route

Accommodations, route planning, & itinerary for Torres del Paine's "W"

WHEN PLANNING YOUR trip to Torres del Paine, keep in mind that a few of the park's accommodations are far from the hiking routes. If your time in the park will be limited, then plan to enter the park from the entrance where you can establish a home base that will put you in the best location for getting to the trailheads at the start of each hike of the "W." (Refer back to maps on p. 168-171.)

All scheduled buses from Puerto Natales stop first at Laguna Amarga #14, continue to Pudeto #15 the catamaran stop, and turn around at Administration #16. There is an early morning bus and an afternoon bus. For Refugios Torre and vicinity #1, get off at Laguna Amarga. For the catamaran to Pehoé (Paine Grande), continue to Pudeto #15. If you stay on until Administration #16, it is a two-hour walk to Campamento Las Carreta with no services, and three hours after that to reach Pehoé.

If your goal is to complete all or part of the "W" route, and you want to do the easiest legs first, you would start with the western leg up to Glaciar Grey, then do the Valle del Francés, and finally the Towers del Paine.

It *is* possible to do parts of the "W" route as *day hikes*, but to do it in its entirety, you'll probably want to do it with overnight stays in either campgrounds or hostels.

The campground/refugios accommodations along the "W" include:

#7 Refugio Grey (VE): Rooms and campground. Lodging, hot showers, flush toilets. Tents/sleeping bags/mats for rent. Restaurant and possibility of box lunch. Store.

#8 Mountain Lodge and Camping Paine Grande (located at site of former Pehoé shelter) (VE): Rooms and campground. Lodging for 100 with 2-3 bunks per room.

Separate shower/bathrooms for men and women. Self-service restaurant; box lunches available. Note that camping here was closed by 2012 fire, so check with VE before planning on it.

#9 Campamento Italiano: Camping only. Often over-crowded, free campground with few tables. No meals or other services. Toilets unreliable.

#10 Campamento Británico: Camping only; no fires.

#11 Refugio Los Cuernos with cabins (FS): Cabins, rooms and campground. Lodging in dorms or private cabins with access to hot tub. Campground with sites nestled among sheltering trees. Restaurant (meals served community style), hot showers and flush toilets. Sleeping bags and tents for rent. Store.

Location #1 has the following four styles of accommodations plus a camping area:

#1 Refugio Torre *Central* (FS): Rooms and camping. Spacious grassy camping area with some tables; showers (timed) and flush toilets. The Refugio has lodging in bunk beds and separate men's and women's restrooms. Restaurant (meals served community style), and bar. Store, but with very few supplies for campers. May have sleeping bags and tents for rent. Credit cards accepted.

#1 Refugio Torre *Norte* is nearby (500 m). An older building, but a decent hostel with bunks beds in dorms. Separate shower rooms for men and women

Note: Refugio Torre Norte and Central are right next to each other, and were not identified separately when we were there. In the text we lump them together with the associated campground as Refugios Torre, or refer to the entire #1 area as Las Torres.

#1 Hostería Las Torres, an upscale lodge with private rooms, dining, bar, and Internet access

#1 EcoCamp Torres del Paine (see page 194) out of sight but nearby.

#12 Campamento Chileno (FS): Rooms and camping. Small camping area. Lodging 8 beds per room. Food served at community tables. Showers, flush toilets. Sleeping bags and tents for rent. Store.

#13 Campamento Torres: Camping only; a shelter in the Valle Ascensio enroute to the Towers, information board.

Campamento Japonés: (4 km north of #13) Officially a camp for climbers and mountaineers only; tarp shelter, no campfires.

"W" Route itinerary with times, distances, and descriptions

THE FOLLOWING IS a plan for managing the days and nights of the popular "W" route, which is 47.18 miles (76.1 km.) Most can hike this in four or five days by doing each of three legs of the "W" as eight- to ten-hour days, and each of the two connecting hikes taking four to six hours. You'll be surrounded by beautiful scenery the entire time and enjoy the major landforms known as the Grey Glaciar, Cuernos del Paine, and Towers (*Torres*) del Paine.

The CONAF (Corporacion Nacional Forestal) map that you should receive when you enter the park gives the distances, times, and degree of difficulty of the most frequently taken hikes within the park. As mentioned earlier, you can find this online at parquetorresdelpaine.cl/maps.html. The park's information is helpful for getting oriented, *but many people have commented on the inaccuracy of the estimate of time needed to walk the various trail segments.*

The following is an *ambitious* five-day plan starting and ending at Puerto Natales.

Day 1: Bus from Puerto Natales to Torres del Paine. Hike to Glaciar Grey (left leg):

THE HIGHLIGHTS OF the first day are the outstanding views of Glaciar Grey and hiking along Lago Grey. Stay at Accommodation #7 **Refugio Grey** (see previous list).

Catch the morning bus from Puerto Natales (2.5 hours) into the park, entering at the *Laguna Amarga* (guard and entrance station) where you will pay your fees and obtain your permit. Get back on the bus for the next stop at Pudeto. Jump on the catamaran at noon (cost approximately US$25) for the 45-minute ride across the Lago Pehoé, which will take you across to the Refugio Paine Grande.

Hike: The hike from Paine Grande to your destination at Lago Grey is on the left (western) leg of the "W". It's 6.8 miles (11 km.) and an estimated 3½ hours to reach **Refugio Grey**.

Going in, this is an uphill hike of moderate intensity the entire way. You go through forests and open lands. You dip into valleys and cross small streams. If it's windy, it's more challenging, but that won't matter because much of the time you are enjoying the outstanding views of Lago Grey, the icebergs floating from Glaciar Grey, and the glacier itself.

If time allows, it's highly recommended that you hike on past Refugio Grey to the mirador (signed) that overlooks the glacier, then return to your accommodations at Grey.

Day 2: Glaciar Grey to Italiano (or to Paine Grande).

IF YOU DIDN'T continue on Day 1 to the mirador beyond Refugio Grey, consider doing so at the start of your second day's hike, if you are prepared to extend an already lengthy day.

Hike: This is a hike that connects the left leg of the "W" with the middle one. From Lago Grey, retrace your steps down to Paine Grande. If time and energy allow, continue on to Campamento Italiano, which puts you in a better position for Day 3's hike into the Valle de Francés. Stay at Accommodation #9, **Campamento Italiano.**

According to CONAF, the distance between Lago Grey and Paine Grande is 6.8 miles (11 km.) and an estimated 3½ hours. From Paine Grande to Campamento Italiano is 4.7 miles (7.6 km.) and takes 2½ hours. Total is 11.5 miles and 6 hours. Italiano has no accommodations other than camping. If you want lodging, stop earlier at Accommodation #8, **Refugio Paine Grande.**

The segment from Paine Grande to Italiano is a beautiful hike and we found it to be the easiest section of the "W" route.

We had some exhilarating moments when the wind kicked up on nearby Lago Skollsberg

Day 3: Italiano to Valle del Francés and Los Cuernos:

THIS SPECTACULAR HIKE is on the middle leg of the "W" route. From Campamento Italiano, you hike into the Valle del Francés (French Valley) past Campamento Británico and on to the French Valley mirador. Then back to Accommodation #11, **Refugio los Cuernos.**

Hike:

Part 1: Camp Italiano to Camp Británico: 3.4 miles (5.5 km.), 2.5 hours. Moderate difficulty.

Part 2: Británico to French Valley mirador. .75-mile (1.2 km.), 30 minutes. (round-trip 1.5 miles, 1 hour).

Part 3: Return to Italiano from mirador: 4.2 miles, (6.7 km.).

Part 4: Italiano to Cuernos: 3.4 miles (5.5 km.), 2.5 hours. Moderate.

Total for day: CONAF: 12.7 miles (18.9 km.), requiring 7.5-8.5 hours. Moderate.

If you leave your backpack in Italiano, you can do your climb into the valley without carrying the excess weight and pick it up on your way out. You start to climb into the valley following alongside a small river and in and out of trees. At times the trail becomes faint, sometimes rocky, but not difficult. A bit before reaching Campamento Británico, you will come to a wide spot with incredible views of waterfalls and hanging glaciers. This is a great place to sit on a rock for a break: hearing and seeing the huge chunks of ice fall is a thrilling experience.

A challenging 800-m climb takes you to the spectacular French Valley, a hidden granite cirque complete with hanging glaciers. Although the CONAF map rates the hike as moderate, it is more precise to say that the initial stage of the hike is moderate, but becomes more challenging after Campamento Británico.

The hike from the French Valley to Refugio Los Cuernos is along the shore of Lago Nordenskjöld, with Paine Massif to your left, until you get to Los Cuernos.

Day 4: Cuernos to Chileno (option of overnight at Campamento Torres):

TODAY'S HIKE CONTINUES along Lago Nordenskjöld and then up through the Ascencio Valley toward the Towers on the third (right/eastern) leg of the "W" route. This adds up to a challenging day! Accommodations #12, **Chileno**, or #13, **Campamento Torres.**

Hike, Part 1: CONAF: Los Cuernos to Chileno: 9.61 miles (15.5 km.), 6 hours. Moderate to strenuous.

The first part of the day—from Cuernos along the lake toward (but not to!) Hostería Torres is gentle. As you begin the climb into the foothills of the Paine Massif and the Valley Ascencio, it becomes a moderately-challenging up-and-down hike. Your destination for the day: either Campamento Chileno (tents or indoor accommodations possible) or Campamento Torres (camping only).

Stopping at Campamento Chileno, which you reach first, will lengthen your final day.

Part 2: Refugio Chileno to Campamento Torres. CONAF: 2 miles (3.2 km.), 1.5 hours. Refugio Chileno has shared bedrooms, a campground, hot showers and a restaurant.

If you want to see the Towers reflect the sunrise in the morning, you can continue on another two miles (3.2 km.), with a 700 ft. climb, to the Campamento Torres campsite, which is free.

See option below for an easier itinerary, but requiring an additional day.*

Day 5: Campamento Torres to the Torres Towers and out.

THIS DAY'S HIKE will take you from your camp to the base of the Torres Towers and then back down the mountain to **Refugios Torres** #1 (and campground). From there, you can take the bus back to Puerto Natales or stay another night.

If you stayed overnight in Refugio Chileno:

Hike, Part 1: Refugio Chileno to Campamento Torres. CONAF: 2 miles (3.2 km.), 1.5 hours.

Part 2: Campamento Torres to the base of the towers. From Campamento Torres, you climb a challenging route to the base of the Towers—the granite spikes of Torre d'Agonsti, Torre Central, and Torre Norte. CONAF: 1 hour (2 hour round-trip).

Allow two hours for this somewhat unnerving 1-mile round-trip. For many, the goal is to be at the Towers' mirador for sunrise.

Part 3: (Part 2, if you camped at Campamento Torres). CONAF: From the Towers' mirador to the Hostería Las Torres is given as 5.89 miles (9.5 km.), estimated 3.5 hours.

It will be an easy descent back down through the Ascensio Valley and out to the refugios or Hostería Torres, where you can catch a bus back to Puerto Natales (or stay overnight in the park).

*Option providing an extra day: Day 4-6.

Day 4: Hike Los Cuernos to Refugios Torre. 6.82 miles (11 km.), 4 hours.

Day 5: Hike Refugios Torre to Chileno, 2 hours; or Camp Torres, 3.5 hours.

Day 6: Return to Refugios Torre and bus to Puerto Natales.

Trekking the Circuit route

Route Planning, accommodations, and itinerary for Torres del Paine's Circuit

When planning your hike, consider where to set up your base camp. As you have read, we entered Torres del Paine through the eastern Laguna Amarga guard station to start and end our hiking trips at the #1 Las Torres campground. The suggested "W" route schedule (given above) also entered the park through the main entrance, Laguna Amarga. However, if you have your own, or hotel arranged transportation, there are other entrances and one of them might work better for your visit.

Accommodations/Camps on the Circuit:

In the list below, note that two different concessionaires run the camps where you will find accommodations: *Fantástico Sur* (FS)[7] and *Vertice Patagonia* (VE).[27]

To complete the Circuit in the usual counterclockwise manner and assuming you started at Las Torres #1, you would encounter campgrounds and hostels in the order below. Most hikers don't stop at all of these camps; further on in this chapter, you will find some recommended itineraries.

#1 Refugio Torre *Central*(FS): Rooms and camping. Spacious, grassy camping area with some tables; showers and flush toilets. Refugio Torre *Central* (also called Lodge Torre *Central*) has lodging in bunk beds and separate men's and women's restrooms. Restaurant (meals served community style), and bar. Store, but with very few supplies for campers. May have sleeping bags and tents for rent. Credit cards accepted.

#1 Refugio Torre *Norte* is nearby (500 m). Older building, but a decent hostel with bunk beds in dorms. Separate shower rooms for men and women.

Note: as mentioned earlier, in the text we lump Norte and Central together, along with the campground as Refugios Torre, or just Las Torres.

#1 Hostería Las Torres is a full service hotel about half a kilometer west of the Refugios Torre. (information at lastorres.com)

#2 Campamento Séron (FS): Camping only. Large grassy camping area with some tables; showers and flush toilets, meals, store.

#3 Refugio Dickson (VE): Rooms and camping. Large camping area with tables; some sites tucked away in sheltered spots. Lodging. Shower rooms for lodge guests. Campers' showers have varying temperatures. Flush toilets. Meals (including possibility of box lunch), store, tents/bags/mats for rent.

#4 Campamento Los Perros (VE): Camping only. Cold showers, flush toilets. No meals. Tents, sleeping bags, and mats for rent. Large shelter for cooking and hanging clothes to dry. Store with limited stock.

#5 Campamento Paso: Camping only; free. A three-sided shelter for cooking. No meals, showers, or store. Privy.

#6 Campamento Los Guardas: Camping only; free. No meals, showers, or store. Privy.

#7 Refugio Grey (VE): Rooms and campground. Large area for camping on the sandy beach of Lago Grey. Tents/sleeping bags/mats for rent. Lodging, hot showers, flush toilets. Restaurant and possibility of box lunch. Store.

#8 Mountain Lodge and Camping Paine Grande (located at site of former Pehoé shelter) **(VE):** Rooms and camping (camping and store closed by fire as of 2012). Lodging for 100 with two or three bunks per room. Separate shower/bath rooms for men and women. Restaurant serving meals at community tables. Comfortable bar. If open, campground has (timed) hot showers, flush toilets, store.

#9 Campamento Italiano: Camping only; free. Often overcrowded with a few tables. No meals or other services. Toilets unreliable.

#10 Campamento Británico: in the Valle del Francés: Camping only. No fires (stoves okay).

#11 Refugio Los Cuernos (FS) with Cabins (and Campamento Cuernos): Rooms and camping. Campground with sites nestled among sheltering trees, lodging in dorms or private cabins with access to hot tub. Restaurant (meals served community style), hot showers and flush toilets. Sleeping bags and tents for rent. Store.

#12 Campamento Chileno in the Valle Ascencio (FS): Rooms and camping. Small camping area. Lodging eight beds per room. Food served at community tables. Showers, flush toilets. Sleeping bags and tents for rent. Store.

#13 Campamento Torres (Towers) in the Valle Ascencio: Camping only. Shelter, information.

Campamento Japonés in the Valle Ascencio: (4 km north of 13) Camping only. Officially a camp for climbers and mountaineers only; tarp shelter, no campfires.

Circuit Route Itinerary with times, distances, and descriptions

THE FIRST MAP of this chapter shows the Circuit route and accommodations along the way. This is a 9-day *hiking* plan that we attempted in 2009, and is a modification of the Lonely Planet 8-day route. The following provides detail about the distances, estimated time for each segment of the hike, and level of difficulty that is given in the CONAF brochure for the Circuit. *Our comments about each segment are given in italics.*

Day 1: Bus from Puerto Natales to Torres del Paine. Hike to Campamento Séron

MORNING BUS FROM Puerto Natales to Torres del Paine and enter park at Laguna Amarga. Take van shuttle from there to Las Torres (#1). Hike Las Torres to Serón. **Accommodation #2, Campamento Serón.**

Hike: Las Torres to Serón going counterclockwise. CONAF: 8.9 km. (5.5 miles), 4 hours. Medium difficulty.

Easy-Moderate. This section of the trail is mostly open with some forest and hills.

Alternate: After arriving in the park, if the weather is good, shift schedule of doing the Circuit by one day and do a day hike from Las Torres to Chileno and the Towers and return. This would be a seven hour trip by CONAF times.

Day 2: Campamento Séron to Refugio Dickson

HIKE: CONAF: 18.5 km. (11.47 miles), 6 hours. Medium difficulty. **Accommodation #3, Refugio/camping Dickson.**

Moderate difficulty. The trail travels through some areas of exposed rock that can be somewhat intimidating. In some older literature, there is mention of Camp Coison—a wild, free campsite—along the way, but we have never seen any sign of this.

We saw other hikers lose the trail through here. They soon found themselves knee deep wading through the bogs. This is a gorgeous stage of your hike: terrific views of the mountains during the day, an outstanding setting with a view of Glaciar Dickson at day's end. Hiking poles were a great aid on the short steep descent just before Dickson.

Day 3: Refugio Dickson to Campamento Los Perros

Hike: CONAF: 8.7 km. (5.4 miles), 4.5 hours. Medium difficulty. **Accommodation/camping #4, Campamento Los Perros.**

Moderate difficulty. The trail initially takes you past glaciers, providing magnificent views. Then it enters dense rainforest where it pays to be attentive to the exposed tree roots in the path. If it is raining, there will also be lots of puddles, even mud, on the trail. You climb gradually to Los Perros. As mentioned earlier, on our 2009 hike, this became a longer day than expected. It took us about seven hours.

We echo Rob Hodges' comments, "The mud in that area was surprising. Of course, we encountered muddy sections throughout Patagonia, but none were remotely as bad as that, which made for slow going. There will be rapidly flowing and splashing glacial streams alongside as you climb, but when you cross them you'll have footbridges."

Day 4: Campamento Los Perros to Campamento Paso

Hike: CONAF: 12 km. (7.44 miles) 4.5 hours. High difficulty. **Accommodation/camping #5, Camp Paso.**

After the initial steep, but short climb out of Los Perros, the ascent to John Garner Pass becomes moderately difficult. You pass through both forested and open rocky terrain. Ducks or paint splashes indicate the route.

Rob wrote, "I'm not good with estimating the percentages, but between Los Perros and Campamento Paso, I would guess maybe a quarter of it was exposed and three-quarters was forested. But who knows?"

After reaching the pass and taking in the incredible views of the Patagonian Ice Field, the descent is difficult. It is steep and often muddy as you plunge through woodland. Ascent is about 2,100 ft.; descent about 2,600 ft. We took six hours.

Alternate: Many hikers, headed for a hot meal, showers, and the option of beds, continue past here to Refugio Grey. For strong hikers trying to cut the number of days out, this would be a good option.

Day 5: Campamento Paso, past Los Guardas, to Refugio Grey

HIKE, PART 1: **Campamento Paso to Los Guardas.** CONAF: 6 km. (3.7 miles), 3 hours. Medium difficulty.
Your descent continues, but less steeply. (Los Guardas is listed above as accommodation #6.)
    Part 2: Los Guardas to Refugio Grey. CONAF: 4 km. (2.5 miles), 2 hours.
Gentle descent continues along Grey Glacier. Probably the easiest part of the Circuit.
    Total for day: CONAF: 10 km. (6.2 miles), 5 hours. Medium difficulty. **Accommodation #7, Refugio/camping Grey.**

Day 6: Refugio Grey to Campamento Italiano

HIKE, PART 1: **Refugio Grey to Paine Grande.** CONAF: 11 km. (6.82 miles), 3.5 hours. Medium difficulty.
Trail follows an up-and-down course. Vegetation changes. Excellent views of Lago Pehoé.
    Part 2: Pehoé (Paine Grande) to Campamento Italiano. CONAF: 7.6 km. (4.7 miles), 2.5 hours. Easy.
You're now away from the glacier and (mostly) out of the forest as you hike along the shore of lovely blue-green Lago Pehoé.
    Total for day: CONAF: 18.6 km. (11.52 miles), 6 hours. About 900 ft. ascent/descent. **Accommodation/camping #9, Campamento Italiano.**

Day 7: Campamento Italiano, side trip to Valle del Francés, Refugio/Campamento Los Cuernos

HIKE, PART 1: **Campamento Italiano to Campamento Británico in the Valle de Francés.** CONAF: 5.5 km. (3.4 miles), 2.5 hours. Medium difficulty.

The side trip climb into the Valle de Francés and to the Campamento Británico provides (approximately) a 900 ft. ascent alongside a rushing stream/river to reach viewpoints of nearby hanging glaciers.

Part 2: Campamento Británico to Refugio/Campamento Los Cuernos. CONAF: 11 km. (6.82 miles), 5 hours. Medium difficulty.

You descend (900 ft.) from your side trip to Británico and continue on to Refugio/Campamento Los Cuernos. As you hike along this stretch of the trail, you are in and out of a few stands of sheltering trees. Depending on the wind and weather, Lago Nordenskjöld can be a calm body of aquamarine water or a wind-whipped steely gray. Moderate.

Total for day: CONAF: 16 km. (9.92 miles), 7.5 hours. **Accommodation/camp #10, Refugio/Campamento Los Cuernos.**

Alternate: If you want to linger longer in the Valle del Francés, stay overnight at Británico.

Day 8: Los Cuernos to Chileno

Hike: Los Cuernos to Chileno. CONAF: Approx. 15.5 km. (9.61 miles), 6 hours. Moderate to strenuous. **Accommodation/camp #12, Chileno.**

As you near completion of the Circuit, the scenery changes once again. In this very open terrain as you cross barren rock, you'll feel like you're on a moonscape. You should keep on the lookout for condors riding the thermals; these impressive black vultures can have a wingspan of more than ten feet. The first part of the day—from Cuernos along the lake toward (but not to!) Hostería Torres is easy-moderate, but as you begin the climb into the foothills of the Paine Massif and the Valley Ascencio, it becomes a moderately-challenging up-and-down hike. There is also a high trail from Cuernos to Chileno, but we've not hiked it.

Alternate: Continue on to the Mirador Torres (viewpoint of the Towers) and return to Campamento Torres. CONAF: (4.9 km.) 1.5 hours to Campamento Torres, plus 1 mile, 2-hour roundtrip to Mirador Torres. Moderate to strenuous difficulty. Total *additional* of the alternate is 3.5 hours (7 km.) . Destination #13, the Towers.

Elevation changes: Chileno to Camp. Torres 700 ft. up, and from there to the Towers 1000 ft. up.

Day 9: Campamento Chileno or Campamento Torres back to Refugios Torres

Hike: Chileno to Refugios Torres (3 km.) or Campamento Torres (8 km.) to Refugios Torre, late afternoon bus back to Puerto Natales.

The circuit distance including the alternate climb from Chileno to the Towers and return is 124 km. or 76.4 miles.

More options:

CHECK OUT APPENDIX #2 to find the details of our 2009 and 2010 trips—including the Circuit trek and the detour into the Valle del Francés. You can use this information as a starting point for your hike, but adjust your schedule according to your personal fitness level and speed as well as expected trail conditions.

Rob Hodges suggests an alternate plan to the usual. "[Kate and I] did the `Q,' which is the Circuit plus a trail that starts down south by the Park Administration and Visitor's Center #16. It was nice starting there because there was no one else on the trail." Their route started from the Serrano entrance and they camped in a small campground nearby.

"At our first campsite [#17 Las Carretas], we thought we had the entire place to ourselves.

Finally, just before dark a solo Austrian hiker showed up, so it was just us three. Another nice thing about starting down there was it felt like the whole park was unfolding before you. When we started, it seemed like Paine Grande and the entire Torres Massif were far away, rather than towering over you like it seems on the 'W' and Circuit."

Entrances to Torres del Paine (Guarderias):

#14 GUARDERIA LAGUNA Amarga. The main park entrance and exit for cars and buses is from highway 9 (north) on the east side of the park. It's 73 miles (116 km.) and approximately two hours from Puerto Natales. Everyone gets off the bus, registers and pays the park entry fees (even if they are going on to Pudeto).

From this entrance station, a van shuttle can bring you to the Las Torres campground, to the Refugios Torre, or to Hostería Las Torres. The #1 Las Torres complex is the most commonly used start and end point for Circuit hikes. If you complete the "W" route with the trek to see the Towers, you'll also end up near the Refugios Torre. From there, you can catch the shuttle back to the Laguna Amarga station and then take the bus back to Puerto Natales.

If you continue on the bus from Puerto Natales, the next stop is the catamaran jetty at #15 Pudeto. This is the best choice for those wanting the catamaran ride over to Paine Grande (NW corner of Lago Pehoé) to begin the "W" route.

The last stop for the bus is #16 Administration Center at Lago del Toro, which is the bus turnaround point.

Porteria and Guarderia Sarmiento. An entrance on the S/SE side of the park and near the Lago Sarmiento. No scheduled buses. No camping.

Porteria y Guarderia Serrano. This is the park's southern entrance, next to Lago Toro, and goes by the CONAF Administration Center. The access road, Highway 290, which formerly required a vehicle with 4-wheel drive, has been paved. Bus or van tours can be arranged from Puerto Natales that will take you to visit *Cueva del Milodon* enroute.

There is a camping area at Rio Serrano slightly before the entrance station. After passing the Administration Center, the road divides: the left branch leads (west) to Lago Grey and Hostería Lago Grey; Campamentos Pingo and Zapata; the right branch leads up the east side of Lago Pehoé to such attractions as Salto Chico and Grande, the Hotel Explora,

Hostería Pehoé, and Pudeto.

Porteria y Guarderia Laguna Verde. This is a lesser-used entrance station on the S/SW side of the park reached from Puerto Natales. The road ends here, but trails into the Laguna Verde sector begin.

Porteria and Guarderia Laguna Azul: This is another lesser-used entrance, on the Laguna Azul, N/NE in the park. It is primarily for those on horseback. There is camping approx. 5 km. from entrance station.

By boat: You can also reach the park by sailing from Puerto Natales (and return) through the fjord of Ultima Esperanza.

The following chart summarizes the hotels as well as facilities not on the"W" Route or the Circuit.

Hotels and other facilities numbers refer to the points shown on the map on pages 170-171	
#1 Hostería Las Torres and EcoCamp Patagonia	
#14 Laguna Amarga entrance station	
#15 Pudeto ferry jetty	the catamaran runs between Pudeto and Pehoé (Paine Grande) 3 times a day during peak season
#16 CONAF administrative headquarters	
#17 Campamento Las Carretas	no services
#18 Hostería Pehoé	
#19 Camping Pehoé	upscale campground just north of Hotel Explora
#19 Hotel Explora	

Hotels and other facilities

numbers refer to the points shown on the map on pages 170-171

#20 Hostería Lago Grey and Grey Lake Navigation Boat Trip	This is where you can catch a boat to Refugio Grey. Departures are once a day.
#21 Hostería Mirador del Paine	
#22 Camp Pingo	no services
#23 Camp Zapata	no services
#24 Pueblito Serrano	

Additional accommodations for Torres del Paine:

BESIDES THE ACCOMMODATIONS along or near the "W" and Circuit trekking trails, there are various other places to stay in, or near, Torres del Paine. Also there are a couple of alternative routes for reaching the park from Puerto Natales (or the Argentine side)—either through the town of Cerro Castillo or along the newly-improved (paved) route that travels past the national monument of Cueva del Milodon. As mentioned earlier, public buses do not presently take the Cueva del Milodon route, but that may change, so check with the bus companies of Puerto Natales if this route interests you and you have time for a stop at the national monument. Note that trekkers of the "W" or Circuit would find accommodations on the south side of the park far removed from the starting points of their hikes.

Some of the upscale accommodations have their own shuttle services. If you are interested in these hotels, hostels, or hosterías, contact them directly for their suggestions for transport or driving options.

Inside Torres del Paine:

ECOCAMP PATAGONIA. LOCATED near the start of the Circuit and Refugios Torre with views of the Towers. EcoCamp offers sustainable accommodations that fall somewhere between a hotel and a camping experience by using geodesic dome tents (high enough to stand in) with beds, private or shared bathrooms, and dining in a large tent. Package deals available with excursions including the "W" and Circuit routes. Phone USA/Canada 1-800-901-6987. www. ecocamp.travel/.

Camping Pehoé. Sites on the south shore of Lago Pehoé by Overland Sodexo. Relatively deluxe campground with sites under three-sided wooden and metal shelters or in five dome tents. Lodging in private rooms, showers, restaurant with private tables. Upscale store with energy bars and similar items for hikers. www.campingpehoe.com/

Hotel Lago Grey. Upscale accommodations with private rooms and baths, restaurants, and full service. Sector Lago Grey/on the shore of Lago Grey. Phone: (56-61) 712100. www.lagogrey.com/

Hotel Salto Chico, Explora. Deluxe accommodations on the shores of Lago Pehoé in the heart of Torres del Paine. 50 rooms. The European plan includes room and three meals a day, transportation to and from local airport, guided excursions. Tours arranged. www.explora.com/explora-patagonia/ Phone: (56-2) 3952533.

Hostería Pehoé. On Lago Pehoé. 45 rooms. Phone: (56-2) 2961238 www.pehoe.cl

Hostería Las Torres. Upscale accommodations. Beautiful setting and close to the Towers of Paine. Restaurant, bar, lounge. Tours arranged. Phone: Punta Arenas office (56) 61 363636; hotel: (56-61) 617450. www.lastorres.com

Outside the park:

HOSTERÍA MIRADOR DEL **Paine.** Located just outside the park boundary on the *east* side of the park, but remote from major hiking trails. On the Estancia El Lazo in the Laguna Verde sector. Phone/Fax (56) (61) 228712. www.miradordelpayne.com/.

Rio Serrano Hotel. Located just outside Torres del Paine on the *southern* edge and on the Rio Serrano. Stunning views of the mountains when weather allows. Pricey. $300+. Phone: (56) 61 223158 or (56) 61 223427. www.hotelrioserrano.cl/home_en.html

Hostería Lago Tyndall. Located on the Rio (River) Serrano, just outside the park's *southern* boundaries. Rooms and cottages (most reviewers seem to prefer the cottages). (56-61) 614682. www.hoteltyndall.cl/

Hostería Cabañas del Paine. Located on the *south* side of the park on the Serrano River with views of the Paine Mountain Range. 41 rooms. Phone: (56-61)730177 Punta Arenas; (56-2) 8891138 Hostel. www.cabanasdelpaine.cl

Guanaco

13 • Packing List for Patagonian Backpacking Trips

When I went on my first backpacking trip in 1989, I wore the same kind of clothing and carried much the same kind of gear that hikers had taken the previous 20 years: flannel shirts, blue jeans, leather boots—all carried in a four-pound backpack. My pack weighed about 35 pounds and I thought I would die.

Luckily for all of us who backpack and don't enjoy struggling, Ray Jardine came out with a book in 1999, entitled *Beyond Backpacking*, which advocated lightening what you carry and relying on your skills more than on heavy equipment. We aren't ultra-light backpackers—we want more of a margin for error—but we have systematically reduced what we carry.

Clothing

We use layers and wear lightweight synthetic clothing or wool. Layering provides insulation and allows easy adjustment with changing weather conditions. Synthetics promote *wicking* (transporting moisture generated when exercising and sweating away from the body). When possible we wash clothing daily: synthetics dry quickly. Cotton should be avoided: it is comparatively heavy, tends to hold moisture, and dries slowly. In the mountains, it is a liability.

Everyday wear

Long pants: Two pair. One pair is the convertible type with zippers allowing you to change them to shorts. (In general, since legs have big muscles and generate a lot of heat, you need fewer layers on your bottom extremities than your top.)

Shirts: Three. Two are short-sleeved; one is long sleeved. I like to start the day wearing a long-sleeved shirt over a short-sleeved one and I remove the outer one if the temperature warms up.

Underwear: One bra, three pair of briefs

Long underwear: Smartwool top & bottom. They don't itch, are warm, and don't retain odors like most synthetics do. I also often wear these as sleepwear.

Cold and wet weather gear

Down jacket for warmth

Fleece layer(s)

Rain jacket (Goretex by Mountain Hardware)

Rain pants (Marmot with full-length side zippers)

Packa: This is a special rain parka that zips up the front. It has sleeves with underarm zippers for ventilation, and a big hump to fit over the backpack. It worked fine, but only protected to about the crotch. I found it worked best when worn over my rain jacket and rain pants. If you carry a pack cover, be forewarned that it and any other loose items can easily be ripped off and sent sailing in the wind.

Footwear

Leather hiking boots: Although on most backpacking trips, I wear trail runners (currently Brooks) because they are light, give good traction on most rocky surfaces, and are cooler, on both Patagonia trips I opted for Lowa Renegade GTX boots and was happy that I did. Whatever you do, buy your shoes well before your trip so that you have time to break them in if necessary and to know that they are comfortable. When you buy them, be sure to get at least a half size larger than your usual size because feet swell when hiking with a backpack.

Socks: Four pair. I wear different kinds of socks on different hiking trips, but in general I carry two pairs of double-layer Wright Socks, a pair of liners, and a pair of heavy wool. (On trips where I expect it to be hot, I often choose Injinji toe socks, worn with a pair of liners on top. Because the toe socks keep your toes separated, they help prevent blisters). Ralph has evolved to mostly wearing liners (Coolmax) only, though he carries a pair of light hikers in case he needs more cushioning. He sometimes has to tape a toe or two for the first few days, but he has found that hot feet cause most of his foot problems, and wearing just the liners resolves that. The toe socks are thin, lightweight and he likes them, but they often develop holes in a week or so of hiking.

Waterproof socks: Sealzskin, 1 pair. These keep your feet warm and dry even when walking through slush, rain, and (to some extent) streams.

Footcare

Tape for feet: When hiking the Camino de Santiago in Spain, we discovered Hartmann Omnifix elastic breathable tape for wrapping feet, which has been very helpful for dealing with my bunions. We also sometimes cut smaller pieces for wrapping toes and covering hot spots. It has a peel off backing that exposes the adhesive. It comes in rolls two-inches by 10 yards. In Spain it's available in pharmacies, but when we finally ran out, Ralph looked for a U.S. source. He found it only online and ordered two rolls for US$24 including shipping from www.medco-school.com. (Just enter "medco" and "omnifix" in

Google and you will find it.) Kinesio-Tex is a similar highly recommended tape that we have used, but it does not stick quite as well as Omnifix. We also carry a roll of three-quarter inch breathable cotton tape from the local drugstore. It is segmented so it can be torn by hand, and is handy for quick taping of toes. Johnson & Johnson is one brand.

Headgear and hand protection

Fleece cap that converts to a balaclava. Note that our rain jackets and packas have hoods.

Gloves: alpaca (knit) gloves; liner gloves

Sun protection: Sunday Afternoons sun hat with a full brim

Backpack

Granite Gear Vapor Trail. This is a well-constructed two-pound pack with padded waist belt and built-in back support. I have used this pack for thousands of backpacking miles and love it. Granite Gear's current version of this pack is called the Crown. Ralph has an assortment of packs. On this trip he carried a Gossamer Gear G4 because it's light, has a waist-belt, and held enough equipment for the length of our trip. Line packs with trash compactor bags.

Shelter

Tent: Four-season tent weighing three pounds. Although we usually carry a Henry Shires Tarptent that weighs two pounds, on this trip we wanted more protection from the anticipated wind, rain, and low temperatures.

In both 2009 and 2010, we took a Stephenson's Warmlite 2R tent and were quite satisfied with it. It set up fast, handled fierce winds (mostly without problems), and we stayed dry. The exterior panel and bug netting interior each had their own zippers.

We observed that many other campers had a problem with wet sleeping bags and other gear. One thing we forgot to do that would have been helpful was to coat the floor with some wide diagonal strips of seam sealer. The tent's silnylon (silicone-impregnated nylon) floor was very slippery, and if we weren't on a level area, we ended up on one side or the other by morning.

If we ordered the Stephenson's 4-season tent again, we would make some changes. First, we would not order the optional side window panels. We plan to use this tent only for severe conditions and don't need the windows. They are just extra weight.

Second, we would get double-wall end panels. Although the main body of the 4-season tent is double wall, the end panels are just a single layer of silnylon. We stayed dry because of the body, but got some condensation during mild conditions, and mist in driving rain. (We think that in snow, the single panel would have been okay.)

Finally, we should have ordered wind stabilizers, which add little to the weight, but are supposed to help the tent withstand stronger winds. If we had had stabilizers on the 2010 hike, it's likely that the tent would have been able to handle the severe wind gust that snapped the tent's pole.

We met another hiker who was carrying only a tarp. He ended up cancelling the hiking part of his trip because he was too cold. We think that taking a tarp is an extreme risk; the wind frequently changes direction and could easily blow a tarp away.

All in all, we feel the Stephenson's Warmlite performed well under extreme wind and driving rain conditions.

Groundcloth: Tyvek (homewrap material) cut to fit the footprint of the tent (use with printed side down).

It's very sturdy and lightweight. You can buy this in large rolls at a home improvement store, but you might be able to get a small piece from a home builder near you.

Sleeping bag: REI sub-kilo down bag, which weighs two pounds. Rated to 20 degrees Fahrenheit, which as Ralph points out, will keep you alive, but not necessarily comfortable. We also carried vapor barriers (four ounces). Vapor barrier are lightweight silnylon (or similar) sleeping bag liners that keep you five to ten degrees warmer, prevent your sweat from reaching your sleeping bag and thereby reducing the bag's loft, and reduce the condensation inside the tent.

We keep wondering if we should get sleeping bags with synthetic filling so they will be warm even if wet, but hate to pay the weight penalty. We do all that we can to make sure our down bags stay dry including carrying them in turkey oven bags, which are lighter than commercial stuff sacks.

Stove and cooking kit

- Snowpeak GigaPower canister stove and isobutane fuel canister combination (more info next page).
- Nesting titanium pots: 1.3-liter and .9-liter
- Pot cozies
- 2 plastic spoons
- 2 titanium cups
- Matches (we each carried one pack of book matches in snack Ziploc bags). There are airline regulations on matches; currently one set is allowed and only in carry-on.)
- Biodegradable dishwashing soap
- and a nylon stuff sack to hold all of the above.
- Folding plastic bucket (for dish and clothes washing), optional.

We bought a canister of isobutane fuel in Patagonia.

The large canister contains 7.76 oz. (220 grams). Other people use the MSR Whisperlite International stove that burns any type of fuel. The GigaPower stove and fuel combination is lighter and less fuss because you don't have to pour the fuel.

Hardware stores and some pharmacies in the gateway town of Puerto Natales sell white gas. It's called *bensina blanca* and works well. Since you can't fly with fuel, you can either bring a used fuel canister or buy new ones when you arrive in Patagonia. If you bring the canister from home, wash and air it out before you pack it. It should be carried in checked luggage aboard flights.

We found that the isobutane canisters (brand-named Doite, from Korea) are available in Punta Arenas, Puerto Natales, and the Refugio Torre Central (the big refugio that you first get to if entering from Laguna Amarga).

Ralph has our water use for meals down to a science, which allows us to carry the appropriate amount of fuel for trips. At breakfast and suppertime, we boil 1½ liters of water for food, beverages and cleanup. If we use a large canister, we get about 14 boils of our 1.3 liter pot, which would be a seven-day supply.

We fill the 1.3-liter pot with water, boil, and then scoop out enough for the freeze-dried meal or tea and coffee, and then the pot goes into its cozy for additional beverages and cleanup later. The freeze-dried meal goes in the .9-liter titanium pot, and it goes into its cozy as soon as water is added.

We use cups for our beverages and don't take bowls. Ralph uses the cooking pot and I rinse out my cup to use for dinner.

Food

BECAUSE WE PLANNED to eat in the refugio camps when possible, we didn't need food for all the days of the Circuit hike. We carried nine lunches, but only three *complete* days of backpack food.

It's important to have a "Plan B" in case any of your food is confiscated at the airport. As mentioned earlier, our beef jerky was seized by Chile customs. There are restrictions against bringing in fresh fruit and vegetables (there can be heavy fines for trying to sneak forbidden items in!). The agency, *Servicio Agricola y Ganadero* (SAG), has a list of approved foods to import into Chile at sag.cl; click on "Declara de todos," then click the plant thumbs up and the animal thumbs up. Translate the resulting list. In short, declare all plant and animal products.

Nuts, dried/cooked fruits and veggies, flour products, canned cooked meat, cured meat (not jerky), pasteurized milk products, cheese aged over 60 days, are listed as okay. However, even though raisins and almonds are listed as being okay on the SAG list, a friend traveling in early 2012 had to relinquish her supply. Other recent travelers have reported having trail mix and other dried fruits and nuts taken, so it is advisable to leave the GORP (Good Old Raisins and Peanuts) home. Comments indicated that home-prepared food is particularly vulnerable, so it's advisable to stick to pre-packaged, sealed, clearly labeled, brand-name food packages of items that might raise red flags.

Although whether or not your food is taken away may depend on the agent you encounter, it is not being taken because of someone's meanness—it's because of concern about *Phylloxera*, a plant disease caused by an aphid, which is a serious threat to Chile's vineyards. Luckily, stores in towns such as Chile's Puerto Natales or Argentina's Mendoza have suitable replacements.

Breakfasts: Oatmeal packets (or similar) and Nido (powdered whole milk). Freeze-dried fruit or similar.

Lunches: Slices from a stick of dried salami purchased in a Chilean supermarket. Various crackers and granola-type bars.

Dinners: freeze-dried commercial meals.

Snacks: Tang, Pop-Tarts, granola-type bars.

Repackaging backpacking food, our typical menus, and Pilot Biscuits

We've also learned a few more tricks on lightening our pack and reducing the volume. For weight, we have replaced dried fruit with the tasty but pricey freeze-dried offerings from Sensible Foods®. (You can get them at a discount at Amazon.)

We've gained space by repackaging the freeze dried dinners, the GORP (when we dare carry it!) and the jerky in Ziplock bags. Food repackaged won't keep forever stored this way, but it works for the length of time we're out. We also use snack-sized ziplock bags (commonly used for kid's lunches). We measure out daily portions of breakfast cereal. We don't like generating the extra trash, but bags used for multiple days tend to develop leaks after several days of use. And finally, having the daily portions already measured out saves quite a bit of time.

Sometimes we like to fortify our drinking water with electrolytes—particularly when we are in arid climates. Tang, for example, gives the water a pleasant fizzy zing and improves the taste. When we go that route, we follow the directions on the Tang's container to make the two liters that we'll use per day. To that, we add one-half teaspoon table salt, one-half teaspoon baking soda, and one-quarter teaspoon lite salt for electrolyte replacement. We found this "recipe" in the 1994 Kaiser Health Handbook and although they have withdrawn this recommendation, we sometimes still use it. Mostly, however, we now buy prepackaged electrolyte drink products such as Nuun tablets.

Breakfast: We use high-density cold cereal, such as Grape-nuts, Cheerios, and granola. Snack baggies hold one serving. We sometimes use instant oatmeal—one serving is two packets (one regular and one flavored). If you use two flavored, by the end of the trip you will never eat that flavor again. We don't bother to premix the Nido (dried whole milk), just dump the desired amount of powder on the cereal, stir & add hot or cold water. Most thru-hikers just eat an energy bar and start walking, but we take the extra hour for a hot beverage, multivitamins and cereal.

Mid-morning snack: A Poptart wafer; i.e., one two-wafer packet for the two of us. Sometimes we also have a freeze-dried fruit packet. If not, we have the fruit at noon. Afternoon snack is the same. If we have GORP, we munch it bit by bit as we hike along or grab a handful at a break. We use two parts mixed and salted nuts to one part raisins and one part plain M&Ms. For two people out eight days, that works out to sixteen ounces of nuts, eight ounces of raisins, and eight ounces of M&Ms.

Lunch: One cracker or equivalent per person, ½-oz. jerky (or other meat), and one bar. The cracker or equivalent means about one and one-half ounces and varies from canned potato chips, to stone-wheat crackers, to cheese or peanut butter sandwich crackers. (The cracker equivalent term came because about 20 years ago we used pilot biscuits, which were big, hard and almost indestructible. These are no longer available. You can order things called pilot biscuits from the Internet, but they are flimsy imitations of the original.) We take a variety of granola, protein, and energy bars to add interest and we look for high calories per ounce.

Dinner: The couple of times that we cooked our own dinner while on the Circuit, we used freeze-dried dinners, using pot cozies as described earlier to conserve fuel and water.

Water

All of the refugios had water from a faucet, and we drank it unfiltered with no problems. When a storm knocked out Campamento Serón's water supply, we had to treat it. Our pump filter clogged repeatedly.

We've tried many filtration and purification systems over the years. For Patagonia, we suggest carrying a SteriPen and purifier tablets as backup. The SteriPen uses an ultraviolet (UV) light ray system to purify against viruses, bacteria, and protozoa (including Giardia and Cryptosporidium). The SteriPen requires that the water be clear—which is why the company also offers a *pre-filter*. Any water treatment system can fail and glacier melt water carries a lot of sediment, which can easily clog filters. Pouring the river water through a bandanna can help filter out some of the particles.

I also highly recommend that you also carry a multi-day supply of Katadyn *Micropur MP 1 Water Purifier Tablets*. The downside of relying on tablets is that though they kill most things in thirty minutes, you must wait four hours in order for them to be fully effective.

Food storage

Ursacks: Since we had heard that mice could be a problem on the Circuit, we decided to carry our food in Ursacks. They are drawstring bags made of Kevlar (bullet-proof material) and have odor-proof liners. Ursacks are used by backpackers in some areas of the U.S. where bears might be a problem (though they are not on the approved list in such areas as Yosemite and other National Park Service or Forest Service lands). These might be considered optional, but since we needed some kind of stow bag for our food and already had the Ursacks, we carried them.

Medical and toilet kit, personal grooming

Everyone has their own list of needed medical supplies. Our basic list includes:
- Ibuprofen, aspirin, and something stronger

- Pepto-Bismol and Cipro
- Ace bandage
- Nail clipper
- Small Swiss Army knife
- Prescription meds
- Assorted bandages
- Bandanna; earplugs
- Matches (book matches in separate dry locations)
- Toilet paper
- Comb
- Toothbrush, paste, floss
- Small mirror

Misc. other

- Hiking poles: carbon fiber, lightweight and adjustable
- Sunglasses
- Reading glasses
- Glacier glasses: (optional) I had some, so I carried them
- Pee container: empty plastic container (such as qt. size yogurt) with lid for night use
- *Dirty girl* gaiters (optional)
- Thin cord for clothesline
- Duct tape or tent patch kit
- Micro (pinch) flashlight and headlamp
- Whistle
- Lipbalm (such as Chapstick®), which I carry on a cord around my neck)
- Security belt (around-the-waist, or other style)
- Notebook paper and pen for journal keeping
- DEET. Some locations had quite a few mosquitoes, not clouds of them, but bring DEET. We also sprayed our hiking clothes beforehand with *Sawyers Clothing Insect Repellent* (which is permethrin-based) and brought headnets (which were not used).
- Trash compactor bags to line backpacks.

Guidebooks carried

Lonely Planet Trekking in Patagonia, and a current Torres
   del Paine Trekking Map

Electronics and camera gear

To be sure, these are optional, but we wouldn't leave
   home without them!

Cellphone: Even though there was no service in Torres
   del Paine and limited service elsewhere in Patagonia, it was useful at other places (see Chapter 11
   for details).

GPS: We carried a Garmin Vista C, but did not find it
   necessary or particularly useful. The trails are well
   marked.

Compass: Silva

Cameras: This is still evolving for us, but on this trip
   we took a Nikon Coolpix P80 with 18x zoom and a
   Canon Powershot SD870IS.

border of Argentina

14 • Patagonia and Beyond

As a practical matter for travelers, keep in mind that Patagonia is the southern region of South America and most of it lies far south of Santiago and Buenos Aires. Defining Patagonia is difficult because its political-economic and geographic boundaries differ.

Argentina's political boundaries of the *region* of Patagonia include the *provinces* of Neuquén, Rio Negro, Chubut, and Santa Cruz. Wayne Bernhardson in Moon Handbooks *Patagonia* says, "In Argentina, it is agreed that Patagonia contains the territory south of the Rio Colorado." That adds the Argentine portion of Tierra del Fuego. A few sources also include the southwestern corner of the *region* of La Pampa because it has topographic and climatic characteristics similar to that of the rest of Patagonia.

Of *Chilean* Patagonia there is even more complexity because its boundaries are not an official political region. Here we will cover three *regions*—*Los Lagos* (the Lake District), Aisén, and Magallanes. That takes in the *provinces* of Palena, Chiloé, Llanquihue, Osorno, Coihaique, Puerto Aisén, General Carrera, Capitan Prat, Magallanes, *Ultima Esperanza* (Last Hope), Tierra del Fuego, and Antarctica Chilena.

Argentinean Patagonia Provinces (north to south)

THE PROVINCE OF La Pampa, which is west of the province of Buenos Aires, is *not* part of Patagonia. It is a sparsely-populated area of 55,382 *sq. mi* (143,440 sq. km.) that sees relatively few tourists. Its chief economic activities are agriculture and the raising of cattle.

However tourists and archeologists do visit the Lihue Calel National Park in south-central La Pampa. Lihue Calel has many attractions—a beautiful mountain range surrounded by arid tableland, many petroglyphs, and wildlife including puma, guanacos and vizcacha (a type of chinchilla). When the *Conquest of the Desert* campaign took place in the 1870s, isolated Lihue Calel became a refuge for many indigenous peoples.

A visit to Lihue Calel is not for wimps; the weather is highly unpredictable. For most people, spring (September-October), when shrubs are in bloom, would be the best time to visit, or in the fall when summer's scorching temperatures have subsided. However, bird-lovers who can deal with the heat would find summer the best time because that's prime time to see the approximately 150 varieties of birds that visit.

Lihue Calel is remote. The nearest village is Puelches, which is 21 miles (33 km.) distant and has few services. Most people get to the park via Santa Rosa. There, you can rent a car or embark on a 3¾ hour bus ride. The bus runs daily and stops about three miles from the park's entrance.

Adventurers willing to make the long trek and deal with the weather are rewarded with the solitude of the desert, the beauty of the park, the uncrowded trails and (free) campgrounds.

Neuquén Province is 36,324 sq. miles (94,078 sq. km.). The western edge of Neuquén is in the Andes and visitors come to such villages as Junín de los Andes and San Martín de los Andes for trout fishing, kayaking, and hiking in the summer, and skiing in the winter. In the eastern section of the province are wide valleys—many filled with fruit orchards. One famous apple orchard is believed to have been planted by the Jesuits in the 17th and 18th centuries. Another intriguing fact: this region is nicknamed the *Steepe of Dinosaurs* because of the numerous fossilized findings.

Although the main economic activities of the Neuquén Province are currently petroleum, cattle, forestry, and mining, that may well change in the days ahead if its energy sources are further developed. Although the Neuquén River is not navigable, it can be dammed, and it's of great interest because of its potential for the production of hydro-electric power.

Rio Negro Province is 78,383 sq. miles (203,013 sq. km.). As described earlier, Ralph and I visited several cities and towns in the Chilean Lake District, including Puerto Montt and Puerto Varas. Just over the border in Argentina, there are also many towns and resorts that draw visitors because of their scenic beauty and outdoor activities.

Probably the city best known to tourists is also the province's most populous, San Carlos de Bariloche, which sits on the edge of the Andes and also on Lake Nahuel Huapi. Bariloche is often called the "American Switzerland" not only because of its setting and skiing (mid-June through September), but also because of its attractive Alpine-style wood and stone architecture and its rich chocolates. It also draws visitors during other seasons for its hiking and mountain climbing, golf, rafting, and fishing.

Chubut Province is 86,751 sq. miles (224,684 sq. km.) and has a population of about 412,000. Its cultural and scenic attractions include the towns that are still home to a population of Welsh heritage: that includes Gaiman, Trelew, Trevelin, Esquel, and Puerto Madryn (on the Peninsula Valdés).

The estimated 25,000 people in the region who still speak Welsh are concentrated in the original Welsh settlements of Trelew and Trevelin. Trevelin was founded in the 1860s by a group of colonists from Wales who left their homeland because they thought Patagonia offered fertile farmland and greater personal freedom.

Visitors are also drawn to Trevelin because of nearby Los Alerces National Park, which is a forest composed mainly of the Alerce tree—a Patagonian cypress. Some of these trees are nearly 3,000 years old.

Finally, tourists visit the Peninsula Valdés, near Puerto Madryn, which is a UNESCO World Heritage site that is known for its Southern Right Whales (generally present May-December) and for its large population of birds, elephant seals and Magellanic Penguins. Outdoor enthusiasts can also go windsurfing, scuba diving, deep sea fishing, and kayaking.

Santa Cruz Province is 94,206 sq. miles (263,993 sq. km.), and the largest province in the Argentinean Patagonia and second largest in the country. Santa Cruz Province is home to the Jamarillo Petrified Forests National Monument, one of the world's most important sites with remnants of Jurassic-era forest. It's also the site of Laguna del Carbón, which lies 344 feet (105 m.) below sea level, making it the lowest geographic point in the Western Hemisphere.

Santa Cruz's most well-known park, however, is Los Glaciares National Park, home of the Glaciar Perito Moreno and Mount Fitz Roy. Ralph and I were not the only ones who wished we had had more time to spend in Los Glaciares. When I interviewed Rob Hodges to compare his hiking there compared to Torres del Paine, he had this to say,

"I loved it! I wish we had spent more time there and less in Torres del Paine. I thought it was more beautiful overall, and there were far less crowds. The Fitz Roy range is one of the top landscapes I have ever seen in the world."

However, it wasn't all easy going. Rob continued, "The worst part of our [Patagonia] experience was probably the hellacious weather we experienced one day in Fitz Roy. Overall, we had spectacular weather. Eleven out of the thirteen days we spent backpacking in Fitz Roy and Torres del Paine were glorious, which is quite unusual. But there was one day in Fitz Roy when we got caught in pounding, freezing rain that almost knocked us off our feet.

"We had to walk in those conditions for a couple hours before arriving in camp, and we were completely disoriented, cold and disheartened. That night was insanely cold, and the winds were unrelenting; we skipped dinner just because we were too cold to cook. The next day was supposed to be our sunrise viewing of the Fitz Roy summit, but we woke up before dawn to find it snowing and still miserable. But, fortunately, the bad weather cleared by mid-morning, and we ended up having some wonderfully clear weather for the summit viewing."

Tierra del Fuego (Land of Fire) is an archipelago off the southern tip of South America. Both Chile and Argentina claim part of Tierra del Fuego and have provinces so named. The Argentine province is separated from the South American mainland by the Strait of Magellan.

The *Isla Grande de Tierra del Fuego* (commonly called either "Tierra del Fuego" or "Isla Grande") is the largest island of the archipelago and it is also divided between Chile and Argentina. Isla Grande is home to Porvenir (the capital of Chile's Tierra del Fuego Province) and of Ushuaia, Argentina, which is the hub for touring the southernmost attractions of Argentina and of Antarctica. Ushuaia is at the end of the Andes Mountain chain and on the Beagle Channel.

Ushuaia, with its population of approximately 38,000, is often described as the "Southernmost City in the World." Even though the Chilean town of Puerto Williams is farther south, its population of 2,000 is not large enough to be considered a city by Chilean authorities (defined as an urban entity of more than 5,000 inhabitants). This is not an easy region to reach.

Visitors to Ushuaia ski, mountain bike, or go horseback riding, depending on the season. Approximately six miles away, at the southern end of the Pan-American Highway, is Tierra del Fuego National Park, which can also be reached by tour bus, rental cars, or the narrow-gauge *End of the World Train.*

When collecting information about Ushuaia, I talked with a former classmate, Bill Whiting, who spent a short time in Ushuaia while on a tour of Patagonia in 2009. "Flying into Ushuaia was an interesting experience. Shortly before we landed, the captain came on to say, 'The runway's been extended, but be prepared for a steep descent and to hit the ground at the end—but we won't go into the water.'

"The port itself is pretty hectic with restaurants and shops serving the tourists, so we stayed in a Bavarian-style lodge about two miles away from the docks." Staying at the higher elevation was a world apart. Bill continues, "We hiked further uphill along the windy access road to the lodge and in about two miles were above tree line and began to see patches of snow. We came to a clearing and found traces of an old tow-rope."

There are frequent cruises through the Beagle Channel and those looking for even more adventure can sail through the Drake Passage and into Antarctica.

Chilean Patagonia (north to south)

CHILE IS DIVIDED into regions, then provinces, then communes. There are almost two dozen national parks in Chile; the descriptions below of a select few in the Patagonian regions should whet your appetite for exploring many of them.

Los Lagos (the Lake district)

LOS LAGOS IS the northernmost region of Chilean Patagonia and includes the *provinces* of Palena, Chiloé, Llanquihue, and Osorno.

Because it is a transportation hub for the province, the town of Chaitén in *Palena Province* is well known to travelers to Chile. Chaitén is also the province's former capital. However, things changed dramatically in 2008 when the town had two major natural disasters. In May of that year, a nearby volcanic eruption forced residents to evacuate the town. Soon after, the accumulated ash and other sediment from the volcano caused a major river to change its course, which in turn caused extensive flooding and damage to the town.

The seismic activity, however, did nothing to turn tourists away. They flocked to the area to see what had occurred causing further concern to officials. The capital of the province was moved to Futaleufú for what was to be a temporary measure. Chaitén is being relocated and whether it will again become the capital is unsettled.

Also in the Palena province is the private nature reserve, *Parque Pumalín* (Pumalín Park), which was created and is headed by the American entrepreneur Douglas Tompkins (co-founder of Espirit and North Face). The reserve is almost 750,000 acres and is of considerable interest not only for its recreational offerings, but also for its missions to educate and to preserve the rainforest in all its diversity. Although it also was briefly closed by the 2008 earthquake, it has since reopened to visitors. Admission to the park is free.

Considering the remoteness of the park, most people don't just drop by. However, there are many ways to get there: by car, bus, or ferry. Once in the rainforest, you can hike the many trails and relax in the visitor center, cabanas, campgrounds, and restaurant. www.parquepumalin.cl/content/index.htm

Best known to most visitors to the province of *Chiloé* is undoubtedly Chiloé Island, which has an important penguin preserve and a temperate rain forest. Chiloé Island is the largest island of the Chiloé archipelago.

Although many parts of Chiloé are difficult to reach, it has had its share of exploration by foreign interests. Explorer Magellan sailed by Patagonia in 1520. The Jesuits came in the 17th century, hoping to convert the indigenous groups—the Chono, Caucahué and Huilliche—to Catholicism. They built at least 80 churches and schools. Sixteen of the beautifully-weathered wooden churches that remain in the islands have been designated World Heritage sites by UNESCO.

The city of Puerto Montt, which serves as an important hub city to visitors to Torres del Paine and other more remote Patagonian locations, is in the *Llanquihue Province.*

Osorno Province, nestled as it is in the Chile's Lakes District, is well suited to cattle production and agriculture.

Its more temperate climate, compared to much of Patagonia, may be why so many European immigrants—including those from Spain and the Basque regions, Germany, Switzerland, Austria, Britain, and Holland—decided to settle here. Chile's Osorno is connected to Argentina's Lake District cities, such as San Carlos de Bariloche, by the important mountain pass Cardenal Antonio Samoré.

Aisén

AISÉN (ALSO AYSÉN) is the middle *region* of Patagonia. It's by far Chile's least-populated sector. A glimpse at a map explains much about why development has been slow: it is composed of mountains, lakes, rivers, glaciers, and hundreds of tiny islands. Compounding the difficulty of completing a road through the region is the unpredictable and often harsh weather. The entire *Carretera Austral* (Southern Highway) is only open a few months of the year (December to February) because it is only during those months that the ferries that provide access to remote sites can operate.

However the region is popular with tourists who want to visit the Northern Patagonian Ice Field. Those who want to experience *Laguna San Rafael* National Park, which holds the entire Northern Patagonian Ice Field, must arrive by boat or plane. Most look forward to a cruise on the lake with towering glaciers alongside. Among other options, the Navimag ferry company offers a five-day cruise leaving from the city of Castro on Chiloé Island and into the Patagonia fjords up to the San Rafael Lagoon.

Hiking, mountain climbing, and kayaking are also popular activities. Because of the relative remoteness of the park, much of it is still unspoiled habitat and home to numerous endemic species such as albatross, dolphins, elephant seals, and *chungungos* (small otters).

Another park in Aisén, is the remote *Queulat* National Park, near the near the village of Puyuhuapi. Queulat has several hiking trails leading through the verdant mosses and forest to scenic views such as the *Salto del Cóndor* (Condor Fall) and *Ventisquero Colgante* (Hanging Glacier).

Magallanes (Region XII) and Chilean Antarctica

THESE ARE THE southernmost, largest and second-least-populated *regions* of Chile. As mentioned previously, Punta Arenas is the hub city of the Magallanes Region. This region has such important tourist destinations as Torres del Paine (in the province of Ultima Esperanza), Cape Horn, Tierra del Fuego Island, and the Strait of Magellan. Sheep ranching and oil are also important parts of the economy. The region also includes the Antarctic territory claimed by Chile.

Cape Horn is on the southern tip of Hornos (aka Horn) Island, which is part of the archipelago of Tierra del Fuego. Chile has two national parks in its *Antarctic Region: Parque National Cabo de Hornos* and *Alberto de Agostini.*

Parque National Cabo de Hornos is on Hornos Island. Adventurous travelers desiring to round Cape Horn, virtually guaranteed to be a ride on the wild side, can help crew on a sailboat while taking in the wonders of this subpolar point.

Alberto de Agostini, named after the Italian missionary and explorer, Alberto Maria De Agostini, is composed of glaciers, fjords, and mountains including the Cordillera Darwin mountain range. There are no roads into the 5,637 sq. miles (14,600 sq. km.) park. To visit this area, ships and other boats typically leave from Puerto Williams, the largest town in Tierra del Fuego.

On the inland passages north of Torres del Paine

15 • Human History

Native peoples and explorations by Magellan, Fitz Roy, Darwin, Moreno

Early Peoples

Humans have inhabited Patagonia for more than ten thousand years and seen many waves of migration, but the precise details of which people were in which areas are lacking. It appears that there was human activity at Monte Verde in Llanquihue Province, Chile around 14,800 years ago, but that the huge expanses of ice fields and amount of surface water would have made settlement difficult.

In 1999, the *Cueva de las Manos* (Cave of the Hands) in Santa Cruz Province, Argentina was named a UNESCO World Heritage Site. Visitors to this Patagonian site south of Glaciar Perito Moreno can explore caves with images of hands, human figures, symbols, and indigenous animals such as the guanacos and rhea painted on the walls. The largest cave, which contains hundreds of images, has hunting scenes dating to 8,000 years ago.

Most of the imprints of hands are of left hands and many are negative images indicating that the painters probably held the painting devices in their right hands and sprayed the paint at their left hands to leave an outline. Experts speculate that remains of small hollow bones found in the cave point were used to direct the spray. Local mineral deposits were most likely used as pigment for the paint. Red dots on the ceilings of some of the caves may have been made by dipping the weighted balls of the hunting *bolas* in paint and then tossing them overhead.

Bolas have been found in many pre-Columbian sites. This popular weapon is made by tying together (generally) three braided leather ropes and attaching a weight to the end of some of the braids. Then, the hunter swings the bola in a circle overhead, releases it to go flying ahead, and waits while the ropes wrap around and entangle the legs of the prey. Bolas, in varying forms, have been used not only in Patagonia for thousands of years, but also in parts of the (present day) U.S. and among the Inuit of Canada and Alaska. (A Sources' link[28] may help sort out the groups.)

The Tehuelches group

THERE WERE MANY indigenous groups in Patagonia when European explorers started exploring the region. There was much that amazed the crews: the people's size, clothing, ornamentation, and customs. When Magellan and his men first explored the region, his official chronicler, Antonio Pigafetta, wrote of one of the men they met on shore, "He was so tall that we reached only to his waist."

It's now generally agreed that Pigafetta's and others report of "giants" is based on encounters with the Tehuelches, who were generally tall. In Charles Darwin's *Voyage of the Beagle*, he estimated the Patagonians' average height at about six feet, which, compared to the five foot, two inch average height of Spanish males at the time, may have seemed tall.

The name *Patagonia* (land of big feet), according to many sources, was given by Magellan, and may have come about because the Patagonians often wrapped their feet in guanaco skins, which would have left very large footprints.

The Patagonians colored their faces and sometimes their bodies with bright paints. The people wore little clothing beyond guanaco skins during the most severe conditions. When engaged in warfare, they would often wear several mantles (armor made of skins) for protection.

Their huts had a framework of tree limbs that was covered with skins. These simple huts, which allowed the people to migrate continually in search of fish and meat, were frequently open to the windward side, but the fires that they kept constantly burning provided needed warmth. When early sailors came around the horn and saw the fires burning on shore, they named the island *Tierra del Fuego*—Land of Fire.

Although the numbers of the Tehuelches group declined after contact with Europeans, descendants remain in both Chile and Argentina. The 2001 census [INDEC] recorded 4,300 Tehuelche in the Argentine provinces of Chubut and Santa Cruz, and an additional 1,637 in other parts of the country.

Darwin describes three major groups

IN HIS *A Naturalist's Voyage Round the World* published in 1860, Charles Darwin described three major aboriginal groups that they saw while on the Beagle: the Fuegians (people of Tierra del Fuego), the Chonos people of the west (the Chonos archipelago and Chiloe), and the Patagonians (probably the Tehuelches). Each of these groups had many subdivisions. According to Darwin's writing, the Patagonians traveled by horses, but not canoes. The Fuegians and Chonos had canoes, but not horses.[29]

The Fuegian (aka Yahgan and Yámana) people were encountered by Magellan, Cook, Darwin, and others. Once again, the journals of the European explorers make it clear that the men did not know what to make of the indigenous people's clothing and customs. Like the Patagonians, the Fuegians wore little or no clothing other than guanaco skins for warmth. This amazed the visitors because of the frigid conditions of Tierra del Fuego. It has been noted, however, that the Fuegians sometimes covered themselves with fish or seal oil and that may well have helped them with the bitter temperatures.

Among the Fuegians best studied during the period of the Beagle's voyages were the four that were captured by Captain Fitz Roy and crew during the first voyage. Their captivity followed an incident where one of the explorers' boats was stolen and members of the suspected thieves' families were taken on board the Beagle. Most were released, but the expedition moved on with Boat Memory, York Minster, 14-year-old Jemmy Button, and an eight or nine-year-old girl, Fuegia Basket (names given by crew) on board. Although some sources suggest that there had originally been plans to leave the four captives behind, they were taken back to England. Most reports agree that Fitz Roy was very interested in learning more about them and took great care that they were well treated. The plan was to "civilize" them and then return them to their home as missionaries.

The arrival of the Fuegians in 1830 caused quite a stir in Victorian England, but the reception and fate of each varied. Boat Memory died of smallpox. The two youngest, Jemmy and Fuegia and Jemmy were "well-fed and feted," and enrolled in elementary school. Twenty-seven-year-old York Minster was less welcome: no one knew what to make of this stranger.

In George Weber's *Captain Fitz Roy's Fuegian Captives*, Weber suggests that there may have been some sort of sexual episode between York and Fuegia and that Fitz Roy was not only shocked that such a liaison had taken place, but also concerned that his own reputation would be ruined if word had gotten out.[30]

However, Fitz Roy held onto their high hopes for educating and converting Jemmy Button. When the Beagle set out from England on the vessel's second voyage in 1831, York, Fuegia, and Jemmy were onboard. When the three Fuegians were returned to Patagonia, along with a missionary, Richard Matthews, it was expected that they would work together to establish a mission.

However, when the Beagle returned a year later, they

could not find York and Fuegia. They learned that the two had married. Jemmy greeted them in English, but had also married. He told Fitz Roy that he preferred to return to his old way of life.

The Chonos People

It appears that the Chonos, a name given to the people of the Chonos Archipelago on the western coast of Chile, were the major group in the region for about two hundred years. Diaries of members of the Spanish Conquistadors record battles with the inhabitants in the mid-1500s, but by the time the Jesuits came in the mid-1600s, the Chonos had largely disappeared. The group is now considered extinct.

By the time that the second voyage of the Beagle arrived in 1834 to spend six months exploring the island of Chiloe and the Chonos Archipelago, there had been so many migrations of the indigenous peoples and so many encounters with European explorers, that it was difficult to trace the exact origins and characteristics of the earliest peoples. It does appear, however, that there was human habitation dating back more than 7,500 years.

As with the other indigenous peoples, it appears that the Chonos used what they found nearby for their food, shelter, and transportation. They built open wooden canoes called *dalcas,* and used stone and wooden anchors. Their homes were either caves or box-like structures framed by sticks and covered with leather. They lived on shell fish and other sea life; their clothing was made of sea lion skins or seaweed.

Ferdinand Magellan

Ferdinand Magellan was born in Portugal in 1480, and is known for being the first explorer to lead an expedition around the world. At the age of 25, he first went to sea. At the time, the Spice Islands (part of Indonesia) were of interest for spices and for other trading purposes. Magellan became intrigued with exploring the region. He first went to the king of Portugal for support, but was refused. He then went to King Charles I of Spain and found his funding.

At that time, Spain was looking for a new trade route to Asia. The 1494 Treaty of Tordesillas had granted the Cape of Good Hope trading route around Africa's southern tip to Portugal. This meant Spain needed to find a different route to Asia, one that did not sail around the Cape. Although Spain was the world's strongest nation at the time, they still did not want to antagonize neighboring Portugal. Sailing west, if it could succeed, would give Spain a strategic advantage.

Sailing west may also have been considered for economic reasons. Although Christopher Columbus's voyages to the New World had revealed more about the North American continent, there was much of the world that had not been mapped. Little did anyone know when Magellan's set out that this first circumnavigation of the world would turn out to be a 37,560 mile voyage.

Magellan had found the funding for his exploration, he had another major difficulty—putting together a crew. Because he was Portuguese, many of the Spanish sailors would not sign on. Eventually a crew of 250 was assembled, including many prisoners who were given early release in exchange for their service. They set sail in September 1519 with five ships: the flagship *Trinidad*, the *Santiago*, the *San Antonio*, the *Concepcion*, and the *Victoria* (*Vittoria*).

Things went well initially for Magellan and crew. They reached South America and resupplied; then headed farther south looking for a route through the continent. Supplies began to dwindle and it became increasingly cold. Mutiny was attempted, but put down. The leaders were captured. Gaspar Quesada, the captain of the *Concepcion*, was executed. Some accounts state that Luis de Mendoza, the captain of the *Victoria*, was also hung. Juan de Cartagena, the captain of the *San Antonio*, was left on the shore in Patagonia near Puerto San Julián, Argentina.

The search for a passageway through the continent continued, but the *Santiago* sank in a storm. Estaban Gómez, who had been appointed to command the *San Antonio* after the mutiny, deserted and sailed the ship back to Spain. Finally, in October 1520, 13 months after their launch, Magellan's remaining vessels found a strait—which we now call the Strait of Magellan. It took 38 days to sail through the 350-mile passageway. They reached the ocean that Balboa had discovered only seven years previously and named the *Pacific* because it was so peaceful.

Things turned even worse—they found themselves sailing across the Pacific for weeks with no land in sight, little food, and drinking water turning bad. The crew turned to eating rats. Scurvy, from lack of Vitamin C, took its toll. Finally, in March 1521, they reached the island of Guam.

With their three ships, they continued on to the Philippines where a war was being waged. One of the islanders shot Magellan in the foot with a poisoned arrow and a spear was put through his heart. He died on April 27, 1521. The crew burned the *Concepcion*. Sources give differing motivations: Was it to keep it out of enemy hands? Was it because of the dwindling number of crew? Perhaps it was both.

The two remaining ships continued on toward the Moluccas (also known as the *Spice Islands*). When they reached their destination, they loaded the holds of the *Trinidad* and *Victoria* with spices, including the highly-valued cloves and cinnamon, and headed back toward Spain.

The Portuguese, who had claimed the Spice Islands, intercepted the ships and claimed the *Trinidad*. Finally in 1521, the *Victoria* made it back to Spain. There were only 18 survivors.

Sir Francis Drake

IF FIGURING OUT which peoples lived where and when throughout Patagonia is difficult because of few original source materials and conflicting interpretations since that time, deciding who were the heroes and were the villains in various battles is equally daunting.

Whether Sir Francis Drake was a pirate as the Spanish believed, or a hero as the English thought, is largely a matter of perspective. Non-debatable is that when Sir Francis Drake, who was the first Englishman to sail around the world, sailed through Tierra del Fuego in 1578, the Spanish took notice.

Drake led numerous raids and was involved in numerous battles against the Spanish in the 1560s-1580s. One of his earliest raids, against the Spanish in Mexico, resulted in his capture, and later escape. In 1572, he sailed to the town of Nombre de Dios (of what is now Panama) to capture the silver and gold that the Spanish had brought from Peru. He was injured during the attack, and withdrew, but he remained in the area for more than a year making several successful forays.

In 1577, England's Queen Elizabeth 1 sent Drake on an expedition against the Spanish off the Pacific Coast of South America. Drake had five ships under his command: his flagship, the *Pelican*; the *Mary* (also known as the Marigold and as Santa Maria); the *Swan*; the *Christopher* (aka the Benedict); and the *Elizabeth*. Two ships turned back early on; the *Mary* was destroyed because it was no longer seaworthy; the *Christopher* was turned back by the rough seas near Patagonia. Only the *Pelican*, which Drake renamed the *Golden Hind*, made it through the Strait of Magellan in 1578.

After the Golden Hind entered the Pacific, it continued up the west coast attacking Spanish port towns along the way. Two Spanish ships carrying vast treasures—one near Lima, Peru, the second further north—were captured by Drake and crew. They collected jewels, tons of silver, and gold coins worth (in today's currency) approximately seven million pounds.

Drake and crew reached Northern California. The exact landing spot is unproven, but most experts believe that it was what is now called Drakes Bay, in Marin County. Then they turned west and sailed through the South Pacific. They returned as heroes to England on September 26, 1870.

Queen Elizabeth accepted her share: one-half of the precious metals, jewels, and spices collected during the voyage. Drake was knighted by the queen on April 4, 1581, for being the first Englishman to circumnavigate the world.[31,32]

Pedro Sarmiento de Gamboa

DRAKE'S SUCCESSES PROMPTED Spain's Viceroy Don Francisco de Toledo to send Pedro Sarmiento de Gamboa to explore the Strait of Magellan and the coast of Chile. Gamboa proceeded to make accurate surveys of the region and to look for places to establish military installations to prevent future invasions by the English.

In 1584 Gamboa guided approximately 300 Spanish settlers to establish the first known European settlements in Tierra del Fuego—Nombre de Dios and Rey Don Felipe (alternately as San Felipe). He established military colonies in the strait to fortify it.

However, most of the settlers of Rey Don Felipe died of starvation or frigid temperatures during the first winter. Gamboa was taken prisoner by the English and taken to England. Rey Don Felipe became so desolate that when English explorer Thomas Cavendish arrived there in 1587, he renamed it Port Famine (*Puerto Hambre* or *Puerto del Hambre*).

Gamboa was later captured by the Huguenots and ransom demanded. He was released at the end of 1589, and returned to Spain where he died in 1592. Port Famine later became a military base used by the British Royal Navy.

Fitz Roy, Darwin, and the Voyages of Discovery aboard the Beagle

FAR, FAR SOUTH in Patagonia lies the Strait of Magellan, which is a natural waterway running roughly east to west linking the Atlantic and Pacific Oceans. It's north of Argentina's Isla Grande de Tierra del Fuego and south of mainland Chile.

Although passage through the strait was difficult for sailing ships because of the narrowness of the passage and the oft-harsh weather, it was an important navigational trade route until the Panama Canal was completed by the United States in 1914.

First voyage

THE HMS (HER Majesty's Service) Beagle, on which Robert Fitz Roy and Charles Darwin were later to sail, was ceremoniously launched on May 11, 1820 on the Thames River near London, but then sat for more than five years before being sailed. Her first voyage, which began May 22, 1826, had a mission to survey the passageways near Patagonia and Tierra del Fuego. It is interesting to note that the Beagle was just over 90 feet long.

With Captain Pringle Stokes in command of the Beagle's first sailing, the ship reached *Puerto Hambre* (Port Famine) on the Strait of Magellan in March 1828. As his journal reveals, he was becoming disheartened by the challenges of the attempted survey. On May 29, 1828, he wrote, "'Nothing can be more dreary than the scene around us. The lofty, bleak, and barren mountains which compose the inhospitable shores of this inlet, are hung, low down their sides, with a dense cloud of mist, upon which the fierce squalls that assail us beat, apparently without at all disturbing it.'"[33]

The situation was made worse by dwindling food supplies, illnesses among the crew, and severe storms. Stokes became increasingly depressed and locked himself in his cabin for two weeks. On August 1, he shot himself, and died on August 12, 1828. His gravestone near Port Famine, weathered by time, reads "died from the effects of the anxieties and hardships incurred while surveying the western shores of Tierra del Fuego." Lieutenant W.G. Skyring, Executive Officer of Beagle, was temporarily named captain, and then Flag Lieutenant Robert Fitz Roy assumed command.

During this first voyage, the channel now called the *Beagle Channel* was identified. The Beagle Channel is south of the Strait of Magellan and north of Drake's Passage around Cape Horn. The Strait of Magellan, even though it offered some protection from the wind once within the channel, was still treacherous because winds and currents would change. Drake's Passage frequently has icebergs and sea ice, but has more room for sailing ships to maneuver. The Beagle Channel, like the others, is narrow and subject to weather; it was considered the least safe of the three.

Second voyage

ROBERT FITZ ROY was only 23 when he was named temporary Captain of the Beagle in December 1828, but by the time the expedition returned to England in 1830 with the four Fuegians, he had established his abilities and was given command of the second voyage of the Beagle.

When planning for this second expedition, Fitz Roy, concerned by the fact that the hardships and loneliness of the Patagonian explorations had led to Stokes committing suicide as well as the knowledge that his own uncle, Viscount Castlereagh, had killed himself, took steps to avoid a similar fate. He looked for a "gentleman companion"— someone who had a scientific background and an inquiring mind with whom he could dine and converse. Charles Darwin, then 22, was selected to go on what would become a five-year voyage of discovery.

As on the first voyage, the purpose of the second one was to survey and chart the coastline and waterways of Patagonia and Tierra del Fuego, but during the five-year expedition much more than the depths and locations of waterways were studied. Darwin, with the encouragement of Fitz Roy, ventured far and wide collecting and carefully noting where fossils were found and the distribution of the native plants and animals. The flora and fauna of South America (and the Galapagos Islands and Australia later visited) were little known to European naturalists at the time.

Third voyage

THE BEAGLE'S THIRD voyage, from 1837-1843, was under the command of John Clements Wickham. Its mission was to survey part of the coast of Australia. Wickham, who had sailed on the second voyage with Darwin, honored him by naming Australia's "Beagle Gulf" and "Port Darwin," after him. Port Darwin was just a tiny outpost at the time, but is now the City of Darwin and the capital of the Northern Territory.

From *Voyage of the Beagle* by Charles Darwin

EXCERPTS FROM CHAPTER 10; Tierra del Fuego[34]

"December 21 [1832] —The Beagle got under way: and on the succeeding day, favoured to an uncommon degree by a fine easterly breeze, we closed in with the Barnevelts, and running past Cape Deceit with its stony peaks, about three o'clock doubled the weather-beaten Cape Horn. The evening was calm and bright, and we enjoyed a fine view of the surrounding isles. Cape Horn, however, demanded his tribute, and before night sent us a gale of wind directly in our teeth. We stood out to sea, and on the second day again made the land, when we saw on our weather-bow this notorious promontory in its proper form—veiled in a mist, and its dim outline surrounded by a storm of wind and water. Great black clouds were rolling across the heavens, and squalls of rain, with hail, swept by us with such extreme violence, that the Captain determined to run into Wigwam Cove. This is a snug little harbour, not far from Cape Horn; and here, at Christmas-eve, we anchored in smooth water. The only thing which reminded us of the gale outside was every now and then a puff from the mountains, which made the ship surge at her anchors.

"December 25th—Close by the Cove, a pointed hill, called Kater's Peak, rises to the height of 1700 feet. The surrounding islands all consist of conical masses of green-stone, associated sometimes with less regular hills of baked and altered clay-slate. This part of Tierra del Fuego may be considered as the extremity of the submerged chain of mountains already alluded to. The cove takes its name of 'Wigwam' from some of the Fuegian habitations; but every bay in the neighbourhood might be so called with equal propriety. The inhabitants, living chiefly upon shell-fish, are obliged constantly to change their place of residence; but they return at intervals to the same spots, as is evident from the piles of old shells, which must often amount to many tons in freight. These heaps can be distinguished at a long distance by the bright green colour of certain plants, which invariably grow on them. Among these may be enumerated the wild celery and scurvy grass, two very serviceable plants, the use of which has not been discovered by the natives.

"The Fuegian wigwam resembles, in size and dimensions, a haycock. It merely consists of a few broken branches stuck in the ground, and very imperfectly thatched on one side with a few tufts of grass and rushes. The whole cannot be the work of an hour, and it is only used for a few days. At Goeree Roads I saw a place where one of these naked men had slept, which absolutely offered no more cover than the form of a hare. The man was evidently living by himself, and York Minster said he was 'very bad man,' and that probably he had stolen something. [Being ostracized for any length of time in such a harsh climate was most likely a death sentence.}

"On the west coast, however, the wigwams are rather better, for they are covered with seal-skins. We were detained here several days by the bad weather. The climate is certainly wretched: the summer solstice was now passed, yet every day snow fell on the hills, and in the valleys there was rain, accompanied by sleet. The thermometer generally stood about 45 degs. but in the night fell to 38 or 40 degs. From the damp and boisterous state of the atmosphere, not cheered by a gleam of sunshine, one fancied the climate even worse than it really was.

"While going one day on shore near Wollaston Island, we pulled alongside a canoe with six Fuegians. These were the most abject and miserable creatures I anywhere beheld. On the east coast the natives, as we have seen, have guanaco cloaks, and on the west they possess seal-skins. Amongst these central tribes the men generally have an otter-skin, or some small scrap about as large as a pocket-handkerchief, which is barely sufficient to cover their backs as low down as their loins. It is laced across the breast by strings, and according as the wind blows, it is shifted from side to side.

"But these Fuegians in the canoe were quite naked, and even one full-grown woman was absolutely so. It was raining heavily, and the fresh water, together with the spray, trickled down her body. In another harbour not far distant, a woman, who was suckling a recently-born child, came one day alongside the vessel, and remained there out of mere curiosity, whilst the sleet fell and thawed on her naked bosom, and on the skin of her naked baby!

"These poor wretches were stunted in their growth, their hideous faces bedaubed with white paint, their skins filthy and greasy, their hair entangled, their voices discordant, and their gestures violent. Viewing such men, one can hardly make one's self believe that they are fellow-creatures, and inhabitants of the same world. It is a common subject of conjecture what pleasure in life some of the lower animals can enjoy: how much more reasonably the same question may be asked with respect to these barbarians!

"At night, five or six human beings, naked and scarcely protected from the wind and rain of this tempestuous climate, sleep on the wet ground coiled up like animals. Whenever it is low water, winter or summer, night or day, they must rise to pick shellfish from the rocks; and the women either dive to collect sea-eggs, or sit patiently in their canoes, and with a baited hair-line without any hook, jerk out little fish. If a seal is killed, or the floating carcass of a putrid whale is discovered, it is a feast; and such miserable food is assisted by a few tasteless berries and fungi.

"They often suffer from famine: I heard Mr. Low, a sealing-master intimately acquainted with the natives of this country, give a curious account of the state of a party of one hundred and fifty natives on the west coast, who were very thin and in great distress. A succession of gales prevented the women from getting shell-fish on the rocks, and they could not go out in their canoes to catch seal. A small party of these men one morning set out, and the other Indians explained to him, that they were going a four days' journey for food: on their return, Low went to meet them, and he found them excessively tired, each man carrying a great square piece of putrid whale's-blubber with a hole in the middle, through which they put their heads, like the Gauchos do through their ponchos or cloaks. As soon as the blubber was brought into a wigwam, an old man cut off thin slices, and muttering over them, broiled them for a minute, and distributed them to the famished party, who during this time preserved a profound silence. Mr. Low believes that whenever a whale is cast on shore, the natives bury large pieces of it in the sand, as a resource in time of famine; and a native boy, whom he had on board, once found a stock thus buried."

And later, "Captain Fitz Roy could never ascertain that the Fuegians have any distinct belief in a future life. They sometimes bury their dead in caves, and sometimes in the mountain forests; we do not know what ceremonies they perform. Jemmy Button would not eat land-birds, because 'eat dead men': they are unwilling even to mention their dead friends. We have no reason to believe that they perform any sort of religious worship; though perhaps the muttering of the old man before he distributed the putrid blubber to his famished party, may be of this nature. Each family or tribe has a wizard or conjuring doctor, whose office we could never clearly ascertain.

"The different tribes have no government or chief; yet each is surrounded by other hostile tribes, speaking different dialects, and separated from each other only by a deserted border or neutral territory: the cause of their warfare appears to be the means of subsistence. Their country is a broken mass of wild rocks, lofty hills, and useless forests: and these are viewed through mists and endless storms.

The habitable land is reduced to the stones on the beach; in search of food they are compelled unceasingly to wander from spot to spot, and so steep is the coast, that they can only move about in their wretched canoes."

[The "useless forests," and "wretched canoes" of which Darwin writes in the previous paragraph, and the "inhospitable countries" and "miserable country" that he mentions in the following paragraph, reflect his ethnocentric views. Yet it is illuminating that Darwin considers that other people, though living very differently from those in his own country, may be equally happy and well-adapted.]

"Whilst beholding these savages, one asks, whence have they come? What could have tempted, or what change compelled a tribe of men, to leave the fine regions of the north, to travel down the Cordillera or backbone of America, to invent and build canoes, which are not used by the tribes of Chile, Peru, and Brazil, and then to enter on one of the most inhospitable countries within the limits of the globe? Although such reflections must at first seize on the mind, yet we may feel sure that they are partly erroneous. There is no reason to believe that the Fuegians decrease in number; therefore we must suppose that they enjoy a sufficient share of happiness, of whatever kind it may be, to render life worth having. Nature by making habit omnipotent, and its effects hereditary, has fitted the Fuegian to the climate and the productions of his miserable country.

"After having been detained six days in Wigwam Cove by very bad weather, we put to sea on the 30th of December. Captain Fitz Roy wished to get westward to land York and Fuegia [who had been captured in the previous sailing] in their own country. When at sea we had a constant succession of gales, and the current was against us: we drifted to 57 degs. 23' south. On the 11th of January, 1833, by carrying a press of sail, we fetched within a few miles of the great rugged mountain of York Minster (so called by Captain Cook, and the origin of the name of the elder Fuegian), when a violent squall compelled us to shorten sail and stand out to sea. The surf was breaking fearfully on the coast, and the spray was carried over a cliff estimated to 200 feet in height. On the 12th the gale was very heavy, and we did not know exactly where we were: it was a most unpleasant sound to hear constantly repeated, 'keep a good look-out to leeward.'

"On the 13th the storm raged with its full fury: our horizon was narrowly limited by the sheets of spray borne by the wind. The sea looked ominous, like a dreary waving plain with patches of drifted snow: whilst the ship laboured heavily, the albatross glided with its expanded wings right up the wind. At noon a great sea broke over us, and filled one of the whale boats, which was obliged to be instantly cut away. The poor Beagle trembled at the shock, and for a few minutes would not obey her helm; but soon, like a good ship that she was, she righted and came up to the wind again. Had another sea followed the first, our fate would have been decided soon, and forever.

"We had now been twenty-four days trying in vain to get westward; the men were worn out with fatigue, and they had not had for many nights or days a dry thing to put on. Captain Fitz Roy gave up the attempt to get westward by the outside coast. In the evening we ran in behind False Cape Horn, and dropped our anchor in forty-seven fathoms, fire flashing from the windlass as the chain rushed round it. How delightful was that still night, after having been so long involved in the din of the warring elements!"³⁴

And of the Patagonian people³⁵

"During our previous visit (in January), we had an interview at Cape Gregory with the famous so-called gigantic Patagonians, who gave us a cordial reception. Their height appears greater than it really is, from their large guanaco mantles, their long flowing hair, and general figure: on an average, their height is about six feet, with some men taller and only a few shorter; and the women are also tall; altogether they are certainly the tallest race which we anywhere saw. In features they strikingly resemble the more northern

Indians whom I saw with Rosas, but they have a wilder and more formidable appearance: their faces were much painted with red and black, and one man was ringed and dotted with white like a Fuegian. Captain Fitz Roy offered to take any three of them on board, and all seemed determined to be of the three. It was long before we could clear the boat; at last we got on board with our three giants, who dined with the Captain, and behaved quite like gentlemen, helping themselves with knives, forks, and spoons: nothing was so much relished as sugar. This tribe has had so much communication with sealers and whalers that most of the men can speak a little English and Spanish; and they are half civilized, and proportionally demoralized."[36]

On the *Origin of Species*

IT SEEMS CERTAIN that at the time, no one could have foreseen that the Beagle would be written about in history books 180 years after its voyages. Nor is it likely that Darwin or anyone else connected to the voyages of discovery would have predicted that Darwin's theories on evolution, which he later wrote about in the *Origin of Species* (1859) would still be hotly debated (primarily in non-scientific settings) almost 200 years later. At the time of the voyage, he did not yet see himself as an evolutionist, but later he wrote, "The voyage of the 'Beagle' has been by far the most important event in my life, and has determined my whole career."

Francisco "Perito" Moreno

GLACIAR PERITO MORENO of *Glaciares* National Park is today justifiably a top tourist destination in Argentina. It was named for a man whose contributions to Argentina went far beyond climbing and exploring the Southern ice cap of Patagonia.

Francisco *Perito* (expert) Moreno was born in Buenos Aires in 1852. From an early age, he shared his father's interest in science, particularly collecting fossils and artifacts. After the Conquest of the Desert campaign occurred (a military campaign carried out against the remaining indigenous people in the 1870s) overland explorations of Patagonia by non-natives had begun to open the region, Moreno went to the Patagonian region to begin a survey of Río Negro Territory. He was the first white Argentine to reach Lake Nahuel Huapi Lago Argentino (Argentine Lake) and the (later named) Glaciar Perito Moreno. On his first trip, he found El Chaltén, which he renamed Mount Fitz Roy.

On his second expedition, he was captured and con-demned to death by the Tehuelches, but managed to escape. In the mid-1880s, he returned to the Rio Negro territories. He disproved the Chilean claims to various lakes in the Andes by finding that drainage in many places along the Continental Divide had originally been to the Atlantic rather than the Pacific. Those findings were of great benefit to Argentina when the Boundary Treaty of 1881, between Chile and Argentina, was negotiated.

In 1877, he established the Buenos Aires Archaeological and Anthropological Museum, which displayed thousands of artifacts that he had collected during his surveys, and which later was incorporated into the museum at the University of La Plata in Buenos Aires.

In 1903, Moreno donated 50 square miles (75 sq. km.) of land to the government for the creation of Nahuel Huapi National Park in the Andes. This, Argentina's first national park, is part of the Rio Negro and Neuquén provinces and surrounds the popular Lake District town of San Carlos de Bariloche. The park has now grown to more than 2,720 sq. mi (7,050 sq. km.), making it the largest park in the region.

Francisco Perito Moreno died on November 22, 1919 and was first buried in Buenos Aires' famous La Recoleta Cemetery, but his remains were later moved to the shores of Centinela Inlet on Lake Nahuel Huapi.

Increased contact with Europeans

ALTHOUGH THE PEOPLES of Patagonia had endured periodic raids from pirates and plunderers for hundreds of years, there had not been massive assaults by foreign powers, primarily because gold or silver and other riches that were found elsewhere in Latin America, had not been discovered in the southern regions.

However, after Chile and Argentina gained their independence from Spain on September 18, 1810 and July 9, 1816, respectively, foreign interest and settlement in Patagonia increased. Anglican missionaries came to convert the indigenous people to their brand of religion. Cattle and sheep ranchers began to view the windswept grasslands and pampas of Patagonia as suitable for the raising of livestock. What had been open land began to be fenced off and huge estancias established.

As Southern Patagonia became of more interest to both, the newly independent countries of Chile and Argentine began to have border disputes. Chilean president Manuel Bulnes sent an expedition to the Strait of Magellan and they founded *Fuerte Bulnes* (Fort Bulnes) in 1843. The climate was so inhospitable that the settlement could not be maintained and so in 1848, the Chilean government moved the main settlement about 40 miles north to the current location of Punta Arenas; this established a presence that later allowed Chile to claim the Strait of Magellan.

When the railroads came in, the regions that had been home to gauchos, guanacos and rheas were even more accessible. The governments of Chile and Argentina welcomed foreign settlement in the remote lands and throughout the 19th and 20th centuries, European missionaries and settlers arrived. One of the largest colonizations was the Welsh settlement of the Chubut Valley.

Great numbers of the native peoples were killed or pushed further and further south. The Conquest of the Desert (which is pictured on Argentina's 100-peso bill) of the 1870s was labeled genocide by some, others claimed that it was to subdue those who were raiding the newcomers' settlements.

In 1885, a mining expeditionary party under the Romanian adventurer Julius Popper landed in southern Patagonia in search of gold, which they found after travelling southwards towards the lands of Tierra del Fuego. This further opened up some of the area to prospectors.

Magellanic Penguins on Magdalena Island

The shuttle to Las Torres

16 • Patagonia Today

Sheep ranching, although it has had peaks and valleys, has remained an important economic activity in Argentina. Increasingly, the activity has moved south. Estimates are that half of the sheep farming is in Patagonia, particularly in the Argentine provinces of Chubut and Santa Cruz.

Tourism is an increasingly valuable source of revenue for both Argentina and Chile. It's no longer just the hale and hearty backpackers that set out for these exotic destinations; it's upscale tourists visiting Argentina's Iguazu Falls, Glaciar Perito Moreno, the Valdés Peninsula, the Lake District, Ushuaia and Tierra del Fuego. In Chile, they come to Torres del Paine National Park for the excellent hiking and climbing; to such wine-growing regions as the Valle Central where the Maipo Valley produces Cabernet Sauvignon and the Curicó Valley produces Chardonnay; and to the Punta Arenas and Chiloe areas for Mapuche traditional crafts. The island of Chiloe remains very rural—small farms overlooking salmon and shellfish farms in the bay.

The largest ethnic group of Chile today is the Mapuche, with sources giving an estimate of four-to-ten percent of the country's population. The Mapuche group, composed of several smaller tribes, includes those who are of mixed Spanish and indigenous ancestry. Originally, they lived in large numbers throughout both Argentina and Chile; today it's estimated that they number 250,000 in Argentina and approximately 1,000,000 in Chile. In Argentina, they live mainly in the provinces of Buenos Aires, La Pampa, Neuquén, Rio Negro and Chubut. In Chile, they live predominately in the major cities of Santiago, Valapariso, Concepcion, and in the southern half of the country.

Keeping their culture alive has been difficult. The earlier efforts toward eliminating or moving them to reservations, the taking of their traditional lands and forcing them off their lands and onto reservations, and the insistence that they give up their language and customs and assimilate into the mainstream culture, have taken their toll. Although there has been increased interest in preserving the Mapuche's handicrafts such as weaving and leather-making, those that wish to live in their homeland see many of the recent developments as threatening.

As efforts to access natural resources—forests for lumber and rivers to construct dams and produce hydroelectric power plants—increase, roads that the crisscross Mapuche areas are built. In addition, when foreigners such as Doug Tompkins, Ted Turner, Sylvester Stallone, Christopher Lambert, and notably, Luciano Benetton have purchased huge tracts of land, there has been concern in the local communities.

Questions arise about how the native people will be treated. Will their traditional lands be developed, or protected, in the years ahead? When one considers the history of interactions between foreigners and indigenous people worldwide, one can hardly fault the Mapuche for watching the increased interest of foreigners with suspicion and distrust.

LUCIANO BENETTON, WHO *Fortune Magazine* placed #396 on its list of world's billionaires in 2008, with an estimated worth of $2.9 billion, has also been called a "Green Billionaire." He owns Compañia de Tierras Sud, and is Patagonia's largest land owner. Whether Benetton's involvement in Patagonia has been a good or a bad thing remains controversial.

The United Colors of Benetton, in a December 2010 news release, stated that, "In 1991, Edizione Holding [holding of the Benetton family] bought Compañía de Tierras Sud

Argentino from three Argentine families, revitalizing this historical company which, despite a past stretching back one hundred years, was at that time in total decline. It currently provides work for more than 600 people on a modern farm dedicated, above all, to breeding sheep."[37]

The Benetton Group reportedly has brought new techniques to the declining sheep-breeding and-rearing industry and built community centers and museums. The Leleque museum in Chubut, for example, was built to showcase the history, arts, and crafts of Patagonia. Its ongoing archeological research, as well as its exhibits open to the public , include the indigenous people.

However, the local Mapuche communities have been critical of the Benetton Group's acquisition of traditional Mapuche lands. Though Benetton may be correct in their statement that they "almost a century later, found itself unwittingly involved" in the creation of Argentina and its relationship to the native populations, this does not negate the concerns of some within the local population about recent changes. There have been complaints that the Compañía de Tierras Sud Argentino property has been fenced off and that the people now lack access to traditional water supplies. They assert also that they are being pushed onto less desirable land.[38] *Mapuche Lands in Patagonia Taken Over by Benetton Wool Farms*

ANOTHER OF THE new landowners, Doug Tompkins, appears to have gained greater acceptance. Tompkins, with his ex-wife Susie, co-founded two companies, North Face, selling outdoor gear, and Espirit, offering clothing, in the United States in the 1960s. North Face's tents, which were the earliest tents to feature bendable support poles instead of the traditional pole in the middle, were an instant success. Espirit got its start in a van—selling children's dresses out the back.

Then in 1968, the adventurous Tompkins, with three other climbers, decided to take a six-month road/adventure trip from California to Patagonia. (The film, *180 Degrees South: Conquerors of the Useless*, portrays their adventures.) One of Tompkins' companions was Yvon Chouinard, environmentalist and founder of the outdoor gear company, Patagonia. The group established a new route on Mt. Fitz Roy and produced a film, *Mountain of Storms*, about their experience.

While North Face and Espirit flourished and became multi-million dollar international businesses, Tompkins grew increasingly concerned about the impact of the clothing industry on the environment. He and Susie separated and in the late 1980s he sold his share of the companies back to her. He moved to Chile, married Kristine in 1993, and began to purchase major property with the intent of keeping it pristine and away from developers.

His first purchase was of 42,000 acres (170 sq. km.) in Chile's Palena Province. The Conservation Land Trust was formed and another 700,000 acres was added to create what is now Pumalín Park.

When Tompkins first arrived, he was an outsider and his motives were suspect, but the fact that the private preserve was opened to the public won him needed support. In 2005, when the Chilean government declared the site a nature sanctuary, it provided increased environment protections as well as important official sanction. Together Doug and Kristine Tompkins have been instrumental in protecting more than two million acres (8,100 sq. km.) of wilderness in Chile and Argentina—more than any other private individuals.

Yet there have been conflicts. For decades, Tompkins has protested the planned route for the Carretera Austral in southern Chile. The Carretera Austral is a 770-mile (1,240 km.), mainly unpaved, gravel road connecting Puerto Montt to parts of Aisén region to the south. The government wanted to run the extension through Pumalín Park; Tompkins proposed building a highway along Chile's coast rather than through the preserve.

There are various sides to this issue including: communities that would like to have a transportation system that would allow goods to be brought in more economically; environmentalists and local residents that would like Pumalín Park and points further south sheltered from more development; companies that would like to open up new territory to harness its natural resources.

In September 2011, Chile's public works (MOP) announced that they would expropriate land in the private national reserve. Work was slated to begin in 2012, and be completed by 2013. The project, if it proceeds as proposed, would take over 30 hectares (74 acres) of land to construct the 6.65 mile (10.7 km.) section between Palena Province's towns of Leptepú and Fiordo Largo.

In September 2012, word came that construction work in Pumalín Park was underway, but was limited to widening existing roads and fixing existing bridges. No new roads through the fjords were under construction at that time.

Though Ted Turner's holdings in Argentina are considerably smaller than Benetton's, there have also been protests involving access to water on or near Turner's properties. Although large tracts of land often contain water sources such as lakes and rivers, there are also often laws that grant certain rights to others to access that water.

Unfortunately, there have been charges that the employees at Turner's Estancia La Primavera (5,000 hectares), which is inside Nahuel Huapi National Park, have harassed, or denied access to, nearby residents attempting to get to the Minero and Traful Rivers and to Traful Lake. Similar complaints have been made about treatment at Turner's estancia Collón Cura.[39]

Of perhaps even more significance is that a consortium of Chilean, as well as foreign companies, continue their efforts to construct dozens of dams throughout Patagonia in order to bring water to the various irrigation projects and major cities, and to produce hydroelectric power for mining interests and cities far away.

This means that the remoteness of Chile's Aisén Region may well become a thing of the past if a plan, approved by the Chilean government in May 2011, comes into being. Five dams are planned, which would dam the wild Pascua and Baker rivers.

The Rio Pascua comes out of Lago O'Higgins. Rio Baker is also a glacier-fed river and is presently popular with sports fisherman and river rafters. Environmentalists, such as the *Patagonia Sin Represa* group, point out that not only would the local area be affected—scarred landscapes, flooded valleys, and dislocated peoples—but also those far away. Transmission lines would cut a wide swath along their routes. A major seaport would need to be constructed to handle the volume of construction materials. In addition, experience has shown that once the dams open up the area, mining and timber exploration will soon follow. The Mapuche claim that massive projects of this sort cross through places sacred to them.

The Chilean government approved the five dam project in May 2011, but nationwide protests—including a 500,000 person march in Santiago—have occurred. In June 2011, a court ruled that the project would be halted for three months to consider objections from opponents. In October 2011, an appeals court in Puerto Montt overturned the blockage.[40,41]

Estimates are that the Aisén project would employ 5,000 and would increase the country's power capacity by 20 percent. Protestors have said that they will take the case to the Supreme Court or the International Court of Human Rights if necessary.

In June 2012, environmentalists received welcome news—one of the owners of HidroAysén had announced that they had suspended indefinitely all work on the 1,200-mile-long transmission line. The Natural Resources Defense Council (NRDC), which has been involved in the fight against this project, issued a statement urging those concerned to write to Chilean President Piñera asking him "to show environmental leadership by overturning the approval of HidroAysén and saving Patagonia from destruction."[42]

ANOTHER ENVIRONMENTAL ASSAULT affects not only the local residents, but also the fishing industry. Salmon, which the Mapuche for centuries fished from the wild rivers using primitive methods, are now raised in huge salmon farms.

"In the last decade of the 20th century, the Chilean State encouraged the expansion of the salmon industry. In regions X and XI, 900 thousand hectares of sea have been declared fish farming areas. 90 percent of salmon production is concentrated in the fiords, channels, lakes and rivers of region X. Chile is now the main producer of farmed salmon in the world, generating US$2 billion per annum.

There have been claims by the Mapuches that "A small group of industry partners has control of 88% of all fish caught, and 90% of sea products from Chilean waters." The Mapuches also claim that their "fisherman located on coastal reservations have had their access to the sea and its resources obstructed by the activities of salmon farming companies."[43]

Patagonian sky

Appendix #1 Preparing for the Extended Trip

Tying up loose ends at home

We have found that no matter how many times we have traveled, without a checklist it is quite easy to overlook some small matter that would have been much more easily handled at an earlier stage.

Looking at the following lists may seem overwhelming, but actually you probably already do most of these things intuitively. If you break the list into even smaller chunks, it makes the tasks much easier to fit into your regular schedule in the weeks preceding your trip. Obviously, not all items will be needed by everyone, or for each trip. For example, if you have a house sitter, you will not need to set the timers and alarms, nor move the indoor plants to one location. Do the chores a bit at a time, and let your trip be one with smooth sailing.

Up to 3 months ahead:

- Purchase airline, ship, or other transportation tickets (check to see if you can get a partial refund if the tickets go on sale after they are initially ordered). Note that airline fares for stays of 30 days and longer usually cost more than shorter visits—and that sale prices seldom apply to long-term stays.
- Make reservations for lodging (we like to know where we will stay the first and last nights—oth-

ers may want to make additional reservations in advance.). To avoid hassles, request confirmations, or at least make a note of who you talk to and when you call, when you make your arrangements.

- Arrange travel interruption insurance, if needed. Check what coverage is offered by your VISA/MasterCard/American Express/AAA. Check that you have adequate medical coverage. If you are going for an extended stay, or into remote locations, consider MED-E-Vac plans. If you want to cover *pre-existing* medical conditions, keep in mind that many policies require that you buy the travel insurance at the same time as you book your flight (or other) tickets. Read the fine print!

- Check the U.S. State Department's website at www.state.gov to get an update on any political, medical, or civil situations in the areas where you are going to travel.

- Order or renew passport if required. Some countries require that your passport be valid for several weeks after your expected return date. Check this out.

- A visa is not required in Argentina or Chile travel.state.gov/travel for visits up to 90 days, but if you are going to other Latin American countries (Brazil or Paraguay at this time) you will need to obtain a visa in advance. For a fee, Chile will grant an extension beyond the 90 days.

- Check with your health care provider to see what medical immunizations are recommended.

- Make necessary doctor and dental appointments.

- Arrange house-sitting or pet care.

- Consider yard maintenance (we have installed a drip irrigation system to simplify watering.).

- If you are buying a new camera, begin your research.

- Consider off premises backup of computer data. (we have a small usb drive that fits in a safe deposit box).

- Revisit your insurance requirements and update

your will.

- Stay organized: create a file folder and keep all correspondence and trip notes in one place (including this checklist).

1 month in advance:

- Purchase footwear and socks. If you are shopping for boots, try them on with the type of socks that you will wear on your trip. Allow plenty of time to break in your shoes. Treat shoes with water repellent at least two times, if appropriate.
- Inventory your clothing and purchase anything additional needed.
- Take special notice of your raingear. If it has lost its repellency, either replace it or revive it by washing, drying, and treating it with appropriate products such as Nixwax.
- Order spare camera batteries and memory cards.
- Select your backpack (or luggage) and related items such as I.D. tags (do NOT put your home address on visible locations), lock, *and* if you have one of the ubiquitous black suitcases, put some unique strap on it so you can spot it easily on the airline baggage conveyers.
- Locate money belt.
- Enlist trusted neighbor to keep an eye on your place: to pick up the mail, to call the newspaper if you forgot to stop the paper, to put the trash barrels back in place as needed, etc.
- Determine watering system for *indoor* plants. (Put them together in a protected spot outdoors? Buy self-watering containers? Give them away? Ask a friend or neighbor to care for them at their place, or yours? Have a house sitter take care of them?)

2 weeks in advance:

- Pre-pay utility and other regular bills (double up) that are not set up for automatic payment.
- Arrange newspaper vacation hold/stop. Some newspapers will deliver to public schools at your request.
- Arrange mail pick-up or hold.
- Obtain foreign currency sufficient to pay for taxis, a middle-of-the-night arrival, and a week of travel. Depending on where you live, foreign currency may need to be ordered by your bank in advance. When deciding how much cash to carry, consider that many foreign countries have limited access to banks on weekends—though ATM machines are available most everywhere. ATMs in both Chile and Argentina charge a transaction fee (currently approx. US$3 in Argentina) for withdrawals.
- Most foreign ATM machines accept a maximum of four characters, and the keys only give numbers. If you normally remember your pin number by letters, be sure you learn the corresponding numbers on the keys.
- Update your address book/personal organizer/electronic data with addresses and emails of personal and professional contacts.
- Make a copy (or copies) of your passport, itinerary (hotel numbers), ATM and credit cards (front and back so you'll have a contact number if needed). Some travelers leave one copy at home with a trusted person and carry one copy separate from those items in case of loss or theft. Another idea is to imbed various coded numbers in an email to yourself.
- Determine how to get from your arrival airport (Santiago, Buenos Aires, or other) to your hotel or other accommodation.
- Put jewelry and valuables in a bank safety deposit box.

1 week in advance:

- Refill needed prescriptions (best to carry in original containers).
- Inventory and fill in needed OTC medications—Lomotil, ibuprofen, etc. (Carry a list of your meds.)
- Purchase sunscreen, toiletries, cosmetics, etc.
- Spray hiking clothes with Sawyers (or equivalent) mosquito repellent if you are going to areas where you might encounter malaria or other serious diseases. www.cdc.gov/malaria/travelers/country_table/a.html
- If you are taking a sleeping bag that has lost some of its loft, put it in the dryer with a tennis ball at the cold setting for a few minutes.
- Consider ear plugs, sleep mask, neck pillow for airline travel and noisy hotel rooms.
- Get needed supply of pet food if pets will be staying home (or leave money in the sugar bowl or some other agreed upon hiding place) for food replenishment by your pet sitter.
- Be certain your security system has up-to-date emergency numbers. Tell them your departure and return dates if warranted. Some communities suggest notifying the local police of your absence.
- Check your freezer compartment—use, or dump, food that will be too old by your return. Fill several liter soda bottles with water and place in freezer to hold in cold in case of short-term brownout.
- Arrange transportation to airport or other terminal.
- Purchase film if you still use it.

Within last week:

- Confirm flights.
- Gather travel documents:
  Passport (and duplicate in separate place)

Record of immunizations as required
Travel tickets
Hotel confirmations
Rental car confirmation number.
- Check watering system.
- Backup computer data and store off premises.
- Wash clothing if needed. (Be certain there is no wet laundry left in the washer or hamper.)
- Clean the perishables out of the pantry and refrigerator.
- Disconnect or switch off TVs, VCRs, and other appliances that consume electricity in the ready-on mode.
- Pack.
- Security Measures:
Set indoor and outdoor lights for self-timing.
Lock windows and doors.
Set radio, or similar, to play at pre-determined times.
Set burglar alarm.

BON VOYAGE!

Appendix #2 The Reality of the 2009 and 2010 Trips

As you've read, *we made substantial changes* as the trip progressed; you'll see how quickly time evaporated.

2009 Days:

#1, 2. Wednesday & Thursday, March 4-5, 2009. Flight San Francisco to Miami International, connecting flight Miami to Santiago, Chile.

#3. Thursday, March 5. Tourists in Santiago.

#4. Friday, March 6. Morning flight Santiago to Punta Arenas (3 hr. LAN Airlines). Afternoon visit by small boat to the island of Magdalena to visit the Magellanic penguins at Monumental Natural Los Pinquinos.

#5. Saturday, March 7. Tourists in Punta Arenas, Chile.

#6. Sunday, March 8. 8:30 a.m. bus Punta Arenas to Puerto Natales. Bus Puerto Natales to Torres del Paine—entering the park through Porteria y Guarderia Laguna Amarga entrance station. Shuttle bus to Refugios Torre & campground.

#7. Monday, March 9. HIKING DAY #1 in Torres del Paine. Because we arrived in good weather, we ascended the right leg of the "W" route to Campamento Chileno, set up camp, went on to Towers and returned to Chileno for overnight.

#8. Tuesday, March 10. HIKING DAY #2. Down from Campamento Chileno to campground at Refugios Torre.

#9-14: Wednesday, March 11 through Monday, March 16. HIKING DAYS #3-8 on the Circuit. Backpacked to Campamento Los Perros and then backtracked to Refugios Torre. (We didn't go over John Garner Pass due to strong winds and weather.)

#15. Tuesday, March 17. Sightseeing tour that included a narrated tour by van on land and a boat on Lago Gray to see the glaciers and the other side of the park. (2nd night at Refugios Torre.)

#16. Wednesday, March 18. Shuttle from the park to the entrance station. Bus travel back to Puerto Natales.

#17. Thursday, March 19. Bus from Puerto Natales to El Calafate, Argentina.

#18. Friday, March 20. Day trip by bus from El Calafate to Los Glaciares National Park (The Glaciers) to see Glaciar Perito Moreno.

#19. Saturday, March 21, 2009. El Calafate to El Chaltén by bus—three hours each way including stops at the La Leona Roadhouse. HIKING DAY—round trip day hike from town of El Chaltén to viewpoints of the Fitz Roy region within Los Glaciares National Park.

#20. Sunday, March 22. Flight from El Calafate to Buenos Aires, Argentina (3 hours).

#21, 22. Monday & Tuesday, March 23-24. Tourists in Buenos Aires.

#23. Wednesday & Thursday, March 25-26. Late night flight home. Buenos Aires to Dallas, change planes to San Francisco. Depart BA 9:45 p.m., Dallas 10:40 a.m. Arrive San Francisco 12:35 p.m. Thurs.

2010 Days:

#1, 2. Monday & Tuesday, February 22-23, 2010. Flight San Francisco to Dallas/Ft. Worth; connecting flight to Santiago; flight to Puerto Montt, Chile; car to Puerto Varas.

#3, 4. Wednesday & Thursday, February 24-25. Exploring Chile's Lake District by rental car.

#5. Friday, February 26. Boarding the Navimag in Puerto Montt, Chile.

#6, 7. Saturday & Sunday, February 27-28. Aboard the

Navimag.

#8. Monday, March 1. Navimag arrives in Puerto Natales, Chile. Overnight.

#9. Tuesday, March 2. HIKING DAY #1. Bus Puerto Natales to Torres del Paine. Start the Circuit by backpacking Refugios Torre to Campamento Serón.

#10. Wednesday, March 3. HIKING DAY #2. Camp Serón to Refugio Dickson.

#11. Thursday, March 4. HIKING DAY #3. Refugio Dickson to Camp Perros.

#12. Friday, March 5. HIKING DAY #4. Los Perros to Campamento Paso.

#13. Saturday, March 6. HIKING DAY #5. Camp Paso to Refugio Grey: camping on the beach.

#14. Sunday, March 7. HIKING DAY #6. Refugio Grey to Campamento Italiano.

#15. Monday, March 8. HIKING DAY #7. Camp Italiano into the Valle del Francés toward Británico as a side trip, and on to Los Cuernos. (We shortened the hike by not going all the way to Británico.)

#16. Tuesday, March 9. HIKING DAY #8. Los Cuernos to Refugio Los Torres for overnight.

#17. Wednesday, March 10. Bus Torres del Paine to Puerto Natales: overnight Casa Cecilia.

#18. Thursday, March 11. Bus Puerto Natales to El Calafate.

#19. Friday, March 12. Flight from El Calafate to Buenos Aires.

#20, 21. Saturday & Sunday, March 13-14. Buenos Aires.

#22. Monday, March 15. Flight Buenos Aires to Dallas, connecting to flight Dallas to San Francisco.

Enroute to Chileno

Resources

Books

Bernhardson, Wayne. Moon Handbook's *Patagonia: including the Falkland Islands*. Berkeley, CA: Avalon Travel, 2008.

Burford, Tim. *Chile: The Bradt Travel Guide*. UK: Bradt Travel Guides Ltd, 2005.

Chatwin, Bruce. *In Patagonia*. New York: Summit Books, 1977. A classic.

McCarthy, Carolyn. Lonely Planet's *Trekking in the Patagonian Andes*. Lonely Planet: CA/Australia/UK, 2009. Highly recommended.

Rudolf, Abraham. *Torres Del Paine: Trekking in Chile's Premier National Park*. UK: Cicerone, 2010.

Salz, Jeff. *The Way of Adventure*. Idyllwild, CA: San Jacinto Press, 2005. Salz is a mountaineer who here relates his year exploring Patagonia on foot: trekking on the Southern Patagonia Ice Cap and climbing Mount Fitz Roy. Equally rich are his conversations with the Mapuche, Argentinean gauchos and Chilean huasos, and Argentine *estancieros* (ranchers).

Shipton, Eric. Land of the Tempest: Travels in Patagonia 1958-1962. New York: E. P. Dutton & Co., 1963. John Garner has sited this book as the inspiration of his own trips and explorations of Patagonia.

Theroux, Paul. *The Old Patagonian Express: By Train through the Americas*. New York: Pocket Books, 1979. Although not much about Patagonia itself, the ancient train plays a part. Classic Theroux: observant, opinionated, and one-of-a-kind.

CD/Video

180 South° (2010) is the story of Jeff Johnson and his buddies heading to Patagonia—inspired by a film clip of the road trip that Doug Tompkins and Yvon Chouinard made in 1968. We meet not only Tompkins, Chouinard, and Johnson, but also several locals who show us beautiful scenes of Patagonia—and explain the environmental threats. (on Netflix)

Mi Mejor Enemigo (in Spanish with English subtitles). An intriguing film about the unexpected meeting of a group of Chilean and Argentinean soldiers during the 1970s war between their countries. They experience their commonalities—we experience the humor of the situation while enjoying the spaciousness and wilds of Patagonia. (on Netflix)

Punta Arenas, Chile

Hostal Patagonia. Magallanes 922, Punta Arenas 6200790, Chile. (not the same as Hostal de la Patagonia). Basic accommodations. We paid $60. www.hostalpatagonia.cl/en phone +56-61-240864.

Tragaluz. An "artsy" guesthouse/Bed & Breakfast transformed from a 100-year-old town home. Dan Elsberg / Lorena Castex, Mejicana 1194, Punta Arenas, Patagonia Chilena. www.tragaluzpatagonia.com phone +56-61-613938.

Puerto Natales, Chile

Casa Cecilia, Tomas Roger 60, Puerto Natales, Chile, www.casaceciliahostal.com Phone: +56-61-613560/613561. We stayed here on both trips. Friendly, English speaking, have tours, rentals, full travel agency services if desired. email: redcecilia@entelchile.net

Erratic Rock International Hostel, 2 Benjamin Zamora, 732 Puerto Natales Patagonia Chile. Phone +56-61-414317. www.erraticrock.com. One of the best resources for information is the free talk given at Erratic Rock hostel (or their nearby B & B). Many sources have commented that they really prepare you with detailed information about the various hikes. It's about US$18 per night in the dorm, US$48 for double bed with shared bath. Erratic Rock also arranges expeditions and rents equipment.

Buenos Aires, Argentina

Hotel Costa Rica, Buenos Aires www.hotelcostarica.com.ar e-mail: reservas@hotelcostarica.com.ar Tel 54 11 4864 7390 address. Hotel Costa Rica, Costa Rica 4137/39, Palermo CP1176, Buenos Aires, Argentina.

El Calafate (our 2010 accommodations):

Che Lagarto Hostel www.chelagarto.com/index.php/en/hostel-in-calafate.html

Transportation

Bus: March 19. El Calafate to Puerto Natales on Turismo Zaahj. US$32 each, one-way for the 5-hour trip. www.turismozaahj.co.cl

Upscale bus: If you are a guest at the Hostería Las Torres, they can arrange direct shuttle service from El Calafate and Punta Arenas. lastorres.com

Flying from Santiago to Punta Arenas.

The only airlines that fly from Chile's capital, Santiago to the nearest airport to Torres del Paine, Carlo Ibañez Del Campo in Punta Arenas, are Lanchile (www.lanchile.com) Sky (www.skyairline.cl) and Aerolineas del Sur (www.aerolineasdelsur.cl).

The price for a ticket can fluctuate between 89.000 pesos (US$180) to 260.000 pesos (US$500). To make sure you get the flight you want at a low price we recommend making your reservations several months in advance.

How to get to Torres del Paine from Argentina

Lodges in Torres del Paine recommend flying from Buenos Aires to El Calafate, and then bus to Puerto Natales and on to the park. We recommend you make your reservations at least one month in advance in order to get the flight you are looking for at a low price. There are two airports in Buenos Aires and local transportation to and between these airports is found in www.easybuenosairescity.com/airporttransportation1.htm If you are staying at the Las Torres Hostería they can arrange private shuttle pickup instead of bus transportation: www.lastorres.com/our-hotel/how-to-get-here/.

Transportation from Santiago, Chile to the park via Puerto Natales:

The Fantástico Sur Lodge gives excellent transportation information, though hard to find from the home page: www.fantasticosur.com/en/torres-del-paine/how-to-get-here/how-to-get-here-from-santiago-of-chile/.

Transportation from Buenos Aires, Argentina to the park via El Calafate

Also from Fantástico Sur: www.fantasticosur.com/en/torres-del-paine/how-to-get-here/how-to-get-here-from-buenos-aires-argentina/

Ferries:

Navimag ferry: www.navimag.com
Victory cruises Cape Horn, Ushuaia, Antarctica, etc: www.victory-cruises.com

Guides and travel companies:

There are many well-known travel companies in the U.S. and elsewhere that offer guided trips or hikes to Patagonia: some include Torres del Paine. The National Geographic Adventure list of *Best Adventure Travel Companies on Earth* 2009 is definitely worth a visit. adventure. nationalgeographic.com/2009/02/adventure-ratings-text. Then explore the websites of some of the following highly rated tour operators for starters:
Sierra Club Outings: www.outings.sierraclub.org
Wilderness Travel: www.wildernesstravel.com
REI: www.rei.com
Mountain Travel Sobek www.mtsobek.com
Southern Explorations www.southernexplorations.com
Cascada Expediciones: www.cascada.travel. Specializes in Chile, Argentina, and Bolivia travel. Emphasis on Eco-travel

Patagonia websites:

Moon guide article on ATM's www.moon.com/blogs/ south-america/beating-the-bank-atms-argentina-chile

The official CONAF *map* of Torres del Paine. parquetorresdelpaine.cl/maps.html Click on outline map on left to zoom in on a section.

Erratic Rock hostel's website with info about Patagonian adventures including Torres del Paine www. erraticrock.com/expeditions/

A commercial site, but very good information on Torres del Paine: transportation, trails, and organized trips. www.torres-del-paine.org/trekking-info.html

The *Best Hike* website gives a wealth of information about hiking in Torres del Paine. www.besthike. com/southamerica/chile/paine.html

A good website for the entire Patagonia area: El Calafate,

etc. www.interpatagonia.com

Good information on the Los Alerces National Park of Argentina www.southernexplorations.com/adventure-travel-information/travel-articles/patagonia/argentina/national-parks/LosAlerces.htm

Good background info on Argentina as well as links to practical services such as travel insurance. www.amazonadventures.com/argentina.htm

For history on Ferdinand Magellan en.wikipedia.org/wiki/Ferdinand_Magellan

Personal accounts and forums:

Very good pictorial essay of a Torres del Paine Circuit trip. gaylord.smugmug.com/Hikes/Torres-Del-Paine-2009/

A couple, Jon and Rachel, provide an excellent account of their "W" trek in Torres del Paine. www.yesadventures.com/2010/04/17/torres-del-paine-chile-5-day-w-trekking-10-essential-tips-2/

Gear lists:

- We created a Google spreadsheet with our itemized gearlist for the Washington part of the Pacific Crest Trail, then tweaked it for Patagonia: tinyurl.com/torresdelpainegear.

- Andrew Skurka, who has hiked more than 30,000 mile of wilderness trails, has an excellent "how-to" website. andrewskurka.com/how-to

- A great site for following current long distance hikers. In addition to journals, many of the hikers include gear lists with weight and photos. www.trailjournals.com

- Check out the website of Ken and Marcia Powers, who are *grand slammers* (Appalachian, Continental Divide, and Pacific Crest trails ("Triple crown") plus American Discovery ADT). Detailed gear info, weights, etc. www.gottawalk.com

- For an excellent site with reviews o̸
  gear, go to www.backpackgeartest.o̸
  also a Yahoo Group called Backpacking̸
  has useful and lively discussions, usually̸
- John Vonhof's *Fixing Your Feet*. fixingyourfe̸
- Backpackinglight.com - excellent, but annual̸

Products mentioned:

- Sawyer products such as Permethrin Clothing Insect Repellent. It doesn't kill mosquitoes and they
  will still buzz around, but they won't land on your
  clothing. Lasts through multiple washings. www.
  sawyer.com/permFAQ.html
- Nido, a whole milk, powdered product sold in a
  canister, is widely available in Hispanic markets if
  not your local supermarket.

Vocabulary/terminology:

- *bencina blanca* = "white spirit" aka camping stove fuel
- *campamento* = camp
- CONAF = Corporacion Nacional Forestal
- *gaucho* = a highly skilled horseman: Argentine
  cowboy
- *huaso* = a highly skilled horseman: Chilean cowboy
- *plantillas* = insoles/shoe inserts
- *proteccion solar* = sunscreen

Foods

Empanadas, are a popular appetizer found in much of
Latin America, are basically pastries with various fill-
ings. The *empanada de pino* is filled with ground beef,
onion, raisins, a piece of boiled egg and a black olive.
An *empanada de queso* is filled with cheese—sometimes
also with onion—and may be deep-fat fried or baked.

- A *hotdog* may differ from what we are used to in the
  U.S. The Chilean hotdog or *completo* (the complete)
  is served not only with mustard and catsup, but

chucrut (sauerkraut), and *ajf
Un Italiano* (an Italian) uses
ag—red, green, and white
ayonnaise.
e fast food hamburger
lar steak sandwich—
and smothered with the
cheese, mayonnaise, avocado,
n. Those who want to sample the
n Santiago should go to the restaurant
Alemana off of Santiago's central Plaza Ita-
— lomitos allegedly originated there.

Lomo a lo pobre is a beefsteak topped with fried onions and one or two fried eggs and served with fried potatoes (French fries).

- *Sopaipillas,* depending on the fried pastry's ingredients and what it is filled with, can be served as a quick bread, a snack food, or a dessert. It might be an appetizer served with mustard or a more substantial meal when stuffed with ground meat and cheese.

- The *Northern sopaipillas* has pumpkin in its dough and is eaten with *chancaca,* (molasses). Less commonly, you may find it served as in the southwestern United States—sprinkled with powdered sugar or topped with honey, syrup, or ice cream.

Beverages:

- *Pisco sour.* It's a brandy made from the skin of white grapes and it has a pleasant tartness similar to a margarita.

- The German influence shows up in the bars—*Schop* is beer on tap. I couldn't quite bring myself to order *Fan-Schop*—a beer and orange Fanta combo, or *Jote*—wine and Coca Cola. Things change—when we were in Peru and Bolivia in the late 1990s, I couldn't find Diet Coca Cola anywhere, now it's available everywhere.

Acknowledgements

I appreciate and wish to thank the many people who helped us prepare for our trips to Chile and Argentina, lent their support while we were traveling, or helped bring this book into the world.

Thanks to Barbara Lee, Berkeley-based photographer. barblee.zenfolio.com, and Harv and Monica for giving us a preview of what trekking in Patagonia would entail. Gracias, Tom Coroneos and Patricia Schaffarczyk, for sharing your South American travel experiences.

Thank you, Rob Hodges and Kate Ellis, Rose Tomey, Henry E. Leinen, William (Bill) Whiting, Francisca Cervandes, and Annie Gardiner for responding to my requests for information about your Patagonia adventures. It was immensely helpful to collect your stories.

It was especially touching to learn that my son, Scott Cole, had send out an e-mail to my buddies to find out how we fared during the disruption following the major Chilean earthquake of 2010.

Bouquets to Melanie Rigney, editor at large, who looked at my earliest drafts and to Carol Yacorzynski of Encore Design, who provided corrections near the last. I appreciate Fran Alcorn, Melanie Clark, Amy Racina, and Sandy Simmons taking the time to read, evaluate, and edit various drafts of this book.

And finally, my thanks to my hiking partner and husband Ralph Alcorn for not only his indispensable research, editing, and production of this book, but also for his great support and care.

Sources

1. **Donna and Jess Saufley:** www.hikerheaven.com
2. **Reciprocity Tax:** www.chile-usa.org/fastfacts.htm
3. **Patagonian Desert temperatures:** en.wikipedia.org/ wiki/Patagonian_Desert
4. **A stunning 360-degree view from the Punta Arenas mirador:** www.360cities.net/image/punta-arenas-chile-mirador
5. **The Baguales Group bus to Torres info:** www.baguales group.com/English/Regular_Buses_to_Torres_del_Paine.html
6. **Bus time from Ushuaia to Puerto Natales:** tinyurl.com/ BusUshuaiaNatales
7. **Fantástico Sur website:** www.fantasticosur.com/en/
8. **Hostería Las Torres:** www.lastorres.com/
9. **Wikipedia on Mate:** en.wikipedia.org/wiki/Mate_(beverage)
10. **Palermo district.** www.hotelcostarica.com.ar/shop/ index.asp
11. **Evita Peron Museum:** www.evitaperon.org/eva_peron_museum.htm
12. **Nahuel Huapi National Park:** en.wikipedia.org/wiki/ Nahuel_Huapi_National_Park
13. **Chocamo Valley view:** tinyurl.com/ChocamoValleyView
14. **Campo Aventura:** www.campoaventura.cl
15. **Map of Puerto Varas and Bariloche area:** www.visitchile.cl/regiondeloslagos.htm
16. **Capitán Leonidas: the history:** www.ussleahy.com/

Unitas%20X.htm

17. **Capitán Leonidas: photos:** global-mariner.com/index-111Magellan1.html

18. **Che Lagarto Hostel:** www.chelagarto.com/index.php/en/hostel-in-calafate.html

19. **Santiago metro:** metrosantiago.cl/

20. **Santiago buses:** www.transantiago.cl/

21. **El Calafate to Los Glaciares:** www.losglaciares.com/en/calafate/transpor.html

22. **Navimag dormitory rates:** www.navimag.com/sitio/es/canales_patagonicos/acomodaciones_y_tarifas-cabina_a.aspx

23. **Cell phone coverage maps:** maps.mobileworldlive.com/

24. **Program providing internet in libraries:** www.biblioredes.cl

25. **Center for disease control:** wwwnc.cdc.gov/travel/destinations/list.htm

26. **Chile Emergency Numbers:** www.experiencechile.org/health-safety.html

27. **Vertice Patagonia website:** www.verticepatagonia.com/

28. **Patagonian Genealogy:** www.accessgenealogy.com/native/races/patagonians_of_south_america.htm

29. **Fuegians and Chonos transport:** www.literature.org/authors/darwin-charles/the-voyage-of-the-beagle/chapter-11.html

30. **Captain Fitz Roy's Fuegian Captives:** www.andaman.org/BOOK/chapter54/text-Fuego/Captives/Captives.htm

31. **Sir Francis Drake history from the UK view:** www.bbc.co.uk/history/historic_figures/drake_francis.shtml

32. **More on Sir Francis Drake:** www.laughtergenealogy.com/bin/histprof/misc/drake.html

33. **Pringle Stokes journal:** www.sl.nsw.gov.au/about/publications/annual_reports/2009/part1/Pringle-Stokes-journal.html

34. *Voyage of the Beagle* **by Charles Darwin, Chapter 10:** tinyurl.com/BeagleVoyageChap10

35. *Voyage of the Beagle* **by Charles Darwin, Chapter 11:** tinyurl.com/BeagleVoyageChap11
36. **Another** *Voyage of the Beagle* **source:** www.infidels.org/library/historical/charles_darwin/voyage_of_beagle.html
37. **Benetton family:** www.benettongroup.com/media-press/company-position-statements
38. **Mapuche land controversy:** www.corpwatch.org/article.php?id=9189
39. **Ted Turner's estancia:** www.patagonia-argentina.com/en/libre-acceso-rios-lagos
40. **Patagonian Dam report:** article.wn.com/view/2011/05/10/Chile_Approves_HidroAysen_Dam_Project_In_Wild_Patagonia_Desp/
41. **Patagonian Dam court action:** www.terradaily.com/reports/Chilean_court_overturns_ban_on_giant_Patagonia_dam_999.html
42. **Patagonian Dam work suspension:** tinyurl.com/PatagonianDamWorkSuspension.
43. **Mapuche nation link:** www.mapuche-nation.org/english/html/news/n-109.htm

Index

About the Author

Susan Alcorn enjoys being a long-distance hiker. She has hiked nearly 2,000 miles on ancient pilgrimage trails in Europe. In 2001, she and her husband Ralph hiked across northern Spain on the famous Camino de Santiago. After their return home, they vowed that they would return to hike various other Camino routes. They have since completed the LePuy and Arles routes of France; the Camino Portugués from Porto, Portugal to Santiago de Compostela, Spain; a segment of the Camino Mozarabe in Spain; and a segment of the Via Podensis (GR65) from Geneva, Switzerland.

From the original trip—, across Spain on the St. James Way, came *Camino Chronicle: Walking to Santiago,* which combines the author's narrative with legends, history, and cultural information about the trail. *Camino Chronicle* was a Benjamin Franklin Award finalist (category: Travel Essay) in 2007. It has received several five-star reviews including that of Midwest Book Review.

Prior to that, Alcorn published *We're in the Mountains, Not Over the Hill: Tales and Tips from Seasoned Women Backpackers.* In that book, the author describes how she began backpacking at age 48 with the goal of climbing Mount Whitney (California), but with little idea what she was getting into.

She describes bear encounters, the kindness of strangers, the lightning storm on Forester Pass, and the culminating climb to the top of Whitney—at 14,996 feet, the highest point in the lower 48. *We're in the Mountains Not over the Hill: Tales and Tips from Seasoned Women Backpackers* received the

BAIPA Best Travel/Adventure Book 2005.

After Susan and Ralph completed their last section of the John Muir Trail in 2001, they decided to tackle the Pacific Crest Trail and in 2010, they completed their final section of the 2,650-mile national trail, which runs from the Mexican border to the Canadian one through the highest mountain ranges of California, Oregon, and Washington.

In January 2007, the couple tackled their highest mountain to date; they flew to Tanzania and were successful at reaching the summit of Mt. Kilimanjaro—at 19,340 feet, the highest peak in Africa.

They made their first trip to Patagonia in 2009 and fell in love with this fascinating region. They were only too happy when the circumstances described in this book led them to return in 2010 to backpack again in Torres del Paine.

Susan Alcorn is a member of several professional organizations: Independent Book Publishers Association(IBPA); Small Publishers Association of North America (SPAN); Bay Area Independent Publishers Association (BAIPA); Bay Area Travel Writers (BATW).

The Alcorns are Oakland residents who have lived in the San Francisco Bay Area most of their lives. Susan attended local schools, and received her B. A. from U.C. Berkeley. After raising her children, she returned to school to become an elementary school teacher and after earning her credential, taught for more than 15 years. Nowadays, when she is not hiking or traveling, she enjoys spending time with friends and family as well as gardening, dancing, and painting.

◆◆◆◆◆

You can contact the the author at backpack45@yahoo.com; visit her website at backpack45.com and Susan's blog at backpack45.blogspot.com; and get her monthly hiking newsletter by emailing her.

If you enjoyed this book, please post a review on amazon.com and mention it on your favorite social media sites. Thank you.

37420723R00175

Made in the USA
Lexington, KY
01 December 2014